P9-DFB-293

"This important book illuminates many unknown chapters of Canadian history in Jim Dubro's significant crusade to make this country unsafe for big-time criminals." – Peter C. Newman

"A crisp, well-researched account." – *The Vancouver Sun*

"Plenty of pace and dash and much more interesting than the rubbish that is now habitually published about Chicago and New York cops and gangsters." – Michael Coren, *Law Times*

"The story of Frank Zaneth is steeped in mystery and intrigue and provides for a fascinating and exceptional character." – *Calgary Herald*

"[**Undercover**] is a valuable historical work . . . but it's also an exciting ride along with a man who rubbed shoulders with . . . some of the biggest crime figures of the day." – *Halifax Daily News*

"Intriguing . . . meticulously researched . . . There are a half-dozen screenplays ripe for development in [**Undercover**]." – *The StarPhoenix* (Saskatoon)

JAMES DUBRO
AND ROBIN ROWLAND

Undercover

Cases of the RCMP's Most Secret Operative

An M&S Paperback from
McClelland & Stewart Inc.
The Canadian Publishers

An M&S Paperback from McClelland & Stewart Inc.

First printing October 1992
Cloth edition printed 1991 by Octopus Publishing Group

Copyright © 1991 by Beacon Hill Productions Inc.
& Eridani Productions Ltd.

Canadian Cataloguing in Publication Data

Dubro, James, 1946-
Undercover: cases of the RCMP's most secret operative

"An M&S paperback."
Includes bibliographical references and index.
ISBN 0-7710-2902-0

1. Zaneth, Frank.   2. Undercover operations - Canada - History.
3. Royal Canadian Mounted Police - Biography.   I. Rowland, Robin F.
II. Title.

HV7911.D83 1992   363.2'32'092   C92-094754-9

Excerpts from "Conspiracy Cases" by Frank Zaneth, copyright by the
RCMP Quarterly, are used by permission of the RCMP.

Cover design by Tania Craan
Photoframe artwork by Avril Orloff
Back cover photo: Rivers Family Collection
Book design and imaging by ECW Type and Art

Printed and bound in Canada

McClelland & Stewart Inc.
The Canadian Publishers
481 University Avenue
Toronto, Ontario
M5G 2E9

Table of Contents

A Note to the Reader

THIS BOOK IS THE STORY OF FRANK ZANETH, the RCMP's most secret operative from 1917 until the 1940s. It tells in detail for the first time the extent of police undercover operations from the radical labor movement in 1919 up to the Conscription Crisis of 1945. The story is based on secret files hidden for up to seventy years in the RCMP archives.

Undercover is both history and investigative journalism. Nothing fictional has been added. All scenes and conversations are based on accounts in police files, trial transcripts, letters, newspaper reports and other accounts. All material in quotation marks is accurate.

When Zaneth was undercover, he assumes another character, for example, the labor agitator Harry Blask. During our account of undercover operations, the name of the character is used. Where Zaneth is himself, a police officer, his own name is used.

There are still gaps in the record. Whole files were routinely destroyed years ago and there are documents missing within existing files.

Much of the material in this book is based on files obtained under the Canadian Access to Information (AIA) and Privacy Act, and the United States Freedom of Information Act (FOI). Under those laws, certain information is often deleted from the copies that were released. Where there is a deleted portion in quoted text it is represented by a dark ellipsis (■ ■ ■). This may represent a few words or a whole paragraph. Information deleted for editorial reasons is represented by an ordinary ellipsis (. . .).

Where a name has been withheld by the AIA or FOI offices we have written [Name Deleted], but where we have discovered the name by using other sources it has been filled in.

A list of the Frank Zaneth papers is included in the Afterword.

INTRODUCTION

The Silent Force

EARLY ON THE MORNING OF TUESDAY, AUGUST 28, 1990, at the small Cape Breton port of Beleine, north of the historic fortress of Louisbourg, a group of men was unloading hashish from a boat anchored just offshore. A twelve-meter fishing boat was shuttling loads of hash to the beach, where men were filling a trailer.

As the sun was slowly rising out of the Atlantic, a gray-green Canadian Forces destroyer, HMCS *Nipigon* suddenly came speeding out of the early morning mist. Beside it was a red Canadian Coast Guard cutter. On land, members of the Royal Canadian Mounted Police tactical squad, dressed in battle fatigues and flak jackets, surrounded the smugglers. Other Mounties, manning a speedy Zodiac, were soon boarding the boat. The bust was over in a few minutes.

At a news conference in Halifax, Commander Carl Doucette, captain of the *Nipigon*, and Sergeant Gary Grant of the RCMP told the story of a modern, sophisticated drug tracking operation. The investigation had involved the RCMP in Nova Scotia, Newfoundland, Quebec and New Brunswick. Aurora surveillance planes had shadowed the drug boats for five days. Then the *Nipigon* took over, tracking the drug boat with radar. The RCMP seized twenty-five tonnes of hashish, with an estimated value in 1990 of $320 million. Sixteen men were charged with narcotics offenses.

In the 1990s, the RCMP uses all the latest high-tech equipment to fight their battle against crime. Satellites track smugglers' aircraft and ships. Night lenses, infrared cameras, body packs, wiretaps are used; computer databases correlate and collate the mass of apparently unrelated data; undercover operatives are specially trained and can call on half a century of experience.

It wasn't always that way. At one time, one man — and in those days, of course, it was always a man — had to start it all. He had to work undercover, living by his wits as he learned on the job, without the benefit of training or tips from more experienced policemen, without computers and radios and body pack recording equipment.

Eighty years ago, the Royal Canadian Mounted Police was beginning to change from a rural, frontier force to a modern urban police organization. There were a few pioneering detectives in Montreal, Toronto and Vancouver, the men who laid the groundwork for today's police force. In the secret history of the Silent Force, one name stands out from that era. That name was Frank Zaneth, the first officer recruited by the old Royal North-West Mounted Police to be a secret undercover operative. Recruited because he was a short Italian immigrant, who did not look anything like the traditional tall, imposing, often very British Mountie. Frank Zaneth had other advantages, among them a natural ease for languages; he spoke English, French and Italian when he was recruited. Other talents became apparent later: he was also a natural and brazen actor. Frank Zaneth was the RCMP's most secret operative.*

The official record shows that Frank Zaneth was born in Italy and came to Canada from Springfield, Massachusetts, in the spring of 1911. He homesteaded near Moose Jaw and joined the Royal North-West Mounted Police in Regina on December 5, 1917. At first promotion came quickly: he was made detective corporal in November 1919 and detective sergeant in September 1920. Then came the lean years for the RCMP, years of low budgets, a time when the force shrank by half. In January 1932,

---

* In RCMP practice of the day, the term "operative" referred to a member of the force working undercover. "Agent" meant a hired informant.

Zaneth was promoted to detective staff sergeant and on April 1, 1934, he became the first man in RCMP history to hold the rank of detective inspector. During his years as inspector, Zaneth became the RCMP's top troubleshooter and was sent on the most difficult cases. With the beginning of the Second World War, he became an administrator. He was promoted to superintendent in October, 1945 and in May 1949, he became an assistant commissioner. In February 1951, he took the six months paid leave granted a retiring officer and officially left the RCMP in August of that year.

That's the record on paper, but ask a retired Mountie, one who served in the thirties and forties, about Zaneth, and you hear of a legend, a mystery man within the force. A former Commissioner of the RCMP, Len Higgitt, said Zaneth "was a cross between Little Caesar and Columbo; a mixture of Sherlock Holmes and Sidney Reilly." A retired Deputy Commissioner, Jim Lemieux, who was a young corporal in the Montreal of the mid-Thirties said, "Zaneth always had some special duty that very few people knew anything about . . . He was known as a cracker jack detective . . . He was everything a good policeman should be . . . He was most of the time referred to as a BTO — a big time operator." Others have called Zaneth "a master of disguise" and "a man of a thousand faces." Lemieux added, "If something unusual was going on, Zaneth was sent because of his ability to clean up a case. He was noted for his memory and also for his observation tactics. If he went in where a crime had been committed, he had the faculty to see what other people didn't see. He was a natural. I always considered him a model policeman."

The story of Frank Zaneth is one of the best-kept secrets of the Silent Force.

Once he was undercover, Zaneth didn't sign his own name. In the early years reports were signed with Zaneth's regimental number, 6743; later he became the RCMP's mysterious Operative No. 1.

The story of Frank Zaneth is not the familiar adventure of the scarlet-coated Mountie on dog-sled patrol in the Arctic or alone on the prairie; Zaneth was not the movie Mountie. If Hollywood had known about Zaneth and had made a movie, he would have been played by Edward G. Robinson or Peter Falk, not Nelson Eddy.

This is the history of a small, elite force of detectives that enforced Canadian federal laws during the height of the gangster era, the Prohibition twenties and the dirty thirties, a force that had less publicity than its U.S. contemporaries. It's also the story of the political arm of the scarlet force, charged with keeping an eye on the so-called subversive movements of the day. Frank Zaneth was present almost every time Canadian history turned during the years he was a Mountie, from the conscription riots in Quebec in 1918 through the postwar labor trouble, the bootleg era, the first big drug rackets, the discontent of the depression, the safe-blowing days on the prairies and into the Second World War and its conscription crisis.

In 1989, Communism collapsed in Europe, but at one time many people believed Communism could bring a better world. In 1919, Zaneth's first major assignment was to infiltrate the radical unions that operated in the coal valley of Drumheller, Alberta. In 1919, Canada's Communist movement was growing in that valley. Many men thought that new revolutionary Soviet Russia was the guide to the future. Fear of the Communist movement, fear of revolution led to the founding of the Royal North-West Mounted Police Secret Service, the fear led to government abuse of civil liberties and the first political interference in the operations of the RCMP.

Organized crime, as we know it today, was born in those years. The RCMP's fight against the Mafia began when prohibition in the United States and Canada gave birth to the Mob. In those years, Zaneth was undercover, playing the part of a Chicago gangster, a Québécois drug dealer or a bumbling Italian bureaucrat; he was translating intercepted Mafia coded letters and watching for heroin in shipments of sultanas and Dutch bulbs. Frank Zaneth worked in Al Capone's Chicago, undercover alongside the IRS team that nailed Scarface. One of Zaneth's important assignments in the late 1920s and early

14

1930s was neutralizing Rocco Perri, Canada's king of the boot-leggers, the rum lord and the drug boss of Ontario. At Perri's side was his common-law wife, Bessie, the first woman to command a Mafia gang. It was against Rocco and Bessie Perri that Zaneth planned and executed an audacious undercover operation.

In the late twentieth century, refugees crowd into camps the around world. Alien smuggling routes today often lead from Tiananmen Square through Hong Kong and Panama to Canada. In the 1920s, the Mafia charged high prices to smuggle desper-ate immigrants from Italy to Canada. Zaneth juggled under-cover investigation with open sleuthing to discover how the mob was selling forged immigration permits to people who wanted to bring their relatives and friends to Canada.

The RCMP has tracked smugglers in Atlantic Canada for sixty years. The same routes used by hashish smugglers or by the Columbian Medellín cocaine cartel were used by the bootleg-gers of the 1920s and 1930s. Mounties chased bootleggers smuggling liquor from St. Pierre or raw alcohol from New-foundland into the Maritime provinces into the same "isolated bays and inlets" that today hide the hash smugglers.

In September, 1989, in Edmunston, New Brunswick, police intercepted a five-man Medellín cartel hit team, on their way to spring two colleagues from a Fredericton jail. In the 1920s and 1930s, the Albert family of Edmunston ran the lucrative smuggling rackets; the family patriarch, bootlegger Maxime Albert, was dubbed by the press the "Robin Hood of New Brunswick frontier." Although the Mounties had been occa-sionally successful in seizing a fishing boat full of liquor, the force up until then had been unsuccessful in getting the men they thought were behind the liquor smuggling racket, so RCMP headquarters sent for Staff Sergeant Frank Zaneth. Zaneth followed a money trail from a small liquor warehouse in St. John's, Newfoundland, to the headquarters of Sam Bronfman's Distillers Corporation–Seagrams Limited.

Zaneth found he had to define a brand new skill, what in the 1990s would be called tracing laundered money. Canadian bankers, accountants and bootleggers pioneered the laundering of money in the late 1920s and 1930s.

Drugs were headline news then, as now. Cocaine was big in the Roaring Twenties, then that expensive drug almost disappeared during the Hungry Thirties. Morphine and opium were common narcotics; the use of heroin was beginning. In the 1930s, the newly amalgamated crime syndicate turned from bootleg booze to drugs. The Mob was importing heroin, opium and morphine from Paris and selling them on the streets of New York. It was Zaneth who set out to break up the first "French Connection."

Secret files reveal that in 1938, as Canadians joined the Mackenzie-Papineau Battalion to fight in Spain, Zaneth was the investigator in another attempt to round up Communist Party leaders — most of the men doing the recruiting.

With Canada again in constitutional difficulties after the death of the Meech Lake constitutional accord, a new nationalist party *Bloc Québécois* sits in the House of Commons. At the time of Canada's conscription crisis in the Second World War, some anti-conscription Quebec MPS and MLAS broke with the mainstream parties to form *Bloc Populaire*. Zaneth commanded the Mounties in the midst of a draft riot in Drummondville. Later, in the House and the Quebec legislature, nationalist politicians made racist attacks on Frank Zaneth.

Zaneth's name seldom appears in the official histories of the Royal Canadian Mounted Police. Most of his operations remained secret until the passage of the Access to the Information Act. He was an intensely private man; little is known of how he spent his hours when he was not working.

The Mounties who track and intercept drug smugglers in the 1990s and go after Canada's organized crime bosses may never have heard of Frank Zaneth. But the struggle against crime in Canada today owes much of its success to the man who began the fight in the streets of the 1920s then passed on what he knew to new generations of Mounties.

This is Frank Zaneth's casebook.

CHAPTER ONE

Frank Zaneth and the Royal North-West Mounted Police

IN THE FALL OF 1917, the headquarters of the Royal North-West Mounted Police (RNWMP) just outside the prairie city of Regina, Saskatchewan, received a letter:

> Springfield, Mass U.S.A.
> Sept. 28 — 1917
>
> As I would like to be a member of the RNWMP of Canada, I whish you would be so kind to answer me, givin' full particulars.
>
> your oblige
> Frank W. Zaneth
> 128 Eastern Ave.
>
> Springfield Mass
> U.S.A.

Canada had been at war in Europe for three years; the RNWMP was facing a shortage of manpower. An application form was mailed to Springfield on October 2.

Within days, Frank Zaneth sent a second letter asking if there would be a problem about his height; he was about five feet six inches tall. In reply, the adjutant of the RNWMP told him "the matter of your height would not hinder you from being engaged in this Force, provided your references are satisfactory."

The references were apparently satisfactory; the next step was a character check by the Regina District of the RNWMP. That, too, went well. On November 14, 1917, Frank Zaneth was notified that if he reported to Regina "at his own expense" he would be engaged.

Franco Zanetti was born in Gombolo, in Pavia, southwest of Milan, on December 2, 1890, the son of Ambrogio Zanetti, a cabinetmaker, and Christina Carnevali Zanetti. He had three younger sisters, Rose, Angelina, and Josephine.

In 1899, with his older brother, Alfredo, the small boy left the poor village and set out, with thousands of others, for the United States.

Eventually, the boys ended up in Springfield, Massachusetts. The city, home of the famed Springfield Rifle, was an industrial town and railhead west of Boston in a valley carved by the Connecticut River. At the turn of the century, Springfield was "the industrial beehive of Massachusetts": as well as pistols, rifles and ammunition, factories produced candy and chocolate, miles of wire and millions of matches; *Good Housekeeping* was published there.[1]

In 1903, more than four thousand Italians were living in Springfield. Most crammed into the city's South End, an immigrant slum of overcrowded, neglected buildings where, it was said, the police were reluctant to patrol. Most of the Italian immigrants were quickly graduating from laborers' jobs to more lucrative and skilled employment in local industry.

The Zanetti brothers liked Springfield and decided to stay, but back in Gombolo, their mother thought the adventure had gone far enough. She set out to bring Franco and Alfredo home. Christina brought the three small girls on the voyage across the Atlantic to Springfield, but Franco and Alfredo refused to leave. Christina decided that if her two sons were not going to return to Italy, she would stay in America. Ambrogio, joined the family in Springfield in 1905.

Ambrose, as he called himself, soon found a demand for his carpentry skills. He became a leader in his neighborhood and a member of the Italian-American Citizens Club. He joined the local volunteer fire brigade. Alfredo — Freddie, as he was called by his American neighbors — started a confectionery store on Eastern Avenue. The family lived around the corner in a house on Tyler Street.*

Franco became Frank, got a job as a clerk and learned on the job. He was a clever young man, bright, a quick study, with a head for languages. He liked books and read whatever he could get his hands on. For a while, Frank worked in Freddie's confectionery store, but the spirit of adventure that first took him from Italy was still calling. In 1910, Frank eloped. Franco Enrico Zanetti ran away with Margaret ("Rita") Scevola-Ruscellotti, a young woman originally from Pavia and they were married by a justice of the peace in Hartford, Connecticut, on June 15, 1910.

A year later, when Frank Zanetti was twenty-one, his chance came to get away from stacking lettuce. A Canadian citizen named Ernesto Cotti arrived in Springfield. Cotti had been a lawyer in Italy, he had come to Canada and settled in a town called Moose Jaw, in the heart of the Canadian prairie in Saskatchewan, "The Last Best West." Both the Canadian government and the Canadian Pacific Railway advertised that the prairie was wide open to the land-hungry settler. Cotti told the Italians crammed into the crowded, smoky American city, that in Canada, there was a chance to own a farm. A CPR booklet

---

* Josephine Zanetti's son, Bill Rivers, remembers his grandfather Ambrose as a quiet man, a good cabinetmaker, a very neat man who wore a white shirt and white coveralls when most working men wore blue denim. "He was an old country sort, stern," Rivers said. "He spoke Italian in the house, he didn't speak English hardly at all. I remember him as tall and lean, with a moustache and glasses. But then I was young and small. He was a soft-spoken man, a quiet man, but then all the Zanettis were soft-spoken. I saw him as stern because in those days you respected your elders when you were a kid.

"I was closer to my grandmother . . . she tried, at least, to speak English and she spoke some . . . I remember her as a small woman with glasses."

said the Dominion Land Office in Moose Jaw had twenty-three million acres available for an entry fee of ten dollars.

From Springfield came Frank and Rita Zanetti and half dozen more Italian families. Under the Dominion Lands Act, passed in 1872, a homesteader could get an "entry" on a quarter section of land, 160 acres, by paying ten dollars, by staying on the land for six months and by cultivating ten acres each year for the next three years. To receive title to the land, the homesteader had to be a British subject by birth or naturalization. The law was convenient, for it took three years of residency to become a naturalized British subject "within Canada"[2] and to learn enough English to satisfy a judge.

On April 1, 1911,[3] the new immigrants took the train north from Springfield to Montreal, then went west. There were no Pullman berths, just Colonial cars that had benches with no upholstery and a common stove for cooking.

The prospective settlers from Massachusetts arrived in Moose Jaw at the height of the city's boom times. As Frank Zanetti joined the crowds lining up outside the Dominion Lands Office, he spotted something he had come to Moose Jaw to see. Cowboys in wide-brimmed Stetsons, riding boots, vest and leather chaps were clomping along the boardwalks and riding saddle horses down River Street.

Frank Zanetti needed a job until he found his homestead. He became a cowboy. Range land was just beginning to be divided into homesteads and the city was surrounded by ranches whose income came from raising work horses for homesteaders. Each spread had a core of owned acreage, but the stock also grazed on land leased from homesteaders or on unclaimed land. Colts were free to roam for three to four years before being corralled, roped, thrown, branded and saddle broken.

Just east of Moose Jaw, the green, flat prairie gradually turned into small hills and gullies. To the south, near the lakes, the hills were large and rolling. Johnston Lake (now called Old Wives Lake) was then a large salt lake, with ample wetlands for ducks. The Italian settlers from Springfield set down their stakes on the shores of the lake.

On June 18, 1912, Frank Zanetti filed an application for entry on a homestead using the system surveyors used to divide the prairie into squares. His homestead was on the southeast quarter, Section Number 19, in Township 14, on the twenty-eighth range west of the Second Meridian. He also filed a "preemption," or reservation on the neighboring quarter section to the east.[4]

The application listed Frank Zanetti as a United States citizen and said he was accompanied by a wife and a child.[5] The family had been living on the site, three and a half miles north of Johnston Lake, since November, 1911.

To the north and east was a large ranch belonging to William "Billy" Howes. It covered almost four complete sections plus leased lands. To the east was the two and a half section ranch belonging to Patrick Henry "Paddy" Doyle.

Paddy Doyle was an adventurer who liked to tell tales of his days as a Mountie. He had left County Wexford, Ireland, worked as a farmhand in Ontario, then joined the NWMP in October 1885. Doyle spent part of his first winter in a tent near Moose Jaw, temperatures dropped to forty degrees below zero Fahrenheit. The most memorable moment of his nine years in the force came when he was standing guard duty the day the rebel Louis Riel was hanged.

After he purchased his discharge in 1895, Doyle settled on his ranch, married and became a leader of the community. He supervised the building of the area's first school in 1910. Doyle introduced Frank Zanetti to the tales of the adventurous life in the Royal North-West Mounted Police.

In the summer of 1912, Frank Zanetti broke ten acres of land. It was a hard job; the land chosen by Ernesto Cotti for the "Italian colony" was poor farming country.* Zanetti built a

---

* Paddy Doyle's daughter, Kathleen McGinn, just into her teens in those days, later remembered, "We called it the Hills, the Hills are ranching country. All the homesteader had to do was build a little shack and have a couple of animals. A lot of them only stayed a little while. It was mostly grassland, it wasn't fit for farming . . . My dad used to say it was crazy to come up here to farm . . . It was darn hard, plowing, going up and down a

house, ten feet by twelve feet, out of lumber which cost him $115. He also erected a stable, at a cost of $90 and dug a well — its materials cost $25. In the spring and fall, as required by law, he worked the homestead, breaking another fifteen acres in 1913 and cropping all twenty-five.

During the summer of 1913, he worked for a rancher named Thomas Linton, whose spread was five miles to the east, and bought a brown gelding horse from another ranch hand for twenty-five dollars.

Moose Jaw, the nearest town, was called "Regina's Red Light District." It was a wild town of land speculators, cowboys, and new settlers, as well as a stop for railwaymen from both the CPR and the Soo Line. River Street was lined with hotels, well stocked with whiskey and "saleswomen" who waved in customers from upper-storey windows. Clubs such as the Colonial and Pipeline Johnson's offered draw and stud poker and black-jack. The clergy and the temperance movement called Moose Jaw the "Sodom and Gomorrah of the prairies."

Frank Zanetti's homestead was twenty miles to the east, but for a man on a horse, it wasn't too hard to get into town. In Moose Jaw, Zanetti found he was a natural at poker and first mixed with underworld characters.

In November 1913, a tall, broad-shouldered stranger with a small black mustache and a heavy red lumberman's coat arrived in Moose Jaw. He said his name was Dr. Feltas and announced he was going to set up a practice. He offered to coach wrestling at the local YMCA.

If there was one thing Frank Zanetti loved, it was wrestling. He became a fanatical follower of the sport. It is probable that he spent many hours watching or even participating in the matches. Other wrestlers were off-duty members of the city police force whose lessons were paid for by the city council.

---

hill and around . . . You couldn't make a good living at it, so most of them got the heck out unless they had stock."

McGinn was interviewed in Calgary during the summer of 1989 at age 90.

On New Year's Day, 1914, the people of Moose Jaw awoke after their celebrations to a startling headline in the Moose Jaw *Evening News*: 'DOCTOR' FELTAS WAS A PRIVATE POLICE DETECTIVE ENGAGED BY CITY COUNCIL. It turned out that Feltas was employed by Pinkertons National Detective Agency. He had worked successfully in Moose Jaw for six weeks until December 16, 1913, when the local police chief had found out from his barber that Feltas was a Pink. (The report did not say how the barber knew.) "His disguise even down to a well-worn pair of wrestling tights was complete," the *Evening News* reported, "he was no mean opponent, but one well versed in the game."

The mayor had hired Winnipeg's Central Detective Service, a Pinkerton franchise, because the mayor and council had suspected that the police were lax in protecting citizens and businesses and spent most of their efforts patrolling the money-making red light district. The Pinkerton report[6] cleared the police and told the council "the city of Moose Jaw seemed to be as free of criminals . . . as the average city in the Northwest."

In 1914, Frank Zanetti broke another fifteen acres and planted forty acres. He also worked for Billy Howes, and his son, Fred, another rancher.

War came in the late summer of 1914. Many homesteaders left the hills around Moose Jaw to enlist in the Canadian Expeditionary Force and follow the colors to France. Among those who volunteered and died for his new country was Ernesto Cotti, the man who had brought the Italians from Springfield to Johnston Lake.

Frank Zanetti stayed in Canada and on January 7, 1915, became a naturalized British subject. That spring he planted a forty-acre crop and on June 23, almost three years after his arrival at Johnston Lake, he applied for the patent on the homestead land. His friends from Springfield acted as witnesses to swear that he had cleared and planted the land. The patent was granted on February 8, 1916.

But with the grant of the land comes a mystery. In his application for the patent, Frank Zanetti lists himself as single.

Apparently Rita had returned to Springfield. Perhaps she could not face the harsh life on the Canadian prairie.

In 1917, the boom ended. The prairie moved into a cycle of drought. By the fall of 1917, Frank Zanetti was back in Springfield and he mailed his brief letter of application to the Royal North-West Mounted Police.

He arrived in Regina in the cold of the prairie winter, with a new name — Frank Zaneth. Zaneth's younger sister Josephine, would recall years later that someone had once looked at her brother's scrawled "Zanetti" signature and pronounced it "Zaneth." Frank had decided that was the name that would fit best on the day he applied to join the still very British RNWMP.

The headquarters of the Royal North-West Mounted Police was at Depot Division, in the flat, snow-covered prairie west of Regina. Solid, confident Victorian brick buildings had risen out of the windswept grassland; a headquarters, mess hall, stables and indoor riding school.

On December 5, 1917, Zaneth was ushered in to meet the adjutant for the interview. Zaneth, the interviewing inspector saw, glancing between the man and the form on the desk, was as short as he had described himself in the application. The surgeon had fixed his height at five feet, five and three quarter inches. Zaneth was twenty-eight years old, weighed 146 pounds, was muscular, with brown hair, brown eyes and a fair complexion. He said he was a member of the Church of England. His next of kin was listed as his father, Ambrose Zaneth, of Tyler Street, Springfield, Massachusetts.* Frank Zaneth's English, in his speech, his letters, and in the essay he wrote before the interview was awkward, ungrammatical and misspelled. His command of French and other languages and

---

* There was one thing Frank Zaneth did not tell the RNWMP — that he was married. Since 1877, the RNWMP had refused to enrol married men. That rule had been suspended in 1914, at the start of the war, but it was well known that the senior officers of the force frowned on married men.

the fact that he could ride a horse, seemed scant qualifications for the elite force. Nevertheless, the inspector gave Zaneth the usual lecture: life in the force was hard, hours were long, the pay was low — $1.25 a day. The RNWMP was a mounted constabulary, a British idea, and took its traditions and discipline from the cavalry.

Zaneth agreed to the conditions and took the RNWMP's traditional oath of office: "I will well and truly obey and perform all lawful orders and instructions which I shall receive as such without fear, favour or affection of, or toward, any person. So help me God."[7] He was now a member of the Royal North-West Mounted Police, Regimental No. 6743.

Zaneth was thrown into the life (always "on the double") of a recruit. He was issued a uniform of stable trousers, Sam Browne belt, spurs and lanyard, a Lee-Enfield rifle and a Colt .45, but no ammunition. The famous red serge of the Mounties would wait until Zaneth had finished his training and had proven he could wear it. The recruits lived in chilly bell tents; they were drilled daily, and endured fatigue, stable-guard and firearms training. There were a few lectures from training officers on the Criminal Code of Canada, on the duties and responsibilities of police constables and the rules of evidence. There were also formal and informal talks from retired Mounties on what the force had done during the past forty-four years.

After about three months, Frank Zaneth was considered worthy of parading for the first time in the red serge uniform of the Royal North-West Mounted Police.

Then Constable Frank Zaneth was paraded again, this time before the commissioner of the force, A. Bowen Perry. Even in a force as small as the Royal North-West Mounted Police, it was unusual for a recruit constable to have any access to the Commissioner, a tall, dignified, imposing man with a neatly trimmed white military moustache.

The Commissioner told Zaneth that he was the first man specially recruited for the new Royal North-West Mounted Police "Secret Service." Perry personally commanded the new Secret Service; Zaneth would be reporting to Perry.

Perry was the opposite of Zaneth. He was born in Lennox, Ontario, in 1860 and entered Royal Military College in Kingston at sixteen. He had joined the North-West Mounted Police in 1882 and served with many of the heroes of the Mounties' early prairie days. He was chosen to lead the NWMP contingent to Queen Victoria's Diamond Jubilee in 1897, and in 1899, commanded Mountie contingent in the Yukon Territory at the height of the Klondike Gold Rush.

He was named commissioner in 1900 and began to transform the force from a frontier peacekeeping body into a police force. He confirmed the Stetson that most men already wore instead of the cavalry helmet. He founded a Detective Division to handle complicated criminal investigations.

In 1914, when Britain automatically brought Canada into the war, Perry had been handed new responsibilities, what today would be called national security tasks, or in those days called secret service work. It would be the job of the RNWMP to keep an eye on the 173,568 Germans and Austrians living on the Canadian West. The British immigrants thought of the Germans, Austrians and even Ukrainians as the hated "alien enemy."

In the spring of 1918, when Frank Zaneth finished his basic training, the term Secret Service, at least in North America, was a general one, and applied to any person or organization that did ad hoc undercover work for a government. It could mean the police, military intelligence or private detective agencies such as Pinkertons. Domestic security in Canada was split among the RNWMP, the Dominion Police — a federal police force based in Ottawa* — and the Military Intelligence

---

* The Dominion Police did secret service work — Sir John A. Macdonald had used its agents to watch the Fenians, Irish rebels who invaded Canada from the U.S. in the 1870s. In many ways, the Dominion Police mirrored its counterpart south of the border, the United States Secret Service. Dominion Police duties included enforcement of counterfeiting laws and white slave statutes, investigation of postal thefts and protection of government officials on the few times it was necessary in Canada. In later years, the Dominion Police maintained the national fingerprint files and

Division of the Militia Department.[8]

In the spring of 1918, Canada was in the midst of a political crisis over conscription, a crisis that became violent. There were riots in Quebec City. Perry sent Frank Zaneth east; his job was to hang around with the young men of the city, looking for draft evaders and checking out the rumor that many Québécois had fled to the Laurentians, armed and ready to resist the Dominion Police. Zaneth's first attempt at undercover work was a success — he was able to arrest some draft evaders.

For a time, security work was confined to investigating German "plots" and keeping an eye on the "alien enemy." In Ottawa, the government was becoming worried. The Bolsheviks had taken power in Russia in the fall of 1917; in North America unrest was growing as the war drew to an end. The cost of living was rising while wages were going down; yet, employers were reaping huge profits from the war. Strikers could be conscripted but labor leaders were talking about a general strike. A few, the more radical, spoke of bringing the Russian revolution to North America. To fight these threats, Prime Minister Robert Borden's cabinet decided to beef up the Secret Service.

In July, Perry received reports of trouble in the Drumheller coal fields in Alberta. Drumheller was one of the radical spots that the RNWMP had to watch; there had been a strike there in May 1917, and a second, more serious wildcat strike in February 1918. Coal was a key strategic commodity that fuelled the war effort.

A Presbyterian missionary in Drumheller had complained to Ottawa that the leaders of the mine unions were "undesirables," "agitators" and "fomenters of trouble." A uniformed constable was sent to Drumheller to check out the complaint

---

administered the paroled prisoners branch. With the outbreak of the First World War, the Dominion Police was put in charge of "Supervision and regulation of Enemy Aliens" as well as enforcement of the War Measures Act and conscription across the country. In this they duplicated the RNWMP duties in the West.

and reported that five of the union leaders were suspected of being members of the Industrial Workers of the World, the Wobblies.[9]

Giving voice to the xenophobia and racism of the day, the constable reported, "It would seem to the mine operators, and the loyal citizens of the district that the IWWS, the aliens of enemy nationality and the disloyal members of the miners unions, mean to tie up the mines."

The officer commanding* in Calgary, Inspector C.C. Raven, recommended sending to Drumheller plainclothes men who could understand foreign languages. Instead, in August, Perry ordered Inspector Raven to go to the valley and take a look himself.[10]

Raven found trouble, but no outside agitators. His report challenged the conventional wisdom that foreigners, the "alien enemy" were behind the trouble: "The men suspected of being agitators in this district are not 'unnaturalized enemy aliens.'" One, Tony Cacchioni, a leader of the United Mineworkers Union was an Italian (in the war, Italy was an ally). Another leader had been born of Russian parents near Leduc, Alberta. Many were English-speaking men and "not of alien enemy nationality or descent." Raven again repeated his recommendation that an undercover agent was needed:

The nationalities of the employees of the Drumheller area include Italians, Russians, English, Canadians and Americans, but the great majority are Austrians, who speak Gallician, Bukowynian and other Slavic dialects . . . the Italians and IWW English-speaking men are the agitators. The few Russians** there are becoming more troublesome all the time . . . If a secret agent was sent into this district, his best method would be obtain employment in the mine and attend the Union meetings; he should be able to speak

---

* The standard RNWMP and RCMP term for the commanding officer.
** In those days, the term "Russian" was generally used by those of British background to refer to people from what is today Ukraine.

Gallician . . . The agitators must influence the majority of the miners who speak Gallician before they could bring on a strike.

On September 12, 1918, Frank Zaneth was once more facing the Commissioner of the RNWMP in his office in Regina.

Perry ordered a more experienced officer, Constable O.N. Nold to go to the Rosedale mine, where trouble was expected to start, and decided he would send Zaneth to Drumheller. If the young constable kept his eyes open, he might find out something, and Perry would learn whether the recruit was worth keeping for the new secret service.

Together, the constable and the commissioner created a cover story. Zaneth would pretend to be a man from the border between Italy and the Austro-Hungarian Empire, so he could mix and talk to the Italian radicals and the Gallician Austrians.

"Harry Blask" was conceived. Born in a nameless village in the Austrian Piedmont, (the border country on the other side of northern Italy from Gombolo); he had lived for a while in Trieste, then part of the Austro-Hungarian Empire, then immigrated to the United States. There he had become a member of the Industrial Workers of the World. He'd come north to help the IWW in Canada.

Perry handed Zaneth a red IWW membership card, confiscated from a prisoner. There were other bureaucratic necessities: an exemption for Harry Blask from the Military Service Act and the registration as a paroled enemy alien which permitted him to travel.

"Keep a sharp lookout for IWWs," Perry told Zaneth.

Zaneth took the CPR west from Regina to Calgary, where he caught the Canadian Northern Railway for Drumheller. The train headed northeast through level farm and ranch country little different from the Saskatchewan prairie. Soon a deep gash cracked the prairie; the train descended into the badlands along the Rosebud River, crossing drumming wooden bridges at each curve of the river and then entered the Drumheller valley.

The river had carved the hills into cake layers of grayish-white sandstone, dull pale brown mudstone, darker volcanic ash and black or sooty-gray seams of coal. There were small mines and villages strung along the valley — Drumheller, Midland, Newcastle, Wayne, Rosedale, Nacmine, East Coulee, and Sunshine.

Drumheller was little more than a line of shacks and huts scattered around the long, stilted tipples that loaded the coal from the mines into railway hopper cars. Trees were scarce in the Red Deer Valley. Some poplar and willows grew along the riverbank, and there were spruce on the upper cliffs. In between were gray-green sage and tough prairie grasses.

The first step was easy: Harry Blask, a paroled enemy alien, had to report to the local RNWMP detachment, a neat, white-painted shack beside the public library, an almost identical shack, on one of the main streets.

The Drumheller detachment would know nothing, of course, of Zaneth's presence in the valley. His orders were to forward his reports secretly to Calgary, where they would be picked up by Superintendent Fitz Horrigan.

After the corporal in command completed a routine check, Harry Blask went looking for work. That too was simple. Unlike British Columbia and some states, Alberta had no laws demanding skilled qualifications from miners.

Two men in the valley were suspected of being members of the Industrial Workers of the World. One was R.L. Bradshaw, secretary of the United Mine Workers district local in Drumheller; the other was Tony Cacchioni, the local president of the miners in Wayne, a couple of miles downriver. The two men had led the valley-wide wildcat strike in February 1918, which had been aimed at organizing the nonunion Rosedale mine. The volatile manager and co-owner, James Moodie, had refused to recognize the United Mine Workers.

Moodie had demanded that the RNWMP protect him from a mob of union members. Inspector Henry Newson had arrived from Calgary on February 2 to find Moodie, his brother and his foremen, all armed, on a bridge facing Cacchioni and two hundred angry union miners who were yelling "Kill Moodie" and who were determined to cross the river. Moodie had drawn a line in the dirt (a "deadline") and threatened to shoot anyone who crossed it. Newson used his British aplomb to calm the crowd, and they dispersed after accepting an offer to send a delegation to negotiate with Moodie. Moodie still refused to talk and workers at every mine in the valley walked out. The RNWMP in Calgary sent sixteen reinforcements and a machine gun, which caused a political storm until Ottawa ordered it removed.

The Calgary *Herald* had printed a telegram from Cacchioni that told his side of the story. "We have laid down our tools in a just cause and we will not resume work until justice and right is obtained in this barbaric land, where any owner of a concern or monopoly can arrest and beat a peaceable working man."

The RNWMP saw things differently, Superintendent Horrigan wrote to Commissioner Perry recommending action against Cacchioni for voicing his opinion, "Would it be possible to proceed against this man for making a statement calling this 'a barbaric land?'"

Zaneth's first target was the Western Gem Mine. Harry Blask was introduced to the miners' wood frame bunkhouse, locally dubbed the "chicken coop." It was overcrowded, with thirty to sixty men crammed into a single room. A typical bunkhouse might have four hundred square feet, so each man had about fourteen square feet, just enough for a rickety bunkbed. The bunkhouse would have an outside pump, a wash pail, two wash basins, one door, one stove and no ventilation.[11]

Blask quickly discovered that work in the mines was dark, hard, dirty and dangerous. He was assigned to a "room" where the coal was dug. It ran off a "gangway," a passage, with rail tracks for the coal cars, leading from the rooms to the entry. There were two coal seams at the Western Gem. The top seam, five feet, nine inches thick, was being worked.

Harry Blask was assigned a partner, working a face, on alternative shifts. The day shift began at 7:30. At the start of the shift, Blask checked the air for signs of methane, coal gas, and coal dust, which could be explosive and caused black lung disease. When he arrived at his room, Blask had to clean up any loose coal and rubble left over from the previous shift, and then he began the job of filling the coal car.

Blask had to learn how to set explosive powder to blast the coal out of the seam. (If the blast was too large and the coal fell below a minimum size set by the company, he didn't get paid.) He then had to shovel the coal into a small iron-bound wooden car, three feet by six feet, or carry the coal back to the end of the rails and pile it up until a car arrived. If there was no car, Blask had to walk back along the entry to find drivers. The miners always complained that the drivers were loafing around, not bringing the cars back down.

On a typical day Harry Blask loaded eight cars of coal plus one of scrap rock. He also had to drill and shoot two six foot holes and put up two sets of timbers. On another day, he might load the usual number of cars and spend most of his time putting down twenty feet of new rail.

Blask discovered his pay depended on the United Mine Workers checkweighman, the union official who checked the weight of each car of coal when it reached the surface. The checkweighman, like Tony Cacchioni at Wayne, usually also had a top job in the union local and was involved in any disputes over weight or pay. The miners had to pay the salaries of the checkweighman and the company doctor (if there was one) as well as buying their own blasting powder.

Moodie had reluctantly recognized the UMW at Rosedale in the late spring of 1918. The hourly rate there for top rated miners ranged from $1.27 to $1.91 an hour, a good wage for those days. Most of the UMW mines in the valley paid hourly wages, but at some mines, pay for the miners was still dependent on how much coal they dug and got out of the mine, not how many hours they worked. Custom had considered the miner to be a skilled independent contractor, but the United Mine Workers were trying to change the custom.

Wages at the Western Gem, also a union mine, were probably comparable. Harry Blask made more in two hours than Frank Zaneth did in a day. Constable Zaneth was earning $1.25 a day plus a $1.00 a day plainclothes allowance. The RNWMP had ordered Zaneth to turn over to the Crown the difference between his government wage and the miner's salary. Apart from a small expense allowance to help him "get acquainted" with sources of information, Blask's wages money went off to Calgary.*

In Drumheller, most of the radical talk in the bunkhouses came from Great Britain, where unions had first organized semi-skilled workers. Attempts to stop union organizers had led to the founding of the British Labour Party. The "aliens" had some socialist, anarchist or syndicalist ideas of their own, but the most subversive were coming from the mother country.

It was a year after the successful Russian Revolution and the beginning of the Red Scare in North America. In Ottawa, on Wednesday, September 25, the Cabinet used the War Measures Act to forbid the use of fourteen languages considered to be "enemy alien." Three days later, a second order outlawed fourteen associations, including the IWW and the Socialist Party of Canada.

That Saturday, Zaneth attended his first meeting of Local 1746 of the United Mine Workers, chaired by local president Tom Broadhurst and the radical secretary R.L. Bradshaw. After the February strike, more moderate miners had split away from the militant local. An RNWMP intelligence report had noted that "the white or English speaking element have broken away and formed two other Locals . . . and these are recognized by the operators." Zaneth sat at the back of the room and scribbled notes in a little notebook.

Broadhurst and Bradshaw needed the support of the other locals for a strike, to force the mine owners to recognize the original local, 1746. The companies were not paying the union dues withheld from miners' pay to Local 1746, perhaps in hope of boosting the moderate faction.

---

* The loss of that hard-earned money was something Frank Zaneth would always remember. He would mention it in a rare newspaper interview years later and it was one of the few stories he told after he retired.

"We have been played long enough by these coal operators and it's come the time when we must take sudden actions," Broadhurst said. "If our brothers in other mining camps are willing to stand by us, we will not give them two hours notice."

Broadhurst tried to convince the miners to ignore the threat that strikers could be drafted under the Military Service Act. If that happened, Broadhurst warned, "we will throw down our tools and put every mine in the country idle and if they do take one of us they must take us all." The meeting was adjourned until the next night.

On Sunday, Harry Smith, checkweighman at the Rosedale mine, called on the miners to strike at the Western Gem, as a means of gauging the reaction of the coal operators. The miners agreed to walk out the next morning.

That night, Zaneth found a private spot to write his report. He told his superiors that the strike was really an attempt by the radical local to regain prominence in the valley.

He mailed the report to the Calgary detachment. Typed copies were sent from Calgary to the Commissioner in Regina. Perry then sent one directly to Newton W. Rowell, president of the Privy Council in Ottawa.

On Monday, September 30, miners at the Western Gem walked out on strike. None of the other mines followed. Blask met Bradshaw on the picket line outside the mine (Blask was "cultivating his acquaintance").

The owners of the Western Gem quickly settled, agreeing to pay dues to Local 1746 "under protest" until the United Mine Workers sorted the matter out. Work resumed in the mine a few days later.

Union politics dominated the meeting on October 13. Three officers of the United Mine Workers tried to solve the problem of competing locals, but they were faced a more urgent problem. On Friday, October 11, the Borden government had passed an order-in-council under the War Measures Act. Strikes were banned, and heavy jail sentences and fines were imposed for anyone who walked off the job. Some of the Conservatives who made up the Cabinet, and especially a key adviser to Borden named C.H. Cahan, believed that revolutionaries were behind the growing labor unrest in the country.

The events of that week allowed Blask to get closer to Bradshaw, who chaired secret meetings of the most radical miners at the back of "the premises of a Jewish tailor in the center of Drumheller." Bradshaw gave Blask some copies of the IWW literature, which Zaneth in turn passed on to his superiors in Calgary. Most important, Bradshaw taught him the secret IWW "grip." Zaneth's cover was now complete.

Zaneth's second target was Cacchioni, the outspoken radical president of the UMW local at the Wayne mine. The young RNWMP constable was perhaps made over confident by his first success with Bradshaw. The account of what happened when Cacchioni invited Harry Blask to his miner's hut in Wayne for a meal of macaroni is based on Cacchioni's account; Zaneth's report has not survived.

The macaroni was as famous in the Drumheller valley as were its creator's fiery outbursts. Blask accepted the invitation. There was a little bootleg wine. During the evening, Blask pulled out the red IWW card and asked Cacchioni point-blank, "You were in the IWW were you not?"

Zaneth had overplayed the hand. He had the card, knew the grip, but did not show the caution the IWW members had learned south of the border, after years of infiltration by police and Pinkerton agents.

"Nothing doing, I never was and never will be," Cacchioni replied and decided he should find out more about this man who said he was a Wobbly.

The talk turned to Italy, and Zaneth, perhaps confused at first, soon recovered. His accent became rougher, and Cacchioni jumped at that. Harry Blask admitted he was not really Italian, that he was from Trieste, still part of the Austrian Empire, and said he had served for a while during the war in Tripoli.

By the end of the evening, Cacchioni had apparently decided that Blask was too dumb to worry about; at least he didn't communicate his suspicions to anyone. Harry Blask continued to be an active and welcome member of the radical movement.

In late October, Nold was ordered back to Regina. Zaneth became the only RNWMP operative in Drumheller. The situation in Drumheller had become clearer: while there was a core of radicals, their focus was on local conditions and internal disputes.* The Commissioner had more pressing problems. A squadron of RNWMP cavalry, six officers and 184 men, was preparing to leave for Siberia, as the Allies intervened in the Bolshevik Revolution. The RNWMP had shrunk to 303 men, ten divisional posts and twenty-six detachments, thirteen of them in the Yukon and the Northwest Territories. All that was left in the south were a border patrol, the old, and the few men in the Secret Service.

While the miners at Western Gem had been fighting over internal problems, Cacchioni's men at Wayne had been demanding a company doctor, something that was badly needed in Drumheller by late October 1918. The worldwide Spanish influenza epidemic arrived on the Canadian Northern coal trains and was spreading rapidly through the overcrowded bunkhouses. Mine operations slowed to a crawl, only a few men were fit enough to run the pump houses that kept the mines dry and the powerhouses that supplied electricity. There was a wild rumor among the immigrant miners; it was not influenza, they said. It was, they believed, the Black Death, which had been the scourge of Europe again and again.

By early November, ninety men were sick at the Rosedale colliery. Zaneth, probably sick himself, filed a brief report to Calgary noting that all meetings had been cancelled because of the flu. There were just two doctors and they were stretched to

---

* Perry had received a letter from Moodie the read in part:

Re Harry Smith, Checkweighman, at Rosedale.
Can we not have something done regarding this man? It is next to impossible to carry on operations successfully with this man in a position to interfere with the miners.

The memo went on for two pages. It seemed the mine owner viewed the RNWMP as his private union busting agency.

36

the limit. Fanny Ramsley, the local madam, one of the few black people in the valley, toured the mining camps, giving what nursing aid she could and helping the sick with a shot of her best bootleg whiskey. The self-appointed doctor at Rosedale was James Moodie, who went from hut to hut or to the quarantine bunkhouse with food and medicine and advice for the sick.

Then, on the morning of November 11, the telegraph clattered at the station. The War to End All Wars had come to an end. That night bonfires blazed along the cliff tops.

The epidemic continued, slowed, then resumed. Toward the middle of December, the first returned soldiers began to drift into the valley. They demanded that the Austrian and Ukrainian miners be fired so veterans could get jobs. Within days a lot of the "foreign element" in the valley were on a wildcat strike, while the "English-speaking men" (few of them veterans) were hard at work. The war was over, so the supply of coal was no longer a national security issue.[12] The growth of Bolshevism was.

Zaneth was ordered to move on into the Rockies to make a routine intelligence check on the radical miners at Canmore in Rocky Mountain Park, the five thousand square mile park created by the government in 1912 that included the towns of Banff, Canmore, and Jasper. There were two coal mines in the park, one at Bankhead, near Banff, and a second at Canmore, owned by the Canadian Pacific Railway. The miners at Canmore and Bankhead were militant, and relations with the CPR were poor. There had been strikes in 1907, 1909, 1911 and 1916. Many of the miners were Italians; others were from Central Europe. Harry Blask would fit in at a miners meeting.

With the end of the war, government and public attention turned to the problem of Bolshevism. Prices and unemployment were rising; the press was talking about the "Bolsheviki" plans for world revolution and there were stories that V.I. Lenin was sending agents to North America. On December 2, 1918, British intelligence sent a secret telegram to Borden: It had "reliable" information that the Bolsheviks were about to start a propaganda campaign in North America.

The Cabinet ordered an immediate reorganization of Canada's national security agencies. On December 12, by an order in council, the Royal North-West Mounted Police took over policing federal laws and security matters from Thunder Bay to Vancouver. The authorized strength of the force was raised to 1,200 men, and the cavalry contingents were immediately recalled from Europe and Siberia.

On January 1, 1919, Frank Zaneth was officially transferred from Depot Division, Regina, to E Division, in Calgary. Harry Blask's task was not completed, he was still to keep an eye on the radicals. Frank Zaneth's apprenticeship had ended.

CHAPTER TWO

The Calgary Stoolpigeon

THE ROYAL NORTH-WEST MOUNTED POLICE were now after bigger game. In Ottawa, there was a growing fear of a "Red Revolution." The prime target for investigation in the early months of 1919 was the banned Socialist Party of Canada, the SPC. Vancouver, Edmonton and Winnipeg had been identified as centers of radical activity, and a series of labor conventions were planned for Calgary. First the United Mine Workers, then the British Columbia Federation of Labor had moved its convention from Vancouver to Calgary. A large Western Labor Conference was planned for March. Calgary was a vital listening post.

Zaneth's job was to use his IWW credentials to keep an eye on that shadowy group. He also told to become friendly with the socialists. He was assigned an RNWMP controller Corporal S.R. Waugh, who was also undercover on the labor beat.*

The young, eager, versatile, hardworking Harry Blask soon found himself a job as secretary to George Sangster, an iron moulder and a leader of one of the most militant unions in the Canadian west, the International Association of Machinists. Sangster represented machinists, pattern makers, moulders, blacksmiths and their helpers. He was also vice president of the Calgary Trades and Labor Council and a member of the

---

* Almost all of Zaneth's reports to Waugh were oral, transcribed by the corporal and sent to Inspector J.W. Spalding, the officer in charge of the Calgary detachment. See also Afterword.

Socialist Party of Canada. As Sangster's secretary, Blask handled Sangster's correspondence and would be getting his hands on all the radical and subversive literature that was circulating on the prairies. In addition, he would soon get to know all the radical leaders in the province of Alberta.

The Socialist Party of Canada was led by British immigrants and Canadians of British descent who followed unadulterated Marxist doctrine. Party members believed that they should teach the working class about scientific socialism and thus prepare them for the time when "educated" workers would start a revolution. The party appealed to the immigrant miners and factory workers, Italians, Jews, Ukrainians and Slavs and was strongest in Alberta and British Columbia.

Sangster took Zaneth to his first secret meeting of the SPC. The speaker that night was the Reverend William Ivens, a passionate former Methodist preacher who had left his assigned pulpit to found what he called the Labor Church in Winnipeg. Ivens was a strong advocate of labor rights. His church services were based on Methodism combined with an eclectic and radical mixture of Marxism, anthropology and political theory.

Zaneth's report on Iven's lecture to the Socialists may have helped set some wheels in motion or move them faster. Early in January, 1919 the RNWMP set up what they called a Secret Service Department in Winnipeg under the command of Sgt. Albert Reames; the sergeant went undercover each Sunday, to attend Iven's services, sing the hymns and take notes.

In Calgary every Sunday, the Socialist Party had a business meeting, followed by a discussion on Marxist economics, during which converts were taught the basic tenets — that workers had nothing in common with the upper classes and that their doctrine should be "production for use, not production for profit."

Harry Blask was a regular at these party meetings, where he had volunteered sell copies of Socialist books, magazines and pamphlets — *Revolutionary Age*, *The Soviet* (a broadsheet published by the Socialist Party), *The Soviet and the Bolshevik*, *The Soviet at Work* and the *Liberator*.

He also distributed those books and pamphlets that were still banned under the War Measures Act, for example a translation of Lenin's *Political Parties in Russia*. To get around the law, he gave them away, a technically illegal activity that greatly strengthened his cover. Copies of everything found their way to Inspector J.W. Spalding, officer commanding in Calgary.*

In early February, a man dropped in to the Calgary Trades and Labor Council office to see George Sangster. Sangster introduced his secretary, Harry Blask. As they shook hands, Zaneth used the IWW grip he had learned in Drumheller. The grip was returned. "I made it a point to cultivate this man [Name deleted]'s acquaintance, because I knew I could learn from him all that I desire . . . It was not long after meeting [Name deleted] that I had the IWW's in Calgary looking upon me as one of the most active members, due to the fact that I was attending every meeting and supporting their objectives."**

In mid-February, his old colleagues from the mines in Drumheller arrived in Calgary for the United Mine Workers District 18 convention.

One self-appointed delegate was the radical editor of the *District Ledger*, P.F. Lawson, from Fernie, British Columbia. The firebrand Lawson paused to introduce himself to the young man selling literature, became friendly and later chronicled Blask's activities from a radical viewpoint. "Blask was in the convention room every day," Lawson wrote, "and disposed of large numbers of *The Soviet*, *The Red Flag* and other Socialist

---

* Some of the magazines Zaneth sent to Spalding eventually became evidence and are now in the Manitoba Archives. One thick issue of the *Liberator*, (a magazine published in New York) was the Special Eugenics and Havelock Ellis Number, published in February 1919, which included an ad for *The Birth Control Review* a magazine whose goal was the "reconstruction of women through birth control." A back issue from November 1918 contained a report by John Reed, "On Intervention in Russia."

** Three men who said they were members of the IWW in Calgary were Jim Davis, A.H. Bunker, and Samuel Rukin. All three were U.S. citizens. It is not clear from this censored report which of the three men Zaneth is referring to.

literature. He was exceedingly easy to become acquainted with and his ability to talk several languages made it a simple matter for him to converse with the few delegates at the convention of foreign nationality as well with the British born."[13]

On the second day of the convention Zaneth listened in fascination to the oratory of Joe Knight, and though some of the miners may not have agreed with Knight, they listened as he spoke. Knight was an immigrant from England, a carpenter and a leader of the Edmonton Trades and Labor Council. He was a practical Marxist, well versed in theory and at the same time an experienced labor negotiator who believed in the IWW concept of gathering all workers into one big union.

Knight played upon the workers' fear. Unemployment was growing in the winter of 1919 as war industries retooled for peace and returning soldiers demanded jobs. The popular solution among the left was to reduce the work day to six hours. Knight disagreed with this conventional wisdom. He pointed out that as only two members of the Edmonton carpenter's local were employed at the moment, shortening hours wouldn't help much.

The far-seeing Knight zeroed in on the growing competition from Japan and China. Imports of cheap Japanese matches were a threat to E.B. Eddy, the Canadian match manufacturer. If Canada reduced the working day to five or six hours, Knight said, while other countries worked eight hours or more, "under that system by reason of lower cost and greater production of common commodities . . . it seems we must close down the industries within the system."

The answer, Knight said, was Bolshevism. "Reasonableness and moderation" was no good. Only world revolution would help. The mine workers applauded and cheered.*

After a meeting on Friday February 21, Harry Blask got a chance for a chat with Joe Knight.

Socialists must wait for "the falling blow," Knight said. "As

---

* The RNWMP obtained a transcript of the speech, probably from Zaneth. It is now in the Manitoba Archives.

soon as we get the people to understand the psychology of socialism, we will call a general strike."[14]

Despite Knight's eloquence the miners voted in favor of the six-hour day; however, they also sent fraternal greetings to the Soviet government, called for one big industrial organization to represent all workers and endorsed the use of the general strike in deadlocked disputes.

When Zaneth's report reached the Cabinet in Ottawa, it was proof that what they had feared most was about to happen: a Bolshevik revolution in Canada.

In the United Mine Workers election held in Calgary, Phillip Christophers, an outspoken Cornish immigrant and a member of the Socialist Party of Canada, became the president of District 18; but Zaneth's attention was drawn to one of the more charismatic defeated candidates, David Rees. A coal miner based on Vancouver Island and a leader in the movement to increase western Canadian influence in labor movement, Rees had been a delegate to the national Trades and Labor Congress the previous September in Quebec. There it had become clear that whereas the eastern unions wanted a postwar world of union-management cooperation, the western delegates were more radical. Most came from resource industries, where working conditions were often terrible and labor-management relations feudal. They had seen their resolutions defeated again and again. At a caucus, the delegates proposed there be a Western Labor Conference, with Rees as chairman. Rees's aim was to strengthen the western labor movement. The western conference was the product of traditional western Canadian dissatisfaction with domination by the east. But militancy took over and the conference was split before it began between activist but traditional craft union leaders and a growing movement for western secession from the national Trades and Labor Congress.

The Western conference opened on Thursday, March 13 at Calgary's Paget Hall, with 234 accredited delegates in attendance from all across the west. Tony Cacchioni and Harry Smith were there from Drumheller. Harry Blask was one of the

43

hundreds of observers in the hall and hard at work at his usual job of distributing radical literature and keeping his eye on the west's top labor leaders. Rees represented the United Mine Workers from Nanaimo; Joe Knight, the Carpenters Local 1325 in Edmonton; Robert Russell and R.J. Johns represented the Winnipeg Trades and Labor Council; William Pritchard and Jack Kavanagh came from the Vancouver Trades and Labor Council.

Everyone at the conference knew it was the beginning of something. "It was a thrilling and tense period, and blood and thunder and a thousand and one other things all seemed to be mixed up in an atmosphere at one and the same moment," the Calgary *Herald* told its readers that afternoon. At very least, it was expected the western unions could split from the internationals. But the back room strategists had bigger plans.

Moments before the convention was to begin, Rees was on his feet on a point of privilege, pointing at the gallery.[15]

"To come down to brass tacks," Rees thundered, "I want to warn my friends there is a man masquerading here under the name of Smith. At Hillcrest, he was known as Brown and after being there a short time entered the local union . . . he hardly thought it wise for him to come here under that name. The real name of this man is Bob Gosden, and who, in my opinion, is a police spy and stool-pigeon. I would warn the delegates to be guarded as to their statements."

There were shouts to have the man ejected.

Two calmer delegates moved that the man be requested to leave. "It looked pretty ugly for Gosden, who stood up and asked permission to be allowed to make a statement," the *Herald* reported.

Permission was refused. There was a "spirited" debate on the motion, the motion lost and Gosden stayed in the gallery. "We need not be afraid of any Secret Service men," shouted Kavanagh to loud applause.

The Mounties did have an agent at Paget Hall, identified in RNWMP reports only as Agent 10. The RNWMP described Agent 10 as a man who "has for many years taken an active part in

44

the Industrial Workers of the World and kindred associations."
It was probably Gosden, who had a reputation as both a radical
and a stool pigeon.

Rees had lost the fight for moderation. The president of the
Calgary Trades and Labor Council, R.J. Tallon, a member of the
radical machinists union, became chairman of the conference.
Kavanagh, a Vancouver longshoreman originally from Liver-
pool, and chairman of the resolution committee, opened the
first session with a proposal that was to set the tone for the
following days: "Be it resolved that the aims of labor as represented by this convention are the abolition of the present
system of production for profit, and substituting production for
use, and that a system of propaganda to this end be carried on."

Then came another resolution. That the unions sever their
affiliation with the internationals, and form "an industrial
organization of all the workers . . ." That brought heated
debate.

William Pritchard was perhaps the best orator in the labor
movement. He said, "We have been victims of the international
shuffling process long enough but we are not going to have any
more of it." There were questions from the floor. A few delegates demanded "something concrete." Kavanagh promised a
plan before the end of the convention.

When the conference had adjourned for the day, David Rees
and other moderates left for a Mine Workers convention in
Indianapolis. Rees's plan for a strong, independent western
labor movement had been overtaken by the radicals.

The following morning, R.J. Johns of Winnipeg introduced a
series of prepared resolutions calling for an organization to be
called the "One Big Union." After a long debate on the structure
of the union and payment of dues came resolutions and
demands for an end to the restrictions imposed by the War
Measures Act, concluding with a threat:

• That this convention demand full freedom of speech, press
  and assembly and advocate united action by organized labor
  to enforce these demands.

45

- That this convention demand the release of all political prisoners and the removal of all disabilities and restrictions now upon working class organizations.

- That a referendum asking for a general strike to be taken . . . to become effective June 1.

A central committee was named, it included W.A. Pritchard, Joe Knight, A.G. Broach from Calgary and two others.

At the end of the day, Knight picked through the crowd to introduce Harry Blask to Bob Russell of Winnipeg, who had led the machinists union in its drive to bring all metalworkers into the fold. The day ended in a long debate over the role of workers in the so-called "vital industries." Kavanagh defined them as trades that by "ceasing work, compel others to cease by virtue of the fact they cannot carry on without them." He pointed out that in Vancouver, the longshoremen and the metal trades were important. "If the longshoremen at Vancouver, Montreal, Quebec and Halifax ceased work, the CPR would be out of business because their trade is carried from continent to continent. All transport workers come under the head 'basic' . . . If you get a majority of transport workers, the miners and the metal trades, you could force all the others into line." While Kavanagh was perhaps right about the economic clout of the groups, he had also named the most militant unions in western Canada, the ones that would be the main supporters of the One Big Union.

The press had covered the conference, the news quickly reached Ottawa. Apprehension grew in the Cabinet. The reports from Zaneth and Agent 10 were submitted to Mounted Police headquarters in Regina. (Zaneth's has been lost.) Agent 10's report was alarmist. He concluded that the motive of the conference was "to seize the present chaotic conditions resulting from the war to weld together different bodies of labor in a common effort to overthrow the present social order and install a Bolsheviki regime."

He proposed a drastic solution — the RNWMP should arrange for the leaders of the new One Big Union to disappear. "After

46

one or two of these leaders had been picked up at various points in a mysterious manner and disappeared just as mysteriously, the unseen hand would so intimidate the weaker and lesser lights that the agitation would automatically die down; where they were kept in custody, no record should be upon the books."

In Regina, Agent 10's report was first read by a senior officer in the newly formed Criminal Investigation Branch (CIB), which covered both security and criminal investigations. The officer refused to send the report on to the Privy Council in Ottawa, he passed it to Perry. In a memo to the Commissioner, the officer said he found Agent 10's report "considerably over-drawn . . ." assuming as it did, that the men had "actually accomplished something" and the "masses were ready to do their will." He added that in Canada, "private ownership of property by small owners" was so widespread that "if Bolshevik ideas were presented to the public in their true light, there would be unanimous condemnation."

A couple of days after the labor conference, Commissioner Perry requested and was granted a secret meeting with three leaders of the radical movement, including Pritchard and Kavanagh. The men, Perry reported to the Cabinet, were "Rev-olutionary Socialists . . . They are intelligent, well-read men, and are close students of economic and social literature. They acknowledged that they were determined to bring about a revolution in social and economic conditions . . . They stated that the "One Big Union" of labor in western Canada must first be perfected before they could take a forward step. Then they intend to demand a six hour day with the same wages and enforce it by a general strike, which they thought might be possible in June."

Perry suggested a cautious approach. His first recommenda-tion was to not interfere directly against the One Big Union, but instead to strengthen the possible opposition already within the ranks of labor. It would be difficult, despite the demands from some people for the prosecution of "Reds," to secure a conviction for sedition against the One Big Union under current law. In any case, Perry reported to the Cabinet that any arrests would only antagonize moderate labor leaders. The Commissioner noted that there were demands from conservative forces in Canada to suppress what was considered "seditious literature." He said "at present, labor is extremely sensitive as to any interference with free speech and active prosecution may do more harm than good."

In the long term, Perry was pessimistic. If there was a general strike, he believed, the strikers might accept aid from what he called "foreign anarchical societies," which could throw responsibility on "the alien enemy" and spark racial problems across the country.

Perry concluded, "I am forced to discuss the possibility of a successful revolution being accomplished by force."

The key, he believed, was the returned soldiers. The labor agitators realized revolution could only succeed if a considerable number of disaffected soldiers joined the movement; they were trying to draw soldiers in. Perry recommended that the grievances of the returned men be dealt with promptly and that employers should treat soldiers with sympathy.

Perry's report, together with Agent 10's, were received in Ottawa on Saturday, April 12, by the acting prime minister, Finance Minister Sir Thomas White. White also had another document, "A Memorandum on Revolutionary Tendencies in Western Canada," prepared by a civil servant, named C.F. Hamilton. Hamilton, who had been deputy chief censor during the war, believed there was evidence of a plot to set up a Soviet government in Canada, directed and controlled by a group somewhere in Canada.

A month earlier, on the Monday after the end of the Labor Conference, March 17, 1919, Blask was hanging around the Socialist Party offices. A man named Jim Davis came over to introduce himself to Comrade Blask. Over the next couple of days, Blask became very friendly with Davis. Zaneth also passed on detailed reports on their conversations.[16]

"I took part in blowing up a safe in Chicago," Davis boasted to Blask. "Half a million dollars worth of jewelry was stolen, and everything turned over to the iww." Davis also told his new

48

friend that he had blown up a watch factory in Santa Fe and bridges in Kansas.

Three days later, Davis told Blask he was sent into Canada before the war to organize iww locals.

"I worked around the mines of District 18," Davis said, "but in 1916 I received instructions from the headquarters in Chicago to go to the border and organize there. I was receiving a hundred dollars per month. But the Military Service Act came into force and I was obliged to take to the bush."

Later, Davis embellished his story a bit. He told Blask that he had filed a homestead claim on a quarter section in the Bluesky district, west of Peace River Crossing and built a shack near the Heart River. He claimed that he had used the shack to manufacture explosives and hide other iwws who were evading the draft. There had been an accident and the hut burned down. Now, Davis was back in Calgary without any money. Zaneth reported all this verbatim, with little comment on Davis's believability.

On Sunday, April 13, the day after Perry's report reached Ottawa, at the regular meeting of the Socialist Party, Knight showed up. After the meeting he had a chat with Harry Blask and his new friend Jim Davis.

Knight casually mentioned that Military District 13, which embraced the area around Calgary, had just received a carload of rifles. "We should keep our eyes on them," he chuckled, "as we might need them some day." Knight suggested that Harry might have a look at them.

Blask and Davis went to take a look at the Ordnance Stores of the local militia. Here, Zaneth was prepared to take one step beyond the bounds that separate an undercover operative gathering information from the *agent provocateur*. He reported to Spalding:

On the evening of April 13, 1919 Davis and myself proceeded to the Ordnance Department of Militia District No. 13 on 10th Ave. West, Calgary with a view of learning when the watchman, employed in that building, was taking his

49

rounds, so that we could get in and help ourselves to the
rifles which where stored in there . . . However, we did not
enter the building and did not notice the watchman . . .

The RNWMP apparently took no action on the report, nor was
there any investigation of Joe Knight's suggestion.

Two days later, Blask was walking a picket line along with
George Sangster. The management of four Calgary metal shops,
including the Riverside Iron Works and the Union Iron Works,
refused to sign a new agreement while metalworkers in Winnipeg and Toronto were still in negotiations. On the morning
of April 15 they locked out their employees.

Meanwhile, trouble was brewing in Winnipeg. There the
metal trades workers had reached a stalemate with the employers, who refused to recognize the metal trades council. They
said they would negotiate only with individual shops. The
Winnipeg metalworkers voted unanimously to strike. Construction workers were also about to walk off their jobs.

Nineteen nineteen had already been a record year for strikes
and the federal government had resorted to an old tactic to head
off labor unrest: they had appointed a Royal Commission on
Industrial Relations. Its tour had reached Calgary; George
Sangster, accompanied by his secretary, Harry Blask, appeared
on the afternoon of Saturday, May 3.

The main cause of the unrest, Sangster told the chairman,
Justice T.G. Mathers, was the great fear of unemployment.[17]

"Have you any solution?" asked Justice Mathers.

"Well," replied Sangster, "I have the solution of the majority
of my class and that is the only way, that we produce for use
instead of for profit."

The employers' representative on the Commission asked
Sangster, "Is there any actual illustration, one working example, of what you mean by 'production for use'?"

"Well, it has been attempted in one part of the world, that is
Russia," Sangster replied.

Can you give some details, asked a lawyer. Sangster replied,
no, he couldn't; most information was distorted when it came

through "normal capitalistic channels" — the daily newspaper.

Meanwhile, Zaneth had another problem. There were rumors in Calgary that a spotter, a stool pigeon, had infiltrated the labor leaders. Inspector Spalding reported to the Commissioner:

> There is a good deal of suspicion amongst the gentry locally at the present time, although the reputed IWW do not appear to suspect Const. Zaneth in the least, and seem to be his staunchest defenders, when, as it happened sometime ago he was under suspicion . . . To quote an instance he told me of when several of them were discussing the "stool pigeon." [Name deleted] pulled out a knife and drove the blade into a table they were standing by saying "I'd like to cut the heart out of the son of the bitch." Const. Zaneth could not do less than say, "I'm with you Jack . . ."

Perry decided that his operative was perhaps in more danger than he realized.

After the hearing, Zaneth left for Moose Jaw to check on his homestead (he was planning to sell the property) and to report to Perry in Regina. Perry had Blask arrested and charged as an enemy alien who had broken parole by not reporting to police, a tactic to ensure that Harry Blask maintained radical credentials.

On Thursday, May 15, Blask was permitted to send a telegram to Calgary. "Arrested here today. Harry Blask." The same day, Constable Frank Zaneth signed an RNWMP property receipt for "one IWW badge." He was not yet behind bars, but working with his superiors.

Later that week, Blask, the "well known agitator," as the newspapers called him, appeared in court and was duly convicted, fined and sent back to Calgary, where he was welcomed sympathetically by his friends in the Socialist Party and the One Big Union.

While Blask was behind bars in Regina, the Winnipeg Trades and Labor Council had called a referendum for a general strike. The strike's aims were to gain the right to organize and bargain

51

collectively, to work an eight-hour day* and to receive a decent wage. About eleven thousand voted in favor; five hundred were opposed. On Thursday, May 15, about twelve thousand union members walked out, followed by an equal number of unorganized workers. Within forty-eight hours the city was paralyzed and the story was front-page news across the continent.

In Calgary, Zaneth found that a referendum called to unite all unions into the One Big Union had been defeated; but Sangster had won his battle. The metal shops in Calgary had settled temporarily with union after all day negotiations on Saturday, May 17. The agreement called for five cents an hour above any settlement in Winnipeg or Toronto capped at eighty-five cents an hour.

On the evening of Tuesday, May 20, the Calgary Trades and Labor Council met to consider Winnipeg's request for support. Corporal Waugh was there as the council had recommended a general sympathetic strike in Calgary. A source, a freight handler, "a returned veteran, also a moderate man," as Waugh described him, said "It is a fight to the finish between capital and labor. Some remedy has to be found to prevent profiteering and the high cost of living, so that we improve our conditions." The next day, the Labor Council endorsed a general strike and called for a confirming referendum by all union members on Friday, May 23. J.S. Hooley, a boilermaker and a member of the OBU, was named to head the Central Strike Committee, with George Sangster as his assistant. Harry Blask was to help Sangster.

In Calgary, only twenty-five of seventy-four unions took part in the strike vote; eighteen were in favor. On Monday morning, May 26, just fifteen hundred workers walked off their jobs, most of them at the CPR metal shops, where there was already an existing dispute.

In Winnipeg, the city's population had polarized. Some sup-

---

* Although the radical ideal to end unemployment was the six-hour day, many workers were still working twelve or sixteen hours and so union members were still demanding an eight-hour day.

ported the strike; others a Citizen's Committee, led by Alfred J. Andrews, whose aim was to maintain essential services.

In Calgary, Waugh reported that Zaneth and an new agent designated "No. 14," were keeping in touch with the "Red element." The two spent all their time at the Labor Temple and the Socialist Party of Canada Hall. According to Zaneth, George Sangster, R.L. Bradshaw from Drumheller, the iww members A.H. Bunker, Jim Davis and Sam Rukin formed the radical "Sub-Central Strike Committee." Zaneth told Waugh that the spirit of the "Red element" in Calgary was broken because of splits in the leadership of the One Big Union. Meanwhile Blask, Sangster and the metalworkers were back on strike, in sympathy with their Winnipeg brethren.

Both Blask and Agent 14 were at the strike meetings, and reported to Waugh that A.H. Bunker and Samuel Rukin:

> lose no opportunity in spreading Bolshevik propaganda and are continually stirring others up to come out on strike, even at meetings called for other purposes . . . A.H. Bunker at a meeting on Sunday night at the Labor Temple stated that he understood that there were Government spotters and stool pigeons in the hall and he was going to speak loud enough, so that they could hear him, that he would rather die in jail . . . than take a job with and for the Capitalists as a stool pigeon.

Waugh told his superiors that:

> I would like to see these two men [Bunker and Rukin] . . . arrested and deported as undesirables; they are doing more harm at this time than anyone else. Besides, they realize they may be arrested at any time and are laughing at the authorities, thinking the latter fear them. They are American Citizens and PHF's* have been rendered upon them some time ago . . .

---

* PHF was a "Personal History File." The Royal North-West Mounted Police Secret Service had begun the system of keeping files on individuals who were identified as activists.

Jim Davis was also quite busy, as Zaneth reported:

> When the sympathetic strike was called, Davis became a member of the sub-central strike committee . . . and gave his support to all radical resolutions; took a very active part in carrying banners on parades and also made arrangements in painting the same. [Davis] Made statements while a member of the . . . sub-central strike committee to the effect that a revolution was not far off, and before the year 1919 expires, a Soviet form of government would be formed in Canada and the workers would reap the fruits of their labor.

About this time, a man later identified by Zaneth only as a member of the iww, was talking to George Sangster in the Calgary Labor Temple.

The iww asked Sangster what the Secret Service was doing.

"Oh, they're half asleep," Sangster replied. "We never have any trouble with them."

"I want to tell you," the iww said, "that your government and police are too soft. You've got all the free speech you can possibly expect. If the Western Conference of Labor had been held in the States, all the leaders would have been in jail by now."[18]

Harry Blask faithfully attended each meeting of the Labor Council, and according to the radical newsman, Lawson, always carried a small notebook in which "he had the record of his own activities and also the minutes of several labor meetings."[19] On the evening of May 28, Harry Blask was at the crowded Socialist Party of Canada Hall. Afterward, Zaneth reported to Waugh on the contents of a key speech:

> R.L. Bradshaw spoke and pointed out "ever since he became conscious that two societies exist in the world, Capitalist & Slaves, he studied the economic conditions, that for every day that a man works, he produces $15.00 worth of wealth, but the slave only receives about $3.00; the balance

goes to the master class to keep up pimps, such as police, spotters and some bastard that passes orders-in-council to keep us slaves.

Bradshaw was convinced, Zaneth told Waugh, that the day had come "that we can work only two hours a day and produce sufficient to live on decent [sic]."

Later, in the privacy of the Central Strike Committee meeting, Bradshaw was more vehement when he was told the miners should stay at work so they could donate to the strike fund:*

Bradshaw said: — "What in hell do you think I was going to do after agitating around for ten years? I was the strongest agitator in the Drumheller Valley and have been an IWW for many years, waiting for this movement to take place and now I have to keep at work by orders of some of those bastards of the Central Strike Committee. I will not be satisfied until I have killed somebody, especially the spotter we have in the bunch."

The strike committee also had to deal with a group called the Citizens Committee, which had been set up by Calgary businessmen in opposition to the strike. The strikers sent their own "undercover agent" to spy on the Citizens Committee meeting. The agent, "a returned soldier and a postal striker," reported to Harry Blask, who reported what he learned to both to the Central Strike Committee and to Corporal Waugh. The agent told Blask "it [the Citizen's Committee] is formed by people who never work, such as Managers, Floor-Walkers and all that class of men."

---

* In Winnipeg, the strike committee had decided that workers in essential services would continue to work. Milk wagons were seen with signs: "With Permission of the Strike Committee." The strikers in Calgary were thinking of adopting a similar system, but not everyone agreed with the idea.

Waugh himself went to a meeting and reported:

> . . . the Citizens Committee is composed of businessmen, who have not the slightest idea of the labor movement. I heard some of them myself ask these men what collective bargaining meant; what a trade union was etc. When one has a body of citizens asking such gross ignorant questions and at the same time attempt to formulate plans to offset this strike, it does not look very favorable to me.

Waugh was worried about Agent 14, a man neither he nor Zaneth trusted. Waugh had concluded that Agent 14 "learns a lot of his information from Zaneth and peddles it to us as his own." As well, he had found out that Agent 14 had said he had been to meetings he had never attended. The corporal reported, "I would like to see this man transferred from here as I am nervous of him all the time, as to playing a double game and giving false information."

On May 30, the government fired striking postal workers in Calgary and other cities; in Winnipeg, thousands of returned soldiers marched on the Manitoba legislature demanding that the provincial government recognize the right of collective bargaining. In Calgary, Zaneth reported to Waugh that members of the strike committee "realized that they have hopelessly lost [the strike] . . . with the result that they are spreading all kinds of rumors."

By the first week in June, the Royal North-West Mounted Police were intensifying a nation-wide security strategy, prompted by genuine fear because of events in Winnipeg and by a wider paranoia. Across the country, RNWMP operatives and agents, together with local police, went to meetings and scanned newspapers, making lists of men the police and their informants considered dangerous.

The RNWMP sent Inspector F.J. "Freddie" Mead and twenty men from Regina to Winnipeg. Mounties returning from the war in Europe were ordered to Winnipeg as soon as they docked in Halifax.

In Calgary, the RNWMP operation went into high gear. A new

undercover supervisor, a Staff Sergeant Hall, replaced Waugh as Zaneth's contact, because as Spalding noted, "Hall is not well-known here, he is not likely to be followed." Waugh would concentrate on supervising the agents. Spalding rented rooms — a safe house — where Waugh could "talk over matters with Special Agents" and meet with Spalding, who would visit when he could in plain clothes.

In his last formal meeting with Waugh on June 2, Zaneth reported that the radical labor movement appeared "hopelessly split." In one of the first indications of his own political opinions, Zaneth added to his report, "the Socialists believe in political action and the IWW in Industrial Action, in other words 'help yourself and take what you want.'"

The next day, Zaneth met with his new controller, Staff Sergeant Hall, who reported that the people on the Central Strike Committee were still wondering why Vancouver and Victoria had not yet walked out. Zaneth said that the One Big Union leadership wanted to find a face-saving way to settling the strike. In an example of his own attitudes, Zaneth told Hall that "the Central Strike Committee here is camouflaging the public and honest working class, by telling them that they must obtain collective bargaining in order to live." Collective bargaining was the stated aim of the strike, but, Zaneth said, the real aim was revolution, "But the truth is always held back, they are afraid to tell them that this is an OBU movement."

On June 7, Blask was at a poorly attended One Big Union convention in Calgary. Afterward, the labor movement marched to Calgary's Mewata Park. Spalding ordered his men to attend the meeting and also hired an unemployed man ("lately returned from overseas, an experienced news reporter") to take shorthand notes of speeches by William Pritchard and Joe Knight. Pritchard opened by attacking those who called the strike leaders part of the "alien enemy." The strike, he said, was the last resort in Winnipeg. "What happens? Fat boys with bulging eyes and bulging pocket books; the so-called intellectuals of the city cry out 'Bolsheviks! Murder! Call out the militia.'"

Waugh summed up his report, one of several on the speeches, with:

> I have heard this man [Pritchard] speak three or four times, but this was the most venomous speech I have yet heard from him. Underlying his speech all the time, he is cleverly urging revolution by force if necessary. He is a dangerous man, more especially as he is considered a good speaker.

On June 10, there was a leak about RNWMP Secret Service activities in the Calgary *Herald*. "Dominion authorities are swiftly gathering evidence connecting the One Big Union movement with Russian Soviet Propaganda . . . prima facie evidence that the principles of the OBU are the overturning of the constituted government in Canada by force. Such proof would bring the OBU promoters within the scope of the new act recently passed by Parliament providing for a penitentiary term for persons advocating the overthrow of constituted government by force."

By now, there was genuine fear of revolution among all political parties in Ottawa. The government had taken a drastic step. The new act the *Herald* referred to was an amendment to the Immigration Act passed on June 6. It gave the federal government the power to deport anyone not born in Canada who sought the violent overthrow of the government, even if the person was naturalized. The bill had received all three readings in the House of Commons within twenty minutes. (The process normally takes months.) In another twenty-five minutes, the bill had three readings in the Senate and Royal Assent from the Governor-General to become law.

The *Herald* commented directly on Zaneth's activities as Harry Blask, but without naming him: "The federal authorities in Calgary have gathered a great mass of literature, some of which has been prohibited for many months, including one of Lenin's[20] pamphlets, all of which has been distributed in this city under the surveillance of federal officers. A local newsstand has been the center for the distribution of this class of literature, though no specific instance of actually prohibited documents being put out by the owners is on record." The RNWMP files contain no reaction to the leak, but it raised the level of suspicion among the radicals. Fortunately for Zaneth, most of the suspicion was aimed at the newsstand. Harry Blask was busy, attending meetings.

The labor radicals were in for more disappointment. The civic employees decided not to strike and some metalworkers drifted back to work: there were few volunteers to hand out "dodgers," small handbills, or to walk the picket lines.

On Tuesday, June 17, a week after the leak to the *Herald*, came the early morning knock on the door. In Winnipeg, in carefully planned and timed raids, members of the Mounted Police, under the command of Inspector Mead, arrested the strike leaders: Winnipeg aldermen Abraham A. Heaps and John Queen; Robert Russell, the secretary of the Metal Trades Council and leader of the strike committee, George Armstrong of the Carpenters Union and Roger Bray, who had led the march on the legislature. The Reverend William Ivens, editor of the *Western Labor News*, was dragged from his home in front of his crying children. Three "aliens," all born in Russia, were also seized. The men were taken directly to Stony Mountain Penitentiary. Warrants were issued for R.J. Johns and William Pritchard — both had left Winnipeg — and, according to exaggerated news reports, "a number of men prominently identified with the early days of the Soviet government."*

The Labor Temple, the offices of the *Western Labor News* and the Ukrainian Labor Temple were all smashed open and files rifled and seized as evidence. The man behind the arrests was Alfred J. Andrews, leader of the Winnipeg Citizens Committee.

---

* In fact, according to reports filed by Superintendent Cortlandt Starnes, the officer commanding in Winnipeg, the local RNWMP never viewed the general strike as anything more than a local labor dispute with the aim of entrenching the concept of collective bargaining, a dispute that had gotten out of hand. Starnes also never directly connected the strike to the One Big Union. There were never any intelligence reports that outside agitators had anything to do with the Winnipeg strike.

NOTICE TO BUILDING TRADES

Having voted strike by a two-thirds majority in your locals

We call on you as men to act accordingly.

Three o'clock today (Wednesday) will determine whether or not you will ACT as you VOTED.

CENTRAL STRIKE COMMITTEE

A Calgary strike "Dodger" or handbill.

In mid-June, Zaneth reported the increasing desperation of the leaders of the Calgary strike. "The call for volunteers for piquet [picket] duty at various places of employment (where men are now on strike) has met with no success, no one seeming to be very anxious for this duty. . . .

Early this morning the Central Strike Committee got "Dodgers" out to endeavor to persuade the Building Trades to come out. When volunteers were called to distribute Dodgers, out of 50 strikers present, only four offered their services."

A few days earlier, Prime Minister Borden had appointed Andrews a deputy minister of justice. Now he was to be the special prosecutor.

The arrests quickly brought an outcry from labor, radical and moderate voices, across the country. In Calgary, the Labor Council wired the national Labor Congress, calling for a nation-wide strike. Even conservative, pro-business newspapers were shocked by the arrests. The Manitoba *Free Press*, which had opposed the general strike, denounced the government "strong arm methods" in an editorial and "dissociated" itself from the action.

On the evening of June 17, Harry Blask was at the meeting with the radical "sub-central" strike committee. Zaneth reported the radicals were doing nothing. "They only sit around, discussing who will be the first one arrested here . . . they think the police very cowardly to wait to 3 a.m. to make any arrests."

Two days later, on Thursday, June 19, the train from Winnipeg was boarded by mounted police as it arrived in Calgary. William Pritchard was arrested. The *Calgary Strike Bulletin* complained that the member of the OBU Central Committee had been "thrown into jail, along with a lot of snow birds and criminals."

R.J. Johns had gone east to Toronto. He surprised the Mounties a few days later by appearing in court in to give himself up.

The widespread outrage did not increase the support for the striking unions. On Friday, June 20, Zaneth was at the Labor Temple for a Central Strike Committee meeting. He reported that disgruntled metalworkers were demanding an end to the strike. They had been on strike for five weeks, had settled, then had gone back to the picket lines in sympathy with Winnipeg:

. . . most of them are getting good and hungry . . .

The biggest majority of the Metal Trades were . . . telling frankly to the Central Strike Committee that they will go to work on Monday morning in spite of what the Central Strike Committee think or do.

The strike leaders here in Calgary realize that if the Metal Trades are going to go back to work it will have a detrimental effect on the present strike . . . They have been holding these men out by great promises, but most of them are fed up with promises . . .

A metal trade man, when he was informed that Pritchard was under arrest said, "it serves him well right, every one of your 'REDS' that is keeping us from work should be in jail, and I hope you will all get it later or sooner."

In Winnipeg, that weekend is remembered as "Bloody Saturday." Two troops of Mounties on horseback were ordered to break up a banned "silent parade" by veterans. The Mounties rode through the crowd and were met by a hail of bricks and bottles. Three men went down near a stalled streetcar, and the RNWMP charged. A few people heard a shot. The police were again hit with rocks and bricks. They fired, first over the people's heads and then into the crowd. One man was killed. It was never proved who fired the fatal shot.

Commissioner Perry blamed "agitation" in the *Western Labor News*. A.J. Andrews, using his power as a deputy attorney general, ordered the paper banned. Its new editor, an activist Methodist minister, J.S. Woodsworth, was arrested on Monday, June 23 and charged with uttering seditious libels in the newspaper — among the libels were quotes from the Book of Isaiah.

In Calgary, on June 23, Harry Blask was at another meeting. The Federated Trades at the Canadian Pacific Railway were still on strike. Zaneth reported, again voicing his opinion: "The Red element ruled this meeting, but the workers were determined to go back and they made several statements to this effect." When it came to a vote the machinists, moulders, blacksmiths and other men who were not affiliated with the Federated Trades also cast ballots, voting not to return to work. "I noticed J. Marshall, J. Gray and a few others cast as much as six votes each."

There were 215 votes to stay out and 197 to return to work, but Zaneth noted:

"It could be easily seen that they were all willing to return. When they came out on strike it required a two thirds vote in favour of it, but now the chairman made it so that it only required an even vote to stay out.

The Reds fully realized there will be another stampede to the Ogden [the CPR repair] shops in the morning, therefore they need more camouflage by putting a motion to stay out for another twenty four hours.

Zaneth was right: the Calgary Sympathetic Strike was over. Those workers who could return were back at their jobs the next morning, Tuesday, June 24. The striking postal workers had been fired by the government and had no jobs to return to.

In Winnipeg, Fred Dixon, a member of the Manitoba legislature, had continued to get the labor paper out. He renamed the *Western Labor News* as the *Western Star*; then, when that paper was banned, he called it the *Enlightener*. On June 24, the Winnipeg strike committee offered to end the walkout if the provincial government called a royal commission on labor relations. The province agreed. On Wednesday, *The Enlightener* told its readers that the Winnipeg general strike would end Thursday morning, exactly six weeks after it began. Dixon was arrested as soon as the paper hit the streets and was charged with uttering seditious libel during the time he edited the two newspapers.

For five days, the country was quiet. People prepared to relax and celebrate Dominion Day on July 1. But in Ottawa, Regina and Winnipeg, the RNWMP security operation was prepared for its next move.

CHAPTER THREE

Zaneth : Agent Provocateur

IN WINNIPEG, A.J. ANDREWS and his assistants had been working with the Commissioner and the RNWMP. They had been poring over a long list of suspected radicals and subversive organizations. Search warrants were secretly issued in Winnipeg and careful plans were laid for raids in every major city as far east as Montreal. Orders were mailed to each RNWMP detachment, and Mounties dispatched to work with local police in the big cities of the east such as Toronto, where the RNWMP had no jurisdiction. The exact date of the planned raids, which would be carried out some time between June 28th and July 1 was a closely guarded secret. Officers commanding would be notified by cipher wire message of the exact date and time of the raids.

The orders for Calgary listed as targets the Labor Temple, the executive committee office of the One Big Union, the offices of the Socialist Party of Canada, the offices of the United Mine Workers of America and the "abode, offices and premises" of a list of individuals.* George Sangster was at the top of the list.

Frank Zaneth now had a new overall commander, Superintendent A.B. Pennefather. As the RNWMP expanded, it once again changed its division structure. Zaneth was now part of K Division, Southern Alberta District and headquarters were in Lethbridge. In the orders, Commissioner Perry told Penne-

---

* The orders for Calgary have been secret for 70 years. (See the Zaneth Papers.)

father "the papers and documents being sought are of the utmost importance and that nothing except the reasonable certainty of a riot should prevent the execution of the Search Warrants."

In the early hours of Tuesday, July 1, the police moved. In Calgary, George Sangster was awakened from his sleep just after midnight by mounted policemen with a warrant. The blanket warrant said in part, "It appears . . . that there is reason to suspect that certain books, papers, letters, documents, writings and copies of same, plates, weapons and other things which will afford evidence as to the commission . . . of the indictable offense of seditious conspiracy, are concealed in the following places." It was signed by A.J. Andrews acting as a justice of the peace.

In Calgary, other houses were raided. Mounted and local police were busy in Edmonton, where they raided the home of Joe Knight, and Saskatoon, Brandon, Montreal and other cities. In Winnipeg, as many as forty homes were raided. The safe at the Winnipeg Labor Temple was drilled open and its contents seized. Andrews gave the reason for the raids: "in view of the tons of literature seized we are confident of securing a conviction of the men accused."

In Calgary, the raids were not as successful as expected. Apparently the raid in Vancouver had gone off early, and the news had been picked up by Canadian Press.

There also may have been leaks, as Zaneth reported to Spalding:

Reg. No. 6743 tells me that similar talk went on at the Labor Temple on the Monday afternoon and evening and he feels certain that papers etc. were sorted on Monday evening at Trades & Labor Office, and anything of an incriminating nature was either destroyed or taken away.

He also tells me that [Name Deleted] mentioned last evening that it was a good thing the Police did not search his place about a week ago, as up to that time had a lot of stuff on the O.B. Union, but he had burned the lot.

Sent out on 175/1006

Newspapers etc sent to Wpg. 14/11/19

Red Flag		Soviet		Revolutionary Age		New Republic	
of No	Date of Paper	Ref No	Date of Paper	Ref No	Date of Paper	Ref No	Date of Paper
74	12	1/4/19		176	7/4/19	74 (11)	25/1/19	175/103 121	29/2
	19 cuttings	175 67	52	24/3/19		20	18/12/18			
175/53 47	cuttings	67	60	4/3/19		27	1/2/19	81	22/2/19	1041 106	14/6
103 64	15/1/19	67	104	15/3/19	505 169	2/5/19			
— 72	15/2/19	344	117	15/3/19	505 181	2/5			
67 103	8/3/19	— 379	115	27/4/19				
— 112	29/3/19		137	18/4/19				
			138	7/4/19				
379 133	22/3/19	498	129	21/4/19				
461 128	12/4/19		160	27/4/19				
315 { 130 6/4/19		317	161	24/4				
5 12/4/19			146	21/5/19				
6 19/4/19		317	161	24/4				
{ 166 12/4		—	197	7/4/19				
496 { 7 19/4		67	126	6/7-11/7				
8 6/9		12 27	207	18/8.				
769 120	24/5/19							
207 25/6			168	6/3				
500 205 5/8		110	27/3				
510 277 6/7				*Nation*				
318 121 20/8				Ref No	Date of Paper			
1125 131 31/8					120	22/2/19		
17 272 12/9				103	122	24/3/19		
218 296 11/10.				1474 274	20/9			
162	26/4/19							

After the raids, Inspector J. W. Spalding sent to Regina this catalog, in Zaneth's handwriting, listing each edition of the Red Flag, *the* Soviet, Revolutionary Age *and the* New Republic *and a second typed list, showing the* RNWMP *had also seized copies of the* Christian Science Monitor, *the* O.B.U. Bulletin, Liberator, *the* B.C. Federationist *and a list of pamphlets including,* Shall Socialism Triumph, The Russian Land Law *and* Wage, Labour and Capital *by Marx. Many of the magazines, with Zaneth's initials, are now in the Manitoba Archives.*

The arrests did not end Zaneth's undercover work. The Cabinet and the high command of the RNWMP were still worried about the One Big Union and the Industrial Workers of the World.

Zaneth reported that the radicals who called themselves members of the IWW had received a letter from IWW headquarters in Chicago "written in invisible ink . . . instructing members of the IWW not to sacrifice themselves in supporting the OBU."

Apparently the One Big Union was "not sufficiently radical to meet with the IWW views." The letter from Chicago instructed members to make efforts to break up the OBU.

A couple of days after the strike collapsed, Harry Blask dropped by to see his friend Jim Davis:

> I visited Davis's room at 211 – 6th Ave East and found him in possession of a small bottle of liquid of two different colors, red and white, which did not mix. He informed me that only a few drops would be sufficient to blow up any safe, and that I should give him my financial support to rent a shack on the outskirts of the city, where he would be able to work more freely. He further informed me that he had a license from the Ottawa Government to manufacture toilet waters* but his claim was that he would manufacture explosives. I also saw in his possession a printed application form which I would be able to identify as application for license to manufacture toilet waters.

The most radical of the IWW members in Calgary was up to his usual tricks. He had to be watched. Was Davis a serious, dangerous revolutionary or was he a con artist and manipulator, using a radical façade?

---

* A license to manufacture toilet water was a favorite dodge of the bootleggers in dry provinces like Alberta. It gave them legal grounds for distilling alcohol. Davis was probably supplementing his meagre income with some bootlegging.

By mid-summer, Zaneth's cover story was in trouble. He sent an urgent report to Spalding:

> As time went on the very fact I was unemployed lead these IWW's to think that I was receiving funds from the states from IWW's and when I was asked about it, I replied "yes" thinking it was the best out . . . I have told them that my father in Springfield, Mass. is also a Wobbly connected to the Boston Local of the IWW and he has been supporting me financially . . .
>
> Some time ago [name withheld] wrote to my father[21] asking if he could not get funds from the IWW's for him as he thought I was an Austrian with a Certificate of Parole and could not get funds from the States* . . . The way things are shaping up at present there is every possibility of me being uncovered, therefore rendering my services of no further value. It would also place my father in a difficult position as he would not be able to explain in such a way as to protect me.

Zaneth and Spalding put their heads together, and came up with a scheme to cement Blask's radical credentials and protect his father. Zaneth would go to the United States and join the IWW. The plan, which was largely Zaneth's idea, called for him to travel first to Chicago, to visit IWW headquarters, and then move to Boston and Springfield, cementing his cover story.

Headquarters liked the plan, with the usual cautions: "A plan of action with regard to what he will endeavor to accomplish should be carefully worked out. Due regard will be paid to economy and length of time to be spent on the trip . . ." At the same time, headquarters made official what had been the ad hoc practice of the new secret service . . . "As a further precautionary measure, please have Cst. Zaneth sign his reports in future by his Reg. Number."

In the Drumheller Valley, the miners had been out on the

---

* The Calgary IWW was probably Davis who was always short of money.

sympathetic strike since May. Most had joined the One Big Union. The mine owners refused to have anything to do with the OBU. They approached the Great War Veteran's Association with a plan to have returned soldiers join the United Mine Workers, so that the mines could reopen. The association agreed; hundreds of veterans were still unemployed and believed their service in the trenches entitled them to jobs.

On Saturday, August 9, in Drumheller, a local leader of the OBU was pulled from his bed by five vigilantes. He was rescued by a neighbor with a rifle. On Monday, the veterans attacked the miners' huts. There was a battle fought with rocks, miners' tools and firewood. The ex-soldiers soon had the upper hand and drove the miners into the hills. That afternoon David Rees, who opposed the OBU, held a United Mine Workers organizing rally. In the evening the OBU leaders, including Phillip Christophers, were grabbed at a meeting in Wayne and forced out of town. By Tuesday, most of the miners had come back from the hills and the mines were operating. Some veterans got jobs, but experienced men were needed to run the mines.

Many members of the OBU fled to Calgary. Zaneth, still undercover as Harry Blask, offered at least one miner a place on his couch until he got back on his financial feet.

One OBU member was becoming suspicious of Harry Blask. P.F. Lawson had left Fernie, B.C. and the *District Ledger* to found a miners' newspaper based in Calgary called the *Searchlight*.[22]

Harry Blask was one of the *Searchlight*'s most enthusiastic subscription salesman and Lawson began keeping an eye on young Harry. Lawson later wrote about Frank Zaneth's story from the viewpoint of western radicals. What follows is based on Lawson's account.

Harry had never asked Lawson for a commission on the subscriptions and the newspaperman couldn't help noticing that Blask didn't have a job. The roused his suspicions. Harry told Lawson that he was able to get money for his meals, clothes and room rent by playing poker.

Then Lawson saw Blask meeting with Corporal Waugh, who

had broken his cover to take part in the Dominion Day raids. Lawson started asking questions.

Harry Blask went to Lawson's hotel room and asked if the writer knew "the boys" considered him a stool pigeon.

"Even supposing you are," Lawson replied, "it wouldn't make any difference for we have nothing to hide. We are not advocating anything wrong. All we know about you is that when there is any work to do in the way of arranging meetings, or advertising, you are always ready and willing to do the work and not expect pay for doing it."

Blask kept up his cover story, saying his father was a great IWW enthusiast and that he had been sent into Canada to help the cause of the Wobblies.

Lawson replied that in the United States, police stool pigeons, agents provocateurs, were always "starting something" in the labor movement.

Then Zaneth's trip to the United States was postponed because the undercover operative was needed for a much more important security operation. Edward, the handsome, charming, debonair Prince of Wales, was on a postwar world tour, intended to bind the Empire together. Spalding reported on September 11;

> I have been in touch with Reg. No. 6743 [Zaneth] and learn that the alleged IWW are at present out of the City, most of them working in the harvest fields. ■ ■ ■ I deemed it best that he remain here [in Calgary] until the visit of HRH the Prince of Wales is over. Therefore, I have instructed him to cover the 'Red' element while His Royal Highness is here.

After the Royal visit, Blask met with the Calgary secretary of the One Big Union, who thought it was a good idea for Blask to go to the United States "to size up the situation." The secretary even suggested that Blask visit the editors of the *Revolutionary Age* in Boston and of the *Russian Soviet* in New York.

The Socialist Party was planning Blask's trip and the Royal North-West Mounted Police were planning Zaneth's trip to the

United States. Headquarters liked the idea of Zaneth going on to New York after Boston.

On September 24, Zaneth's future as an operative was in jeopardy. An assistant crown attorney named Goldstine had travelled to Calgary to look at the RNWMP files and meet with Waugh, who had been promoted to sergeant. Waugh and Goldstine were searching for evidence of seditious conspiracy. They examined files on the One Big Union, on the Socialist Party, on "Russian Jews in Calgary," on the labor conferences, on a "Bolsheviki Organization-Drumheller" and on the Calgary Sympathetic Strike. The name of Constable Frank Zaneth appeared again and again. Spalding arranged a meeting between Goldstine and Zaneth. The assistant crown was convinced that Zaneth could give valuable evidence at the sedition trial. Spalding pointed out that Zaneth's cover would be blown if he had to testify:

> Unless his evidence is absolutely necessary, it would be to the interest of the continued investigation of labor matters for him to remain undercover, as it would be most difficult to obtain another man who has the knowledge and experience which Const. Zaneth gained during the past six months here in Calgary.

On October 2, Andrews, who as deputy minister and special prosecutor had been granted extraordinary powers in the sedition case, decided that Zaneth should appear at the conspiracy trial, telling the RNWMP that "we would be assuming a grave responsibility if we did not use his evidence."

Three weeks later, Harry Blask was still was at work, and Spalding tried again to protect his operative:

> I can only reaffirm . . . that unless it is absolutely necessary, No. 6743 should not be uncovered.
>
> He continues to attend all OBU meetings and is apparently able to meet with alleged IWW element and OBU leaders . . . he still enjoys the confidence of these men ■ ■ ■

Inspector T.M. Shoebotham, temporary commander of K Division, added as he kicked the reports upstairs:

> It would be a great pity if the prosecution decided that it was necessary to uncover this agent at the Winnipeg trial, ■ ■ ■ to produce him in court I think means the immediate end of his successfulness in this particular work. Of course if the department decides to use this man at the trial, it would scarcely be safe to let him start for the States and then be required here . . .

Andrews promised to go over Zaneth's evidence thoroughly and he would not call him for five to six weeks.

On October 29, Blask attended a fund raiser for the defense of the Winnipeg "conspirators." One of them, Roger Bray, was there. He called the Mounties "skunks" and "rattlesnakes."

On November 10, 1919, Blask had his last recorded meeting with Jim Davis:

> I met Davis on 8th Ave. Calgary, when he informed me that he was out of funds, and said that I should give him financial support in order to make his plant a success. He stated that we should get a shack with a stove in order that he could make his explosives and that the OBU was coming along just as he expected it would."

Spalding, basing his conclusions on Zaneth's reports noted: "I am of the opinion that the majority of these Alleged IWW's who have been reported on, and who have been in Canada for some years, are not active members of any lodge or local of the IWW organization and therefore not in direct touch with the latest movement in the States." The revolutionary threat, at least from the IWW, the organization which Perry seemed to fear the most, had been "considerably overdrawn."

On November 1, 1919, after almost two years as a constable, Frank Zaneth was promoted to detective corporal. Ten days later, Andrews made his decision. He needed Zaneth for the trials.

As Andrews built his case against the conspirators, Zaneth became more important. On November 13, an urgent telegram was sent to Perry in Regina: "Andrews requires all original copies of reports of Sergt. Waugh and Corpl. Zaneth under the following periods be sent here as soon as possible . . . Also copies of publications . . . forwarded to Regina by Zaneth."

On December 5, 1919, Corporal Frank Zaneth walked into a Winnipeg courtroom in the red serge uniform of the Royal North-West Mounted Police. In the prisoner's dock was Bob Russell, the first defendant to appear, considered the most radical. (He signed his letters "Yours in Revolt."*) Russell was charged with six counts of seditious conspiracy and one charge of being a common nuisance. The indictment charged that the conspiracy had begun in Winnipeg and was developed at the Western Labor Conference.

Zaneth's appearance brought shock, consternation and anger to the prisoner and to many spectators; W.A. Pritchard, John Queen, A.A. Heaps and Roger Bray, all scheduled to appear later were in court, taking notes, facing Harry Blask in red serge.

Answering Andrews' questions, Zaneth outlined his work, beginning with September in Drumheller and continuing in Calgary where he was "converted" to socialism by George Sangster. Zaneth testified that Joe Knight had introduced Harry Blask to the defendant Robert Russell in the convention room at the Western Labor Conference.[23]

Zaneth described the meetings he had attended, the discussion of the general strike and revolution, how the members believed that Lenin and Trotsky were the greatest men in the world.

At first, Zaneth said, he had sold books and pamphlets. When they became prohibited literature, they were given away. A

---

* Intercepted letters written by the Winnipeg defendants and other radicals across the prairies were signed "Yours in Revolt," "I am Yours for Bolshevikism" [sic] or "Yours for Socialism" which dreamed of a Soviet Canada. The letters were one reason the government was so sure that was a revolution was being planned.

popular book was Lenin's *Political Parties in Russia*.

Robert Cassidy, the chief defense counsel, objected again and again to Zaneth's testimony. He told Justice Metcalfe that no connection had been proved between Russell and the Socialist Party of Canada.

Zaneth described the meeting that followed the Western Labor Conference.

"Would it not be wise to find out if Mr. Russell was there?" Cassidy asked. The judge did not respond.

Andrews asked about other meetings that followed the conference.

Cassidy objected. "It is an outrage to decency and to law that such evidence be admitted. You could not hang a cat on such evidence!"

"Did you meet Joe Knight in Calgary?" Andrews asked Zaneth.

"That's not a fair question, my Lord," said Cassidy. "The date of the meeting should be stated."

"What meeting was that?" Metcalfe asked.

"It is not a meeting at all," answered Andrews. "I asked if the witness saw Joe Knight in Calgary."

Zaneth said he had told Knight he thought the General Strike was going to start in Vancouver. "Knight told me, 'Oh no, Vancouver is tame in comparison to Winnipeg.'" Zaneth said that Knight had told him that the metal trades in Winnipeg were involved in a dispute.

"Knight said, 'We might just as well come out in sympathy with them and if we start in Winnipeg we shall spread the strike as far as Montreal and Vancouver.'"

Knight then had suggested that if the radicals waited, things might be in such a state politically that they might be facing machine guns.

Andrews turned to the Calgary strike. While he was secretary of the strike committee, Zaneth said, the committee received telegrams that then were changed to read as if Vancouver and every other place was out solid. When the workers found out from the newspapers that the strike was not solid, they began to scrap among themselves, and the strike collapsed.

Andrews returned to questions about Joe Knight. "Have you ever heard Joe Knight talk about the matter of arms?" asked Andrews.

Yes, Zaneth answered, on April 21, Knight had told him the ordnance department of Military District 13 had received a carload of rifles. "Knight said, 'We should keep our eyes on them as we might need them some day.' " Zaneth said he had gone to see them.

"I must object," Cassidy said. "It is most unfair. He ought not be allowed to go into such stuff as this about guns. If there was anything of this sort, we ought to have been told about it. In fact, it should have been a direct personal charge against any person associated with it. If that were true, why was Joe Knight at liberty? Why was he walking about at large if he was such a ruffian and Russell is in the dock?"

That was the end for that day. Andrews's carefully timed bombshell had its effect. The Canadian Press account of Zaneth, "the Secret Service man," and his testimony was headlined across Canada the next day. The CP story did not use the name Harry Blask. The name Zaneth, however, was on almost every front page. Zaneth was now uncovered as an operative and was immediately pegged by the radicals as the villain of the trial.

Zaneth was recalled for cross examination late on the afternoon of December 6. He began by outlining the speech given by William Pritchard in Calgary.

"I take it then that Pritchard was a Socialist?" Cassidy asked.

"Yes and then some," Zaneth replied. He then explained to Cassidy that Pritchard believed in "direct action."

"But he said he desired to avoid revolution?" Cassidy asked.

"He did not." Pritchard talked about revolution in every meeting, Zaneth testified, and was always saying that the workers had nothing in common with the master class.

Cassidy turned to the carload of rifles. Knight had told about their arrival. Zaneth said he had seen rifles, about one thousand of them. The building, he said, was in Calgary on 10th Avenue and was marked "Paint and Glass." He had informed the government of this.

"You reported to the government what Mr. Knight told you about the rifles and no charges have been laid. How do account for this?" Cassidy asked.[24]

"Search me. I'm only a corporal in the North West Mounted Police.

"Then you don't know why Russell is accused?"

"No, I don't."

Russell asked for a conference with Cassidy, and the two men whispered together. Cassidy turned and said, "I am instructed that he never saw you in his life and that he never attended any socialist meetings in Calgary." That was the end of Zaneth's testimony.

Six days later, on December 12, in the *Searchlight*, P.F. Lawson told his readers his side of the story. Lawson claimed that Harry Blask had been fingered early on as a stool pigeon: "we were warned by one or two Calgary men to 'watch out for that Harry Blask . . .' The warning only provoked a smile on the faces of those in the miners' labor movement for we had nothing to conceal from stool pigeons or from anyone else and if Blask saw fit to assist the radical element in the distribution of propaganda that was his privilege." Lawson said Blask had let one young Scottish refugee from the Drumheller riots sleep on the couch in his room. "He had nothing to fear or conceal, so he accepted the proffered hospitality. Blask showed equal kindness to others . . . and paid for more than one meal. With all his assiduous attention . . . he discovered nothing."

Lawson recalled meeting Harry Blask in the hotel room and that Blask said he had made his money by playing "the great American game" of poker. Lawson had some advice for the young undercover operative:

When he bought one of Campbell's hats a number of months ago, a nifty green fedora, he should have had the initials "H.B." perforated in the band thereof instead of "F.W.Z." We might also tell Harry that girls are not to be trusted. Like every young Mountie he had a weakness for a pretty face and in these days when workers have to be constantly on their guard there are many young women who can "put it across" even on a member of the "red coated riders of the plain." Harry won his way into the hearts of a girl or two without having to put on the red tunic with the padded chest and the trousers with the yellow streak.

Lawson told the story of how Blask had met and had macaroni with Tony Cacchioni. Cacchioni had quickly discovered that "by his accent" that Blask "was not really an Italian." Lawson concluded, "The shrewd miner soon had the 'mounty's' stories so twisted he was positive that Blask was a stool pigeon and he passed the word all over the camp and into Calgary." Lawson also claimed that "one of Blask's favorite tricks" was to show his revolver to socialists and boast nobody was ever going to get him. "He advised the boys that it was always safer to go with a gun for one could never tell what might happen, but the boys would not fall for any such rot."

Lawson was outraged that a foreigner, an Austrian, he said — the cover story was still holding — would be a member of the Royal North-West Mounted Police.

The "detective" work done by Inspector Spalding's men has, for the most part, been very clumsy and many a good laugh has been had over some of the attempts of his Austrian stool pigeon to discover crime when crime did not exist ... We do not know that Inspector Spalding instructed Blask to carry a revolver, an IWW card and a button in the same unlawful organization ... How could he countenance what his Austrian stool pigeon was doing in the attempt to cause crime and bloodshed? Trained by the R.N.W.M.P, Blask was not without a certain amount of one kind of intelligence. Being smooth of tongue, and able to speak several languages, he had quite an influence upon some of the foreign workers. That influence was never for good or in the direction of good citizenship or in keeping with the high standard of honor which Inspector Spalding stands for . . . and for which the RNWMP has long been noted . . . That was in the days before German and Austrian and Italian and Slav stool pigeons were taken into the force and set on the trail of honest men . . . British and Canadian born mounties with whom we are acquainted in this western country are endeavoring to uphold the traditions of the force and will not stoop to the low, the mean, the despicable work that is beginning to make the workers believe that the yellow streak is a predominant characteristic of what should be a highly respected body of men.

Spalding did not believe Lawson:

I do not think that Lawson or anyone else ever had the faintest idea as to this man's connection with us. If they had known of this all along as they claim, he would have been exposed before.

Lawson did not know that the RNWMP had an agent on the staff of the *Searchlight*. A few days later, an advance copy of the next issue was in Spalding's hands. The Inspector was concerned about one key paragraph in the galleys:

We already had a mass of evidence against the stool pigeon Blask and two of his crony associates, one of whom has recently been tried at Vancouver on a charge of perjury.* The agent provocateur work by this delectable trio was appalling. It is an actual fact, backed by the strongest evidence, that the three endeavored to interest a number

---

* The two men were agents — informants — inside the Russian Workers Union in Vancouver, one of the organizations banned under the War Measures Act. In June 1919, fourteen members were arrested and threatened with deportation. Supporters of the Russian Workers Union charged the two agents with perjury, claiming the two had lied at the deportation hearings. The case brought a lot of publicity to the RNWMP use of agents. The men were eventually acquitted. Since Zaneth worked in Alberta it is highly likely he never met the two Vancouver agents. Horrall, Canadian Historical Review LXI, 2, pp 176–177.

of workers in Calgary in an explosive manufacturing plant for "revolutionary purposes," that they actually endeavored to get workers in this city to advance some money to buy necessary materials. They also advocated, during the Calgary strike, that the strikers should carry bottles of sulphuric acid to the Calgary Post Office and have it thrown over the clothes of the businessmen and others who went after mail."

Spalding called Zaneth on the carpet and asked for an explanation of the acid incident, which apparently he had never reported.

Zaneth quickly pointed the finger at Jim Davis:

The only time Lawson may have heard of anyone intending use it was by James L. Davis.

A few days after the Western Conference, Lawson happened to be in the S.P. of C. hall. ■ ■ ■ and myself, stated that if the OBU General strike on 1st June, 1919, was going to be advocated he, Davis, had the right medicine for the Police. He said that a few drops of acid on auto tires would burn them up, preventing the authorities from transporting police or soldiers in any points in the city, and the strikers would have the full run of the city.

Zaneth's defense was a bit weak, and it's clear that he at least acquiesced with Davis' scheme:

While Davis was making statements of this nature in the presence of others, I never concurred with him in his statements. As a matter of fact at this particular time I pretended to be reading some book, but I must admit that when I met Jim Davis alone, during our conversations, I used to drift back to his statements of this nature, in order to find out of what material he was made of, and how far he dared to go to carry out his threat.

I am prepared to state that Lawson never heard me speak at any meeting, much less making statements of this nature, nor inciting anyone to use violence on people.

Sergeant Waugh then told Spalding he had seen Davis on the street, so Spalding proposed to Commissioner Perry that the Calgary detachment pick up Davis on a charge of perjury, so that, if necessary, Zaneth could be placed on the witness stand. "This would give the local papers here a chance to write up the case," Spalding wrote, "and in a casual way refer to Corpl. Zaneth's nationality, as the *Searchlight* has made a roar about his being an Austrian. This action would help to lessen the effect of Lawson's articles, which are no doubt written in an effort to discredit Corpl. Zaneth's evidence."*

The next issue of the *Searchlight* contained a racial attack on Zaneth and other non-British mounties, a poem called "The Stool Pigeon" "from the pen of a soldier who spent five years in the fight for democracy . . . It will be read with much pleasure by the Canadian and British born members of the RNWMP who are anxious to keep that force free from alien and other stool pigeons and to keep themselves up to that standard so heroically proclaimed by Ralph Connor, Pauline Johnson and other Canadian writers."

THE STOOL PIGEON

Just a little Austri-Hun, with a yellow streak
Came and saw and settled on the prairie bleak
A well supported stool pigeon, in favor wished to bask —
Corporal or Sergeant, Alias "Harry Blask."

He'd thought he'd be a "Sherlock," it was a merry joke
The way we found his number, we simple mining folks:
We "fell" for all his chatter in a confidential way,
And listened so politely to all he had to say.

---

* There is no record that the RNWMP ever took any action against Jim Davis. Perhaps Perry decided it was better not to force the issue.

He canvassed for the "Searchlight," drummed a lot of trade;
We thank him for his industry, his memory ne'er will fade.
The "Red Flag" and the "Soviet" he sold to all the dubs;
Kept hustling and a-humping and gathering in the subs.

He tried to get the "Hunkies" to bust our good old law,
Then carried all his prattle to brave Detective —;
He surely was a some tough nut, the way he'd flash a gun,
A sorry imitation of Kaiser Bill, the Hun.

He rambled here and wandered there, righting all the wrong
Like old "Johnny Walker," always going strong,
Striving hard to do his bit, and get his little name
Inscribed upon the Mounties' time-honored roll of fame.

He landed in with "Tony" (that's short for Cacchioni)
And sought for inspiration while eating macaroni;
But "Tony" had his number, had him weighed up right;
To him was most attentive and screamingly polite.

The miners are not hard on him, he'll get another chance;
He gave us quite a bit of fun, the first we've had since France;
We would not hurt his feelings, nor fun at him would poke,
But as a police detective he really was a joke.

Should these modest rhymings greet dear Harry's eye,
We'd like another visit, if he is not too shy;
But first we'll make a suggestion, it should not raise his ire
He'd better practice up a bit; he's a novice as a liar.[25]

On December 23, Robert Russell was found guilty of seditious conspiracy and was later sentenced to two years in jail.

There were more trials that winter. In January, Andrews proceeded against the other Winnipeg conspirators while at the same time, the province put Fred Dixon on trial.

The Wisdom of the Poor Fish

The Poor Fish Says:
If he wore a red tunic and trousers with a yellow streak he wouldn't associate with Austrians sent out with I.W. W. cards and guns in their pockets and he sure would be mad if he were told that one of those ginks was a sergeant in the force of which he had been taught to be proud.

The Searchlight ran a cartoon about a "Poor Fish," with a yellow streak, along with the poem attacking Zaneth.

On February 1, 1920, the Royal North-West Mounted Police became the Royal Canadian Mounted Police. After the events in Winnipeg, Prime Minister Robert Borden had decided Canada needed a trustworthy national police force, one that would not go out on strike, as some municipal forces had.[26]

On Thursday, February 5, Zaneth appeared in the trial of the remaining defendants. Andrews once more took Zaneth through what happened in Calgary in the early months of 1919. The defense counsel, R.J. Bonnar, cross-examined. After considerable questioning, he asked if Zaneth was a "wolf in sheep's clothing when he was pretending to be a member of the Socialist Party."

"You might call it that," Zaneth said.

"Isn't that in the order of being a sneak?" Bonnar asked.

"I will not permit a question like that," Justice Metcalfe said. "This man we all know was acting under orders of the Mounted Police. I will not permit him to be called a sneak.

Bonnar commented on how Zaneth pronounced "comrade" making it sound like the German word "kamerad." Metcalfe once more intervened.

"You are accusing this man of being a German," the judge said. "There is no evidence to that effect. I will not have the witness abused or untrue insinuations made." Bonnar then demanded why Zaneth had said he was born in Austria. Zaneth replied it was part of the disguise.

A couple of days later, Zaneth was also called to testify in the Fred Dixon case. Dixon was defending himself. In the summation, on February 15, Dixon addressed the jury for seven hours. He spoke smoothly, rapidly, occasionally raising his voice and banging on the table. And when Fred Dixon turned his attention to Zaneth's testimony, the RCMP operative's place in the history of the Canadian labor movement was fixed:

> I am going to ask you not to pay too much attention to a man like Zaneth. He is the man who poses as a bohunk before the labor organizations. When he was in the box he said he was an Italian, and when I asked him if he had ever

heard of Michelangelo, he said, "No I never heard of him." And Mazzini. "No." He never heard of him. And nearly everyone else in the room had heard of them. I ask if everyone else did not know who they were and if the Italian in the box was not the only one who did not know who I was asking about when I spoke of Michelangelo, Marcus Aurelius and Mazzini. We might forgive him if he did not know of Mazzini, who stood for a united Italy and the doing away of the temporal power of the Pope — perhaps he never heard of Marcus Aurelius, a great emperor philosopher; but do you think he would have gone to school in a convent and not heard of Michelangelo, renowned for his great religious paintings and sculpture?

The next day, February 16, the jury acquitted Dixon, and the provincial Crown immediately withdrew charges of seditious libel against J.S. Woodsworth.

The main trial continued, then the summations. William Pritchard, who was defending himself, was the final speaker. When he rose to speak on March 23, the courtroom was packed. He spoke rapidly but clearly and was called by the Winnipeg *Evening Tribune* "the most brilliant of the galaxy of star orators." For more than an hour, Pritchard turned his attack on Corporal Zaneth. "Are you going to tell me that a man that lied every day consistently for nine months could suddenly pull himself out of that rut and tell you, 'I am telling the truth now'?"

Pritchard maintained that people from northern Italy were natural liars, a trait caused by the "backward and forward movement of the military . . . over that particular district . . . there is bred a people who themselves must resort to lying and who are made cunning and sharp . . . A nation of liars and perjurers arise."

Pritchard then turned to one piece of evidence against him, a pamphlet called "The Social General Strike," published in New York. One copy — and only one — had been found in the nationwide raids.

Use your judgment on this gentlemen. Do you think he just packed that I.W.W card in his pocket and as he met working man after working man, never used it, never said anything about it, never attempted to induce those with whom he came in contact to join him in that organization?

And the Crown uses this one copy of this pamphlet, "Social General Strike." Where did they find it? They found it, as the evidence says, in the Socialist Party hall in Calgary. I let it go at that.

This gentleman that carried the IWW card, sold lots of literature, gave lots of literature away, lied as often as he considered it necessary, every hour in the day, and apparently had access to all kinds of workingmen's homes, had access to that Socialist hall and said in the box he was at every business meeting of the Socialist Party of Canada, a man packing around an IWW card and carrying literature there and reporting day after day to his officer commanding.

Gentlemen, do you think that it would be possible for him to go and put the only one copy that could be found in the Dominion of Canada — for such a man to take one copy of that pamphlet himself — and put it in a place where he or his officer commanding could go and find it?

Despite his eloquence, William Pritchard was convicted and sentenced to a year in jail. William Ivens, George Armstrong, R.J. Johns and John Queen also were sentenced to a year. Roger Bray got six months. A.A. Heaps, who later became a member of Parliament, was acquitted.

The Winnipeg Defense Committee, which had been raising money for the defendants and supporting their families, published four books: *Dixon's Address to the Jury in Defense of Freedom of Speech*, *Russell Trial and Labour's Rights*, *W.A. Pritchard's Address to the Jury*, and *The Winnipeg General Sympathetic Strike*. The books were part of a change in the political campaign for labor rights in Canada — from the streets to the ballot box. They were aimed at the electorate and would soon have an affect.

With the publication of the pamphlets, Frank Zaneth became known as the agent provocateur of the Winnipeg strike. The freed "conspirators" were soon on the road, raising money for their defense. Zaneth was a favorite target.

A.A. Heaps reached Edmonton on April 2nd and an RCMP agent reported that Heaps said: "The spy system was a wonderful thing. Even the Kaiser might be proud of it."

Fred Dixon was also in Edmonton on April 21, speaking to raise funds for the Winnipeg Defense Fund. The RCMP undercover operative in Albion Hall reported:

> Corpl. Zaneth came in for some severe criticism, on the way he had obtained his evidence, and he [Zaneth] admitted in his cross-examination that he had lied when he thought it necessary. Dixon then remarked that he thought the "Royal North-West Mounted Police" would much prefer to get evidence against the profiteers and grafters than against the labor classes; but they had to do what they are told.

Alfred Andrews and the high command of the new RCMP had a different attitude toward Zaneth. In a memo to Perry, Andrews said Zaneth was a valuable asset, "There is nothing I can now say which would be too flattering to this young chap. His evidence in this case was most clean cut and decisive, and the opposing attorneys were not able to shake him."

CHAPTER FOUR

Zaneth and the Communists (I)

AFTER HE WAS "UNCOVERED" during the Winnipeg trials, Zaneth had, at his own insistence, been temporarily assigned to ordinary police duties in southern Saskatchewan. It was a risk, but the magic of the red serge apparently worked. There were no reports of trouble.

In April 1920, Zaneth resurrected the plan to go to the United States and infiltrate the Industrial Workers of the World.

Having been disclosed at the Winnipeg trials, I find it impossible to join any Radical Organization in Western Canada, and in order to get well into these Organizations in Montreal it is necessary that I should have good credentials. Credentials coming from the States will carry more weight than elsewhere and also give me the appearance of a new arrival in this country. I request that I may go to Springfield because I am well known there and would have no difficulty in getting these credentials.

Perry supported the idea. RCMP and military intelligence sources in Montreal had been reporting that there was dangerous radical agitation in the One Big Union, and in communist and socialist circles.

Nineteen-nineteen had also been a turbulent year in the United States. The trouble had begun in February, with a five-day general strike in Seattle, sparked by a shipyard dispute.

In late April, 1919, a mail bomb arrived at the office of Seattle's mayor. In the weeks that followed, terrorists mailed or planted thirty-five more bombs. One was sent to the United States Attorney General, a Pennsylvania Quaker named A. Mitchell Palmer; it exploded outside his Washington home. The press blamed the bombings on the Bolsheviks or the IWW, but the most likely suspects belonged to a fringe anarchist group. It was never proved who was behind the bombings.

The bombing heightened the growing Red Scare in the United States. Many people made no distinction between Wobblies, socialists, Bolsheviks or militant union members. The left did have support — Eugene Debs had received almost a million votes for president in 1912. In 1919, the United States had two Communist parties. The Communist Party of America attracted mainly foreign-born adherents; Americans joined the Communist Labor Party, founded by John Reed and his friends.

Fear of a Red revolution was growing; conservative forces fanned the flames for their own political reasons. Attorney General Palmer warned of revolution sweeping like "a prairie fire" across America.

On New Year's Day, 1920, U.S. federal agents and local police began a series of raids against the left. They arrested suspected radicals, especially "foreigners," smashed their way into union and meeting halls and invaded private homes. There were few, if any, warrants; the Bill of Rights was ignored. In what became known as the Palmer Red Scare Raids, six thousand people were picked up, and many were forced to "volunteer" to leave the United States. No evidence of revolution was found. About six hundred people were found guilty of various offenses. Springfield was a center for radicals in New England, and in the raids at least sixty people in and around Springfield were arrested. Many were called "Russians" by the newspapers of the day.

Ambrose Zanetti was apparently quite ill that spring, and Zaneth spent a few days in Springfield visiting his family, before going to New York City.

He arrived in New York on April 22, 1920 and headed for the headquarters of the Communist Party of America on Grand

Street. It was empty. Zaneth struck up a conversation with the local beat cop and discovered that place had been raided and the officials of the party indicted by the State of New York. One of them, the cop said, an Irish-American named James Larkin, secretary of the Irish Transportation Union and an official of the Communist Party, was on trial at the moment.

Zaneth tried the Social Publication Society on Fifty-fifth Street in Brooklyn, where the Rand School of Social Science held classes. There he met the sole occupant, a Russian Jew who told him he couldn't join the Communist Party "because it had been disorganized by the authorities." The police had taken everything away. The man told Zaneth he had to get two members of the party to endorse his application. "That goes to show," Zaneth reported, "that they are very careful as to who they take into the organization, for they are also aware of the fact there are Secret Agents among them."

Zaneth reported that the Rand School of Social Science was the distribution center for "all the radical propaganda." They printed *The Soviet and the Bolshevik*, *The Soviet At Work*, *The Old Order in Europe and the New Order in Russia*, some of the magazines Harry Blask had distributed in Calgary. The place had been smashed up during the raid. Zaneth commented, in his still somewhat awkward English, "the Authorities during the raid, they disrupted the place so badly, that there is nothing in contact" — meaning nothing was left intact.

Zaneth contacted groups that attracted recent immigrants to the United States, the Brand Komunistich Bolshevickies, the Manifesto First Program Komunistich Internatzonalu and the Nukovi First Utopyine Sotkzializm with headquarters at 222 East Fifth Street. Most of the members of the groups were, Zaneth reported, "Russian Jews, Ukrainians and Slavoniks." All, Zaneth said, were affiliated with the Third International, but he noted, "the authorities had raided the headquarters and most of the officials had been deported." He also tried the headquarters of the Left Wing Section Socialist Party of Greater New York, on West Twenty-ninth. Here Zaneth had his first success, he was offered a membership card in the "Menshevick" or right-wing faction, of the Socialist Party but, he said, "I came to the conclusion that very little benefit I could derive from it, rather it would hinder me from getting in with the Red element so I did not become a member of the Party in question."

Zaneth found out that most of the remaining free radicals were hanging around the court, watching the Larkin trial. At the court, he ran into a man he knew [Name deleted from the report], a fellow Crown witness from the Winnipeg Conspiracy trial. The man was now an "expert" witness. Zaneth approached him "in a casual way" and was soon introduced to the prosecutors. They were able to get the cards he was looking for: ". . . a blank membership card of the Communist Party of America and one of the Left Wing Socialist Section Party Greater New York, which cards I have had filled out and it would appear that I have been a member of the two mentioned parties for a considerable length of time."

Zaneth found out that Joe Knight was busy in New York, trying to expand the One Big Union into the United States. Knight had spoken to the Independent Electricians local in New York, in an attempt to get it to affiliate with the OBU. He was now on a speaking tour of New England.

Armed with his membership cards, Zaneth left New York for Boston. There he found a movement to get the workers to sever their connection with the international trade unions and affiliate with the Canadian One Big Union. The OBU at the time was making an effort to expand beyond Canada, and there were organizing attempts on the west coast and in Chicago, home base of the IWW.[27]

Zaneth visited the Central Labor Union Hall and spoke to a secretary of the International Typographical Union, who told him that an OBU secretary in Vancouver had been writing to union leaders in Boston, urging them to join the One Big Union because, according to them. "as far as the workers of Canada were concerned, the International had become a corpse."

Zaneth returned to Springfield where he was a local boy and had the most success. He attended several radical meetings, and got two more membership cards — in the Machinists Helpers Local 214 and in the Socialist Party of America, Ward 5.

Zaneth reported:"It has been stated at every meeting I have attended that a Revolution is inevitable."

He had a chat with one of Springfield's local radical leaders and asked the man what was the best way to take over industries with little bloodshed.

"If a local go out on strike," the man told Zaneth, "and the rest of the workers belonging to different locals understand the ultimate motive as to why this local went out on strike, they will come out in sympathy with them. Strikes are developing, verging on Revolutionary actions. That is the only method to use establish a proletarian dictatorship." The man warmed to his theme. "Strikes will usurp the functions of industries. We had a lesson during the Seattle strike and the Winnipeg Strike. We did not win because there was too many reactionaries against us. But it won't be long now before the workers will be united and the first strike will decide who is the strongest between the Capitalist Class and the Working Class."

On May 18, Zaneth arrived for duty in Montreal, a new cover intact. He was James Laplante, a New Englander with ancestors from Quebec who had returned to his roots.

In Montreal, he typed out his report on the trip to the United States, a report that also reveals Zaneth's own attitudes toward Communism:

I am fully convinced that all the Radicals are working with only one object in view, whether they are called Socialists, Anarchists, Bolsheviks, IWW's; their principles are identical. They first send a man to plant the seed of discontent, just as soon as the seed begins to take root, there will be someone else along to help it come to the surface, then there will be someone else along to cultivate the discontent, and just as soon as the plant is dry enough to set fire to it, they send a man to burn it. Someone else will fan the blaze of discontent, hoping that the world will be on fire, as the Bolsheviks have done in Russia.

The officer commanding the Quebec Division of the RCMP, Superintendent N. Belcher, read Zaneth's report and that day wrote the Commissioner warning that Zaneth would "have a hard time concealing his identity for any length of time in this part of the country."

The labor movement in Montreal was fractured. There were the traditional craft unions, there was an active unit of the One Big Union, and there was the Socialist Party of Canada which was split into two groups, a new French-speaking *Parti Socialiste Communiste Français du Québec* and the English-speaking Socialist Party of Canada.*

On May 21, 1920, six days after he arrived in Montreal, James Laplante boldly walked into a Socialist Party of Canada meeting. He talked to several organizers and he showed them his American credentials. They suggested that if he wished to join the party, he should go to a meeting later in the week and introduce himself to the speaker, A.A. Heaps, the Winnipeg alderman who had been arrested during the general strike. Zaneth had a problem with this course of action, because Heaps knew him as "Harry Blask."

Laplante did attend the SPC meeting on May 29th and listened to the talk on "Labour Unrest" given by Heaps. Laplante carefully stationed himself in the hallway on a stairway where the speaker and other acquaintances could not see him. Zaneth departed immediately after the speech to avoid an embarrassing run-in with anyone he had met out West, his former radical "colleagues."

Belcher decided that Zaneth should not try to infiltrate the executive of the radical parties in Montreal, but Zaneth was ordered to interview officials in the Socialist Party to find out the organizing goals of the new socialist parties, the extent to which they were really part of the One Big Union and the kind of "propaganda" they were proposing.

---

* RCMP agents and operatives translated the names of French organizations into English, for example the French Socialist Communist Party, in their reports.

On June 6, James Laplante attended a SPC rally where the star speaker was Rebecca "Becky" Buhay, who was later to become a major focus of RCMP investigations into the Communist Party in Canada. The Buhays, Becky and her brother Michael, were Jewish radicals who had emigrated to Canada from England. They had become the leading lights of the far left movement in Canada and ran the English speaking OBU in Montreal. At the rally Becky Buhay went after the labor establishment in the United States and openly and savagely attacked Sam Gompers and the American Federation of Labor. On July 29, at the election of the OBU executive, Becky further split the very splintered left in Canada by launching a salvo at the IWW itself, calling its leadership "weak-kneed."

On August 3, Laplante attended a meeting the new French Socialist Communist Party. Zaneth, fluent in French, bridged the cultural gap in the radical movement in Montreal and was able to infiltrate both wings of the Socialist Party of Canada. The main players in this new group were Ulric Binnette and Albert Saint Martin. The two were fierce rivals and frequently argued at meetings. Binnette was a militant unionist, and his mission seemed to be to encourage the communists to adopt some of the principles of the democratic labor organization. Saint Martin was a doctrinaire communist, and according to Zaneth he claimed to be the one true leader of the Communist forces among the francophones in Quebec. He was a rabble-rouser, a barn-burning type who vehemently denounced the government of Canada. Saint Martin constantly wrote to Communist leaders in Moscow, who, according to Zaneth's informed account, didn't bother to even answer his letters. Saint Martin also had a farm outside of Montreal, which, it was said by his rivals, he ran like an ideal commune, but then kept all the profits.

The Soviet Union itself was apparently also getting involved in the revolutionary movement in New York City and Montreal; on August 12, 1920, Laplante attended an OBU meeting where he learned that the Soviet Bureau in New York were talking about financing and sponsoring the establishment of a labor college in Canada.[28]* He managed to work for five months before several radical leaders became suspicious of Laplante. Military intelligence files on the One Big Union indicate that Lieutenant Colonel G.B. Price, in charge of intelligence operations in the Montreal military district, reported on September 8 that, based on information from one of his own secret agents, "the identity of the Royal Canadian Mounted police Secret Agent named Laplante had been disclosed." Apparently, Harry Blask had been spotted in a leftwing bookstore by someone who knew him from out west.

The RCMP brass in Montreal refused to believe the report. Laplante was still attending meetings and was apparently not being opposed in any manner. The RCMP decided to continue Laplante as an agent.

A September 30 military intelligence report signed by Price indicated that "a great number of people are aware of his being a Government Secret Agent and simply tolerate him and are practically laughing up their sleeve." But Price decided it was better to let him carry on and "lead him to believe that he was not under suspicion." Perhaps Price and military intelligence felt that suspicion on Laplante would help the activities of their own secret agents working the radical beat and helped to distract the leftist leadership from the government's other intelligence activities.

What happened next is one of the few events in Zaneth's career that can be reconstructed from his report and an independent account.

October 17, 1920, was a quiet Sunday afternoon. James Laplante was browsing in a hole-in-the-wall bookstore in the east end of Montreal on rue Ste-Catherine. It was filled with books, many of them paperbound, a few hardcovers, magazines such as *Soviet Russia, Le Soviet, Le Libertaire, The Worker* and the less radical *Nation*; and newspapers such as Montreal's *Revolt*, the One Big Union's *OBU Bulletin* from Winnipeg, and the *B.C. Federationist* from Vancouver.

---

* Zaneth was promoted to Detective Sergeant on September 1, 1920.

At about 2:45, Laplante was chatting with the proprietor, a woman in her late forties, and her daughter, a girl of about ten. A new customer opened the door. When he saw Laplante, the man stopped short.

Then the man walked up to Laplante, nodded and said, "Hello, Harry, what are you doing here?" Then he chuckled, "Oh no, your name is not Harry any more." It was David Rees, of the United Mine Workers Union.[29]

"That will do now, David," Zaneth replied. He put out his hand. Rees, to his own surprise, shook it. He looked around, picked up the latest copy of *The Nation* and went to the counter, where he pulled out a notebook and began to scribble a note.

Laplante glanced back, took a couple of steps to the door, turned and called to the owner. "I'll see you tomorrow," and was gone. The woman asked David Rees if there was anything else she could get him.

"Do you know who that man is?" Rees asked.

The woman hesitated for a moment. "Yes," she replied.

"You don't know me from Adam," Rees said, "but let me tell you he is a spotter. He masqueraded under the name of Harry —" he paused; Rees could not remember Harry's last name — "for long enough in the West."

Rees had stopped over in Montreal on his way to Cape Breton, where there was talk of a strike by the UMW against the Dominion Coal Company. He later reported that the woman nodded and said someone else had told her the man was a police agent. "Her first informant being an ex-spotter, fired for some reason, possibly having a conscience," Rees noted. She said she had had two other warnings in the past weeks.

Each Sunday and sometimes more often, when the weather was good, she told Rees, the *Parti Socialiste Communiste Français du Montréal* held open-air meetings at Market Square. On those days, the bookstore owner and her daughter would carry some of her stock up to the Labor Temple on Craig Street East and sell newspapers and magazines, ask help for Soviet Russia, or tell of the latest labor troubles out west. In July, a charming young man had approached her and offered to help.

"And soon," Rees would later write, "our suave and genial or smooth and slimy 'Harry' was assisting in the sale of literature."

For the past three months, Laplante had had two jobs; when he wasn't "selling insurance," he had acted as sales agent for the bookstore. Just as Blask had been in Calgary, Laplante was hardworking and honest, he turned in every penny. Later, Laplante had told the book store proprietor that he was tired of collecting insurance payments and wanted something better. He asked her to write a letter of reference; despite the tip and her own suspicions, she agreed. Rees wrote:

> He had been trying to get the lady bookseller (by the way, a lady old enough to be his mother and a widow) to give him lessons in the French language. He was very anxious to learn anything and had the happy faculty of asking numerous simple questions for enlightenment. The bookstore was one of his regular calling places, thereby gaining tab, I expect, on regular customers, and the kind of wares they purchased.

On October 19, 1920, the *B.C. Federationist*, the organ of the radical British Columbia Federation of Labour, published a long story by David Rees exposing James Laplante as Mountie secret agent Frank Zaneth, headlined: ZANETH OF WINNIPEG "FAME" NOW BUSY IN CITY OF MONTREAL.

The paper carried a photo of Zaneth, perhaps the first most radicals had seen, with the caption, "Here he is."

Superintendent Demers, the new officer commanding in Montreal, wrote to the Commissioner that the exposure was "what could be expected." He felt that it was "useless for 6743 to continue here on the work he has been doing [as] it would be only a matter of time before he would be uncovered no matter where he went." He suggested that Zaneth had the makings of "a good detective for general investigations."

The new Commissioner, Cortlandt Starnes, agreed that

Zaneth was in danger working with the radicals and that his undercover career in the movement in Montreal was over. Zaneth was given a desk job as the head of the drug squad in Montreal, but he couldn't stay away from undercover action for long. On October 29, 1920 Zaneth was ordered by Ottawa not to take unnecessary risks, but he would be allowed to continue his espionage work in Montreal in a supervisory capacity.

A month after he had met David Rees in the bookstore, on November 16, 1920, Zaneth reported that he ran into his former employer and French teacher in downtown Montreal. He pretended for a moment that he didn't recognize her.

"Laplante," she shouted. "Oh, no, no more Laplante, Zaneth now, *n'est-ce pas*?"

"Zaneth, if you please," he replied.

"I have no hard feelings against you," she said.

Zaneth reported:

as she knew me as a man and not a detective and although she did not agree with the nature of my work, she did not blame me for doing it.

"It is not you who are to blame, but the system. Once we change the system, you and all your officers will be out of a job. We are sorry that out of all the men employed in this kind of work, you were the one sent to Montreal, after all the damage you have done out West, and especially at the Winnipeg trial, we were all under the impression that you had outlived your usefulness, but now we can see the Government has the right sort of men in the right jobs."

She went on to tell Zaneth that W.E. Long, the General Secretary of the One Big Union in Montreal, had become the laughing stock of the local. Long had attended the OBU conference in Winnipeg that February and he had sat in on the sedition trials. Long had told his Montreal brothers he had seen Zaneth and would recognize him "among ten thousand men in ten years time," but Zaneth had got away with being James Laplante until the meeting with David Rees.

Zaneth reported that the woman smiled and asked:

"Now that you have come to the end of your efforts, no doubt the government will get someone else to take over your work, the worst of it is, we don't know whom it might be."

"Why I do not know." ("It was obvious to me that [Name Deleted] was anxious to find out if we had other men on this work"). "There are thousands of applications from good men willing to work, but we do not know who they are. It might be the man the Radicals consider that most class conscious leaders, as you know that the Reds in this country are very much in the minority."

I asked [Name Deleted] if it was true she told David Rees, that she had been told three different times who I was and that I was a government spotter. She denied telling Rees this and said I was the last person in the world they suspected.

As she was about to leave, the woman told Zaneth, to remember that she was still his friend, but warned him to be careful of the others, as they were all very bitter against him.

On November 3, 1920, Albert Saint Martin sent a "Dear Comrade" letter in French to James Laplante, inviting him to an executive meeting in mid-November. Supt. Demers referred the letter to Commissioner Cortlandt Starnes noting that "This is probably intended as a trap, and he is taking no notice of it." Zaneth was now under strict orders from Ottawa and from his commander in Quebec "not to take any risks."

Zaneth continued on his intelligence work on the radical movement for another three years as the RCMP control officer and spymaster for a number of RCMP agents, infiltrators and agents provocateurs in Montreal, interpreting the reports from his agents for the RCMP brass in Ottawa. Many of the reports contain accounts of the repetitious internal wrangling of the radical leaders and endless attacks on the capitalist system, mostly made by Rebecca Buhay and Albert Saint Martin.

On April 21, 1921, Zaneth went to Springfield, where his 1910 civil marriage to Margaret Scevola-Ruscellotti was solemnized at Mt. Carmel Church. Rita joined him in Montreal. Zaneth must have had a hint of a coming change in RCMP policy. Officially, marriage was not allowed until after a man had served seven years. The idea was to save the public money and to keep the Mounties more mobile. By 1921, there had been a considerable relaxation of the marriage rule. Zaneth's timing was good, as in 1922 the RCMP issued a new set of marriage regulations which allowed a marriage only after the Commissioner himself gave his permission. Otherwise, married men were not accepted for engagement.

The Communist movement continued to grow in Canada. In the summer of 1921, Zaneth learned that some of the Montreal radicals had been at a secret meeting in a barn in Guelph, Ontario. At the meeting, the new Communist Party of Canada had been officially founded.

The Communists soon had their first candidates in a federal election. In November, Zaneth reported that Michael Buhay had a good chance of winning a seat as MP for the Montreal riding of Cartier, held by Liberal MP Samuel Jacobs. Jacobs was one of Canada's first civil rights lawyers and became the first Jew elected to the House of Commons when he won the seat in 1917.[30] Jacobs retained the seat in the December federal election, and stayed in Parliament where his contacts with bootleggers would later bring him to the attention of the RCMP.

From time to time, Zaneth went undercover to check up on his agents and survey the situation for himself. In October 1922 he attended a series of meetings and speeches by J.S. Woodsworth, now a Winnipeg MP, and later the father of the CCF, sponsored by the French Socialist Communist Party. Zaneth's analysis of Woodsworth and his speeches which he sent on to RCMP headquarters was both informed and intelligent:

Woodsworth's lectures were of a mild character. There were no utterances made which could be considered of an advanced Radical nature, and on this account Woodsworth does not seem to have been too popular with his audience . . . Woodsworth was particularly careful to refrain from saying anything that might damage his own standing in the House. It is also characteristic of Woodsworth that he seized the opportunity to carry his audience back to the West where he first won his reputation as an agitator and leader of Labour.

Zaneth continued to run his secret agents inside the Montreal radical movement until March 1923 when the government and RCMP decided that the One Big Union and the socialist parties in Montreal were no longer a major security threat. Surveillance would continue without Zaneth.

Zaneth had started with no training. The RCMP intelligence service had also been new and provided little support. Zaneth made mistakes but managed to overcome them and to do the job he was assigned to. Zaneth's focus was narrow, targeted. Was there a threat to society, as suspected by his superiors? He did not ask the larger questions, for example, about why the leftist movement had, at least for a couple of years, found such fertile ground.

Five years of work had proved that Detective Sergeant Frank Zaneth was a dogged, meticulous investigator, but the priorities of the RCMP were changing. Prohibition was in full, leaky force in the United States, and Canada and its gangs were busy filling the orders of that thirsty nation. The RCMP needed Zaneth in a new role.

CHAPTER FIVE

Operative No. 1 and
the Tangled Web

IN MONTREAL, Detective Sergeant Frank Zaneth, nominally the administrative head of the Narcotics Squad, was learning the detective side of the business from his immediate superior, Staff Sergeant Ernest C.P. Salt. They were working out of RCMP headquarters, an old mansion near the McGill University gates on Sherbrooke Street.

It was the first days of the bootlegging era. The racket moved both ways. Liquor flowed south from Quebec, and to double the profit, the gangs came north with other goods, cars stolen in the United States, trucks full of cigarettes, raw textiles, dresses, even men's suits made in a U.S. prison. The drug trade thrived along Boulevard St-Laurent, Montreal's Main, a world of opium dens, brothels and blind pigs where decks of cocaine and morphine were sold.[31] *

In the fall of 1922, Salt picked Zaneth to help him in a counterfeiting case. Counterfeit fifty-cent pieces were turning up in Montreal. Similar coins had appeared in 1916, they had been engraved by a man named Albert Côté. Côté had tipped off the police, and the subsequent raid had recovered dies, matrixes and a bag of phony coins. Six years later, Zaneth and Salt were following Côté from his home in Verdun to Montreal. He was a frequent visitor to a house on rue St-Catherine Ouest

---

* A deck was a folded piece of paper containing a grain of morphine or cocaine; a deck sold for fifty cents. Opium sold for thirty-five cents.

owned by a man named Georges W. Brisson. When they raided the house, Zaneth and Salt found a coining press, a number of dies and some engraving tools. At Côté's house in Verdun, they found more dies and two almost perfect 1912 King George V counterfeit fifty-cent pieces.*

A few days after the Côté raids, Zaneth was posted to Quebec City, where he took charge of the detachment. Andrew Veitch, one of the men Zaneth would later command in Toronto, said that the sergeant's time in Quebec City was a period of "hibernation," between his exposure in Montreal and his emergence as a senior detective three years later.

Smuggling silk into Quebec had become a major racket. The customs tariff was forty percent. The smuggled silk was stolen or purchased in New York's mob-run garment district, then brought into Canada by returning bootleggers. In 1923, Zaneth investigated a woman named Denise Larde who was involved in the smuggling of a large number of dresses near Quebec. Apparently, she once unsuccessfully tried to bribe Zaneth by thrusting money into his hands.

In 1925, the RCMP Annual Report noted: "Sergeant F.W. Zaneth . . . made a very good clean up of the drug situation in Québec City, apprehending a number of doctors and druggists."

In 1926, Zaneth was seconded to the Department of National Defence, for the first of many special investigations in his career. He assisted a court of inquiry into the conduct of Captain Charles Greffard, Superintendent of Camp Valcartier.** The Department of National Defence thanked Zaneth,

---

* The trial took place in November 1923. Brisson had agreed to plead guilty and testify against Côté. Each man blamed the other, Brisson claimed he had rented the press from Côté but never used it. Côté claimed he had forgotten a die from the 1916 racket and had planned to use it to make lockets and ornaments. Côté was found guilty of possession, but acquitted of counterfeiting.

** There are records of two inquiries into Greffard's conduct, one investigating alleged financial mismanagement and the second looking into the cutting down of trees at the camp. Details are restricted until 1996 under the Access to Information Act.

noting that he was "courteous, zealous and at all times ready to fulfil our every requirement and wish."

By the mid-twenties, books and movies had romanticized the adventures of the Mounties and had made the RCMP famous around the world.* The reality was very different. The Mounties were Canada's "feds," a small, elite force of detectives, undermanned and overworked with an inadequate budget. Its mandate was to enforce thirty-seven Canadian federal laws.

One of the main duties was to enforce the Opium and Narcotic Drug Act, which prohibited the importation, sale and possession of opium, cocaine and morphine (and later heroin). Beginning in 1921, Commissioner Cortlandt Starnes pioneered the idea of having the RCMP go after the big men in the dope rings, while leaving the small fry to local police.** In the late winter of 1926, Zaneth requested and was granted a transfer to O Division, Western Ontario District, which had its head-

---

* The Edison Moving Picture Company released *Riders of the Plains* in 1910; in 1919 Tom Mix played a Mountie in a silent moving picture. *Rose Marie* would be filmed at Lake Tahoe and released in 1936.

** No Mountie ever charged a Chicago gangster on horseback. In the overimaginative, fictionalized movie version of *The Untouchables*, writer David Mamet has a troop of Mounties galloping across a bridge to stop a shipment of bootleg alcohol. In fact, export of liquor from Canada to the United States was legal. The Mounties, Canadian "revenooers," would go after those moonshiners who distilled their own stuff — to collect the federal excise tax. Distilling itself was illegal under provincial laws. If the bootleggers tried to "reimport" liquor that had been granted an export permit, the RCMP would go after them under the Excise Act for tax and the Customs Act for smuggling. The RCMP was already doing a job done by half a dozen agencies in the United States. One, the small Bureau of Investigation under its newly appointed director, J. Edgar Hoover, was just beginning to expand. The Justice Department's other agency, the Bureau of Prohibition, was corrupted by the job it had to do — to enforce the Volstead Act which prohibited the sale of alcohol and which most Americans ignored. One division of the Bureau of Prohibition enforced American narcotics laws. The Treasury Department had the Secret Service which enforced counterfeiting laws and the overworked Customs Bureau. Finally, there was Treasury Intelligence Service, an enforcement branch of the Internal Revenue Service.

quarters in Toronto. The RCMP office was on the top floor of a solid stone post office built in 1909 at the corner of Yonge and Charles streets.[32] One of the investigators was Constable Andrew Veitch, who had arrived in Toronto in about 1923.[33] "There were only seven or eight men here," he recalled. "As time went on, we formed a criminal investigation branch. I did the general investigations and Hugh Mathewson did the narcotics end of it . . . gradually, we developed more until we had a real investigative organization going here. Zaneth came along a while after that. He came down as a 'special;' he was a very competent investigator."

From April 1926 to September 1927, Zaneth's official record notes, "He was actively engaged in the enforcement of the Customs and Excise Acts, Opium and Narcotic Drugs Act, and handled investigations involving forged bank notes, counterfeiting, as well as numerous other cases." By December, 1927, when the next surviving case file begins, Frank Zaneth was signing his reports "Operative No. 1." The notation meant that he was on a special assignment.

There are three hints of his activities during this lost 1926–27 period. Zaneth's personnel summary says: "While stationed in Toronto, Zaneth worked in conjunction with the U.S. Secret Service, on cases common to both countries." The Secret Service has no surviving record of working with Zaneth, although the term "secret service" was still used generically in the 1920s and it could refer to any U.S. agency.

The second comes from a Montreal *Star* story published about Zaneth on December 14, 1945:

> Sergeant-Detective Zaneth, as he was known then, came in close contact with the Detroit and Chicago mobs which terrorized the United States in the Roaring Twenties era. Investigating several crimes in Windsor, Ont., he discovered that the gangsters there were merely "small fry" working under orders from across the river at Detroit.
>
> Ottawa authorities decided to give Zaneth a free hand in the investigation. For nine months, his impersonation

worked and the information gathered from within the Detroit underworld led to wholesale arrests of several criminal gangs.

The *Star*'s story is probably accurate, as Zaneth had close contacts with Chicago which he used in later investigations.

The third hint comes from Zaneth's personnel file and is a simple notation from Starnes on December 5, 1927: "The Commissioner further states that the high operating costs of this NCO's car is difficult to understand." There is a cross reference to a long lost file on International Drug Trafficking through Windsor, Ontario.

The missing two years gave Zaneth the reputation as a superb undercover operative, and his next case added to his stature as a detective. It has the most bureaucratic title of any of Zaneth's cases: "Re: Forgery of the name of Thomas Gelley (Division Commissioner of Immigration) Winnipeg." The case made Zaneth the Sherlock Holmes of the Royal Canadian Mounted Police. It was a convoluted web, involving a myriad characters and required a special mind to solve it.

In 1923, Canada had imposed severe restrictions on European immigration. Just three classes of non-British immigrants were permitted to come to Canada: "agriculturists" with sufficient means to begin farming, farm laborers with "reasonable assurance of employment" and female domestic servants.

If a farmer on the prairies wanted to hire a cheap field hand, usually from Italy, he used a labor agent to select the man and was given an "assurance of employment" form, usually just called a permit. A permit was a simple application run off on the letterhead of the Department of Immigration and Colonization. The farmer filled in the blanks with the name he got from the labor agent, then sent the permit to the immigration office in Winnipeg.

Once the permits were approved by Canadian immigration, they were mailed to the Italian consulate in Ottawa. The government of Benito Mussolini demanded exit visas for

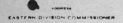

EASTERN DIVISION COMMISSIONER

CANADA

IN YOUR REPLY REFER TO

No.

N.B. - DO NOT WRITE ON MORE THAN
ONE SUBJECT IN ANY ONE LETTER

DEPARTMENT OF IMMIGRATION AND COLONIZATION

COPY.

OTTAWA.

Sir:-

Referring to your application for
the admission to Canada of----------------------,
aged-----, a citizen of-------------------------
and now residing at-----------------------------,
for the purpose of employment with you as a
farmlabourer, I beg to advise you that as a result
of our investigation the material now on file with
the Department will be accepted as satisfactory
assurance of employment as indicated above. It
will be necessary, however, for the said-----------
----------------to pass medical inspection, have in
his possession a valid passport properly vised by a
Canadian Immigration Officer in Europe, and to
otherwise comply with the provisions of the Immigration
Act.

This letter is to be carried by the
said--------------------------and presented to the
Canadian Immigration Officers by whom he is examined.

Yours truly,

Division Commissioner.

emigrants. The consulate stamped the permit with the exit visa and then sent the permit on to the foreign ministry in Rome. The farm laborer would pick up both his passport and the permit from the foreign ministry before leaving for Canada.

Emile Belanger was the Canadian immigration officer at the French port of Cherbourg. His job was to examine prospective immigrants boarding steamships for North America, to confirm that they were eligible for entry into Canada.

One day in early November 1927, Belanger faced a line of more than a hundred Italian steerage passengers.

"Where are you going?" Belanger asked one man.

"Windsor," the man replied, "I go stay with my brother in Detroit."

The answer made Belanger take another look at the man's permit. According to the form, the man was supposed to go to a farm in Alberta.

"Aren't going to work for . . . ?" Belanger asked, naming the farmer.

"No, I never heard of him," the man replied. "I am going to join my brother in the United States."

Belanger suspected that the man's permit was forged. The next permit seemed identical. That day, Belanger rejected 149 men with suspect permits. He sent all the permits to Ottawa. On November 23, the Department of Immigration and Colonization called in the RCMP.

Two weeks later, after a preliminary investigation by headquarters Staff Sergeant C.A. Ramsay, Commissioner Cortlandt Starnes ordered Frank Zaneth to Ottawa to work with Ramsay on the case.

RCMP headquarters suspected there was a wide-spread forged permit racket and believed the most likely suspect was the Mafia. Since 1922, Mussolini had cracked down on the Sicilian Mafia. Don Vito Cascio Ferro, one of the leading Mafia bosses on the island, had organized a network to smuggle men from Sicily to Marseilles. From France they boarded ships to Quebec or New York. From Canada, Italians with connections or enough money to pay off the mob were smuggled into the

United States at Niagara Falls or Windsor.

Staff Sergeant Ramsay had discovered that the permits sent by Emile Belanger were indeed forged. But the Italian exit visas attached to the forged immigration permits by the consulate in Ottawa were genuine. That could mean the forgery was an inside job.

The permits were easy to forge; they could be run off on any Multigraph machine. The greatest challenge for the forger was to duplicate the letterhead of the Department of Immigration and Colonization.

Zaneth and Ramsay met the Italian consul, Eugenio Bonardelli. The consul told the Mounties that in the previous summer he had had a run-in with an alien smuggler named Romolo Bobba. The consul had discovered that Bobba was charging two hundred dollars a head for "helping" Italians bring their relatives to Canada. The consulate gave the same advice for nothing, so Bonardelli had cut Bobba off. The alien smuggler had responded by threatening to kill the consul, then had left Ottawa for more profitable cities. About a month later, the Italian consulate had received a large number applications for farm workers from Winnipeg. There was no reason to suspect forgeries, so the consulate processed the permits and sent them on to Rome. That had been a year ago.

Now, Bonardelli suspected those permits were forged. The RCMP knew Bobba as an Italian mobster based in New York. He was on a look-out list compiled by the U.S. immigration service.

The first lead came from Winnipeg, and Zaneth arrived in the city on December 16. There he discovered some destitute Italian farmers, victims of an earlier, unrelated scam, who had arrived in Manitoba to find the land they wanted was not available. Desperate for help, the men had approached Bobba, who had claimed to have close ties with two members of parliament. But instead of using political influence, Bobba had offered to smuggle the men into the United States. Bobba had a black club bag full of blank assurance of employment permits. The forms were already signed by Saskatchewan farmers and endorsed with (the presumably forged) signature of Thomas

Gelley, immigration director for the prairies and sealed with the departmental seal. Any name could be filled in. The poor farmers had refused the deal, and Bobba was long gone.

Zaneth followed Bobba's trail to Windsor, the prime city for smuggling booze and immigrants. There he learned from gangland sources that Bobba had showed off the permits to colleagues.

As in any good Sherlock Holmes story, a new and important character entered at this point. He was Luigi Maconi, a steamship agent who worked in Windsor. Like many travel agents serving new immigrant communities in Canada then and now, Maconi was a professional go-between. For a fee, he would help a newly arrived Italian with a problem, whether it was bringing a relative to Canada or filling out an income tax form.

On New Year's Eve, 1927, Luigi Maconi arrived in Ottawa to see Eugenio Bonardelli, the consul, about a serious problem. He told Bonardelli that many of the men rejected by Emile Belanger at Cherbourg had been his clients. Now their relatives in Windsor and Detroit, who had paid up to two hundred dollars for the immigration "permits," were demanding their money back.

Bonardelli immediately took Maconi to see S/Sgt. Ramsay at RCMP headquarters. (Zaneth was in Toronto looking for alien smugglers).

Maconi had a strange story to tell the two men. In the fall of 1927, Maconi said, he had met another go-between, a man named Flavio Masi who was based in Hamilton.

Masi said he had a quick way, using his connections, to get Italian immigrants into the country. He was very sure of himself and quite persuasive. He said each permit would cost the family in Canada two hundred dollars. Maconi could take a commission of twenty-five dollars on each permit. Maconi believed Masi because his brother, Nicola, was the Italian vice consul in Hamilton.

Maconi thought it was a good deal and quickly went to work. He soon sent Flavio Masi the names of 148 prospective immigrants, together with $20,400.41.

Everything went well with the first few immigrants, who settled in Windsor. Then had come the interception at Cherbourg and Luigi Maconi found himself in big trouble.

Maconi offered to prove he was on the level. He pulled a letter out of his briefcase to show to Ramsay. To Bonardelli's surprise, it was a letter of acknowledgment for a permit, signed by the Consul's secretary, a young Ottawa man named Paul Edward Clement.

Bonardelli left RCMP headquarters, returned to the consulate and fired Clement.

When Ramsay questioned Clement a couple of days later, Clement claimed he was helping out a member of parliament — unnamed in the file — who had promised him two dollars a sheet for processing each immigration form. But the Staff Sergeant found out that Clement was using his own post office box to handle the permit. It seemed Clement knew both Romolo Bobba and Flavio Masi.

Meanwhile, Luigi Maconi, anxious to save his business and his skin, decided to become his own private detective, and he kept the RCMP informed of his progress. On his way home to Windsor, he stopped off in Hamilton. There he met Ernestina Masi, Flavio's wife, who told Maconi her husband had left for Italy in October. He was in Castellamare Adriatico, near Pescara, on the east coast.

At the beginning of the investigation, Zaneth had signed his reports with his own name "F.W. Zaneth, Det-Sergt. Reg. No. 6743." On January 10, 1928, Commissioner Starnes made the decision to activate Zaneth in his role as "Operative No. 1." for this case. From then on, all reports to the Commissioner, by Zaneth and from other people in the RCMP referring to Zaneth, mention only Operative No. 1.

Zaneth read Maconi's report on his visit to Hamilton, then visited Ernestina Masi. He was posing as a not-too-bright staff member from the Italian consulate in Ottawa. Ernestina told Zaneth that her husband had received permits in batches of two or three envelopes a week and that each envelope contained about ten permits.

Zaneth's next stop was in Windsor to question Luigi Maconi. Operative No. 1 pretended to be an investigator for Immigration and Colonization. Maconi's initial contact had been Flavio Masi, but the first three permits had come from a man named Frank Wise. Wise ran a cod exporting business from an office building near Yonge and King streets in Toronto. Maconi had paid two hundred dollars each for permits for men named Michele Rinaldi, Pasquale Fratarelli and Luigi Bianchi. Everything appeared to go fine: Maconi had sold more permits in the Windsor–Detroit area. After the first three permits, Maconi had dealt directly with Masi on the hundreds more he had sold. Wise, it appeared, was a small-time operator.

Maconi told Zaneth that Rinaldi had arrived a few months after his permit came through and was now living in Windsor. Bianchi had decided not to come to Canada. Fratarelli was somewhere in North America, but his brother, who had tried to come later, had been caught with a forged permit. Maconi had suspected that the first three permits were also forged, and he had written a letter to Wise asking about the forgeries. According to Maconi, Wise replied "in a very unfriendly manner," and told Maconi he did not want to see or hear from him again.

Maconi was still playing his own detective. He gave Zaneth an address for Romolo Bobba in New York, on Barrow Street in Greenwich Village. Zaneth concluded that Maconi was what he claimed to be — a go-between who had got caught up in a racket.

Zaneth returned to Toronto and in a report to the Commissioner, requested that the immigration department supply the RCMP with the names of Italian farm laborers so he could discover how many of the permits were forged and when the forgeries first appeared.

On the evening of Friday, January 20, Operative No. 1 met Frank Wise in his tiny office in a building on 34 Yonge Street. Wise, a man in his early sixties, said he had received three permits from a group called the Italian Aid and Protective Society; the society had got the permits from Ottawa. Wise said he had sold only those three permits to Luigi Maconi.

Zaneth's investigation showed there was a shady system that worked with what customers believed were *genuine* assurance of employment permits. The chain began somewhere in Ottawa; the instigator was likely someone with influence, probably a member of parliament, who obtained genuine permits from someone in the Department of Immigration and Colonization. The permits were sold to an Ottawa go-between, who then passed them on to the Italian Aid and Protective Society in Toronto, apparently an immigrant mutual help group.

The Italian Aid and Protective Society then supplied permits to its members. It also sold permits to men like Frank Wise and Flavio Masi.

Wise bought permits from the society and then sold them to Maconi. The customer who bought the permit had to fill in the name of the friend or relative, then forward the permit to Paul Clement's box number. At the Italian consulate, Clement stamped the permit with a genuine exit visa and mailed it to Rome.

Then *forged* permits had suddenly appeared in large numbers. The forgeries were pre-signed by Saskatchewan farmers and "approved" in Winnipeg with the forged signature and seal of the immigration director, Thomas Gelley.

On January 24, Zaneth was back in Ottawa, and with Ramsay, met with the Immigration Commissioner, A.L. Jolliffe. Protecting his bureaucratic turf, Jolliffe refused to show Zaneth the files on Rinaldi, Fratarelli, and Bianchi, the three men whose permits were obtained by Maconi. He told the two Mounties that, surprisingly, the three permits were genuine. Apparently, that chain was a dead end.

Zaneth and Ramsay discovered that there were at least half a dozen people in the city who dealt in genuine immigration permits. One was a member of the Parliamentary Press Gallery.

Zaneth surmised that they were dealing with at least two rackets and probably more. There were the people selling genuine immigration permits; there were the forgers and there were the alien smugglers. Where was the connection?

Then Zaneth got a tip from one of his underworld sources who said a man from Niagara Falls, Ontario, Giuseppe Biamonte, had bought permits from Mike Trotta, a well-known gangster in the Falls. Trotta was a known associate of Hamilton gang boss and bootlegger Rocco Perri, who called himself "King of the Bootleggers," and who was recognized as the head of the Calabrian Mafia gangs in southern Ontario.

On Saturday, January 28, Operative No. 1 once again used the cover of the Italian consular official.* He talked to Mike Trotta's mobster brother Tony, later noting in the euphemistic language of a police report, "I informed him that it would be in the interests of his brother to have him see me, for I suspected that he was an innocent party and he might just as well tell the truth as shoulder the blame himself."

Zaneth had come up with an interesting angle. Someone may have had the brains and chutzpah to take on and scam the Mafia alien smuggling networks. It seemed the forgers had been selling some of their phony permits to the mob.

Giuseppe Biamonte told Operative No. 1, in his role as the consular official, that in August 1927, Mike Trotta had offered him three immigration permits for two hundred fifty dollars each. Biamonte had later bought four more permits from a Niagara Falls, New York, gangster named Frank D'Agostino.

On January 31, Operative No. 1 finally met with Mike Trotta. The racketeer told Zaneth, still the consular official, that he had bought seven permits from Flavio Masi. He had sold two to Biamonte and used the others to bring friends from Italy. Those friends never arrived. Trotta said he had made no profit on the transactions. Zaneth reported: "This statement can be taken with a grain of salt, as even though Trotta is almost

---

* Zaneth's service record indicates that he spent at least his first year in Ontario living in Niagara Falls. Unless he and his wife were in deep cover, it is likely that two experienced gangsters like the Trotta brothers would have known who the local RCMP detective sergeant was. Yet apparently they didn't recognize Operative No. 1. This may be an indication of Zaneth's ability with disguises.

illiterate and [can] only speak a few words of the English language, yet I cannot believe that he was not recompensed in some manner for his part."

Trotta said Masi had also taken him for two hundred dollars. Masi had borrowed the money from Trotta for a weekend trip to Brooklyn. Before he went, Masi had given four permits to Trotta as collateral. Then Masi had boarded a ship for Italy.

Trotta had two permits left. He gave them to Zaneth. They had been stamped in Ottawa, on October 14, 1927. When he saw the date, Zaneth concluded that Clement and Masi were partners. Masi had left for Italy on the eleventh, three days before the date on the official stamp.

Zaneth then left for New York City, where he began to look for Paul Clement with the assistance of the New York Police Department. His family said he was staying with Romolo Bobba. Zaneth followed Bobba through a series of Broadway nightclubs and staked out his house, but there was never any sign of Clement, Zaneth's prime target. Zaneth concluded that the RCMP could get their hands on Bobba any time they wanted. He returned to Toronto.

Zaneth then spent a few days in Hamilton, where he met and talked with two men who had purchased permits from Masi. Masi had accepted checks from his agents but demanded cash from his local customers. The Italian community in Hamilton believed that the whole Masi family was involved in the fraud. People were using threats to demand refunds from Nicola Masi, the vice-consul, and other members of the Masi family. The Masi family hotly denied any involvement.

Zaneth decided it was time for another talk with Mike Trotta. He drove to Niagara Falls and spotted the gangster on the street. He identified himself for the first time as a Mountie and "requested" that Trotta accompany him to the RCMP office.

This man was a rather difficult person to question owing to the fact that . . . he is inclined to despise all law representatives, I decided to adopt certain unusual methods to extract the truth from him. When I questioned him regard-

114

ing the permits . . . he first denied it but later when I informed him that I had all kinds of time at my disposal and that he would not be allowed to go until he had told me the whole truth, he stated that it was so.

Trotta told Zaneth that Flavio Masi had originally approached the Niagara Falls mob with the idea of bankrolling the permit racket. Trotta had given Masi $150; a second gangster, Mike Surace, had advanced $300. By July 1927, nothing had happened; the gangsters had customers for permits, but Masi had supplied nothing.

Trotta and Surace went to Masi and demanded their money back. Masi coolly replied that he was getting anxious himself as he had not yet received the permits from his supplier in Toronto. Zaneth's reported continued: "Then Surace, who is an anarchist, black hander, bootlegger and a criminal in general, requested Masi to see this man."

Trotta, Surace and Masi drove to the King Edward Hotel in Toronto. There Masi used a pay phone. After a few minutes a man appeared; it was Masi's supplier.

Trotta said the man wore white spats and carried a cane over his arm. Surace and Masi went to the second floor and left Trotta waiting for two hours. When they returned, they told Trotta the permits would be available in two weeks time.

Two weeks later, Flavio Masi showed up in Niagara Falls and gave Trotta three permits. Later, Trotta saw "the Toronto man" give Surace two large envelopes containing two hundred immigration permits.

Mike Trotta did not know who "the Toronto man" was; Surace apparently did, since he was later able to phone him without any help from Flavio Masi.

Zaneth needed to discover who Masi's contact — "the Toronto man" — was.

In early March, Zaneth spent two weeks in hospital. (He suffered from "a slight rupture of the base of his lung which has resulted in his spitting up blood.") While Zaneth was confined to the hospital bed, an Italian who lived in Toronto stopped by the RCMP office and told Staff Sergeant Herb Darling, the head of the Toronto Criminal Investigation Branch, that Flavio Masi had approached him about the permits and then introduced him to a gentleman of about seventy, who was "walking with a stick and a plug hat." Masi had told the Italian, a part-time travel agent, that the gentleman was a member of parliament. The travel agent had refused to deal with Masi.

By March 22, Zaneth was back on the job. He submitted to Commissioner Starnes a list of the victims and participants in the racket. Zaneth had discovered that the last genuine permit was purchased in the spring of 1926. All later permits were forged.

Flavio Masi, Mike Trotta and Paul Clement had sold 233 — some genuine and some forged — for $32,645. All the victims were angry and willing to testify. One question remained. Who was the Toronto man?

The first weekend in April, Zaneth met a Niagara Falls man who had bought two permits from Mike Surace in August, 1927. The man was willing to approach Surace to see if he would talk to the Mounties. Zaneth noted, "I may say that Mike Surace is a man who lives by his wits and bears a very shady reputation around that district."

That evening, Surace arrived at Zaneth's hotel room. To Zaneth's surprise, the gangster was "quite frank and honest about his statements." He said the permits from Flavio Masi were genuine. He also stated that during the last federal election he and Flavio Masi had worked for a candidate, who had been elected, and who later supplied the permits.

Surace's story was similar to Trotta's. He had made a deal with Masi for immigration permits and paid deposits of one hundred dollars per permit. A year had gone by. The customers wanted action. Surace had decided it was time for a talk with Flavio Masi.

Zaneth later translated the story of the meeting into the euphemistically bureaucratic language of a formal statement to the RCMP:

During the conversation, he [Masi] stated [to Surace] that he was expecting the permits every day, that he had telephoned to Toronto and Ottawa in an endeavor to have them rushed.

As we [Surace and Trotta] were very firm in our demand, Flavio Masi invited us to accompany him to Toronto where we would see the man who was getting the permits . . .

Mike and Tony Trotta, Mike Surace and Flavio Masi went to the King Edward Hotel, had lunch, then met with Masi's contact.

"Flavio Masi introduced me to him — he gave the name of Mr. Wise." Surace said.

Wise had claimed that the permits had been held up by the bureaucracy because farmers had made arrangements for a large number of immigrants. Wise promised that the permits would arrive in a few days. It was more than two months before Surace got two more permits. Probably because he felt he was a victim of a racket, the gangster had no qualms about talking or promising further cooperation with Zaneth.

Zaneth, meticulous as always, stayed in Niagara Falls to locate more permit sellers and buyers. He decided he wanted another talk with Mike Trotta, but discovered that Trotta had fled to Italy on March 3.

Zaneth then turned his attention to Frank Wise, who had claimed be a simple go-between. He had sold the permits for Bianchi, Rinaldi and Fratarelli to Luigi Maconi in Windsor. Michele Rinaldi had come to Canada. His permit had come from Wise. So far, the Immigration Commissioner had not permitted the RCMP to see Michele Rinaldi's file. Jolliffe had said all three permits in question appeared to be genuine. Zaneth decided the Rinaldi file was the key that would unlock the mystery. He reported to RCMP Headquarters:

. . . in order that I may get to the bottom of this investigation in an intelligent and satisfactory manner I would like to peruse the file in question myself.

My reason for being desirous to peruse Michele Rinaldi's file is this: — If the three permits in question were issued by the Department and naturally genuine there is no necessity for going further than Frank Wise and we can reasonably assume that he was the instigator and the brains of this whole scheme. On the other hand, if the three permits in question were forged and identical to those in our possession, this investigation will bring in . . . someone in the Department.

On April 11, in Ottawa, Zaneth finally got to see the three files. All three permits were genuine.

Zaneth next had to find out where the forged permits came from. The genuine "assurance of employment," Zaneth noted, "are identical in the form of heading and body of the letter to the forged ones with the exception that they bear the genuine seal and signature."

Zaneth went to the King's Printer. There he discovered that the Winnipeg immigration office had been supplied with ten thousand sheets of stationery produced in late 1924 and early 1925. After 1925, the format changed: the letterhead was smaller. The printing plate for the original letterhead and coat of arms was destroyed in 1925, but in 1927 the Winnipeg office was still using the stationery with the old letterhead for the employment assurance permits.

Wise had had his hands on the three genuine permits in July 1927; he had passed them on to Maconi.

Zaneth concluded that Wise must have used one of the genuine permits as the model for the forgeries:

After examining very closely the Crown which appears on the forged permits, I came to the conclusion that the plate used in the production of the same was made through a photographic copy of the genuine and this is the reason why same is not as clear as the genuine.

Any man could produce a plate through the above mentioned process by placing the film and zinc plate and with

118

acid they could bring forward every letter or design but not quite as clear as the genuine and in view of this it is most difficult to ascertain who produced the plate.

Zaneth had solved the case. It was time to make an arrest. On April 21, in Hamilton, Zaneth laid three charges against Flavio Masi: conspiracy to defraud, uttering forged documents and false pretences. Since Masi was in Italy, there was no publicity. The government began the process of applying for extradition.

Four days later, Zaneth obtained a search warrant and with Staff Sergeant Darling raided Wise's home on Madison Avenue in Toronto. They found envelopes similar to those used for mailing the permits. They took Wise to his office and searched the files.

In Wise's files, Zaneth found letters from a man named Barney Phillips in North Battleford, Saskatchewan. From the letters, it appeared Phillips had supplied the names of the farmers that appeared on the forged permits. Zaneth seized the files and Wise's typewriter. Zaneth and Darling arrested Wise and took him to the Toronto police station, where he was held overnight and charged with conspiracy, uttering and false pretences.

In his report of April 30, Zaneth reconstructed for Commissioner Starnes how the racket worked. It began during the federal election in the summer of 1926. Mackenzie King had been returned to power after the short, ill-fated Conservative government of Arthur Meighen.

During the campaign, Flavio Masi, together with gang-connected Italians such as Mike Trotta, apparently worked for a Liberal candidate in the Niagara region. The candidate was elected.

The Liberals then apparently defied the spirit and the letter of their own immigration restrictions, and gave out handfuls of genuine immigration permits as rewards to Italians who had supported the party. One of those was Flavio Masi. It is unlikely that the Liberals expected the immigrants to go to Alberta or Saskatchewan to work on farms. Some of the prairie MPs, or at least their campaign organizations, were, however, apparently involved in getting the farmers to sign permits. It is likely the Liberals expected the immigrants to end up in Toronto and eventually vote the right way. The MP from the Niagara region was never named in the file, nor is there any indication that the RCMP did an in-depth investigation of this corruption by the governing party.

In December 1926, Flavio Masi had introduced Luigi Maconi to Frank Wise. Wise told Maconi that he could get permits through Liberal contacts in Ottawa.

Over the next few months, Maconi submitted names of prospective immigrants to Wise through Masi. In July, 1927, Wise supplied the three permits for Rinaldi, Bianchi and Fratarelli. At this point, apparently frustrated with the political process, Wise decided to forge the permits and set up his own network using Flavio Masi in Hamilton, Maconi in Windsor, and organized crime figures in Niagara Falls, Buffalo and Detroit.

Wise had the Bianchi permit photographed then reproduced as a plate. He then cut the plate, separating the letter head from the body of the letter. Then the rest of the form was set on the Multigraph machine and run off.

Wise had a corporate seal made that was almost identical to the immigration department seal, with its Canadian Coat of Arms. The corporate name "English Mortgage Company" was added around the outside as camouflage, so the company that made the seal would not be suspicious. Once he had the seal, Wise scraped off the corporate name. Finally, he forged the signature of Thomas Gelley, the immigration director.

Wise needed someone to supply the names of farmers, so he recruited Barney Phillips in Saskatchewan and paid him for the names.

Wise and Flavio Masi then went to Ottawa. The consul was in New York on business and they bribed Paul Clement, who was "an easy subject to approach."

An agent would submit the names of would-be immigrants to Frank Wise. Wise would fill in the form with the name of the prospective immigrant and pick at random the name of a farmer from the list sent to him by Phillips. The agent would take the filled-in form to the sponsors and then get a deposit or payment in full.

Wise or Masi then mailed the forms to Clement at a box number in Ottawa. Clement added the genuine Italian government exit visa to the permits, then mailed them to Rome. (Zaneth reported that some were probably never sent to Italy.) Clement then sent an "official" acknowledgment from the Consulate to Masi or Wise; the agent used the acknowledgment to collect the bulk of the money from the sponsor.

Zaneth took the train to North Battleford. With a local RCMP corporal, he questioned Barney Phillips who quickly confessed that he had recruited some farmers in the district to request "Italian laborers." He had forged the names of other farmers. Zaneth's report showed just how all the crooks in the racket were typically scamming each other:

> I may say that although these farmers denied having received any remuneration . . . after questioning Mr. William Reckel [a local farmer], for a short while I ascertained that Mr. Phillips gave him an old hay mower and an old hay rake and he was to pay other farmers $10.00 if Mr. Phillips could collect the $25.00 for each signature from Mr. Frank Wise, but according to Mr. Reckel, Frank Wise never paid Phillips. However, there is definite proof Mr. Wise paid Barnard Phillips the sum of $300.00 for the applications signed by the farmers.
>
> I am quite positive that none of these farmers are in a position to hire help. The country is not a very good farming district . . .
>
> I can frankly say that Mr. Wise was kidding Mr. Phillips and Mr. Phillips was kidding Mr. Wise. It is a physical impossibility to quote even the most interesting assertion made by either man during the correspondence which started sometime in June, 1926 and ended in August, 1927 . . . Mr. Bernard Phillips . . . advised Mr. Wise that they had a great amount of land at their disposal for settlement and

121

that by putting this proposition before the Department of Immigration and Colonization, they would be able to obtain permits to bring Italian immigrants into this country.

On the other hand, Mr. Wise . . . informed Mr. Phillips that he had a Count in Italy who had at his disposal 18 million lire to put into the scheme.

While checking more of Phillips's correspondence, Zaneth found that Wise was in the permit game much earlier than he had suspected. Zaneth found proof of direct political influence and indirect proof that the Liberals were running their own immigration racket. Phillips had wired his member of parliament, Cameron McIntosh, and requested help with two of the permits. Within a few days, Thomas Gelley issued two genuine permits and sent them to Phillips, who sold them to Wise for two hundred dollars.

Zaneth discovered a second note that showed that in June 1927 the Mussolini government had issued a proclamation closing emigration from Italy. The forged permit racket began soon after. And in January, 1928, after Zaneth first talked to Wise, the forger had written to Phillips warning "there is a grand investigation going on in Ottawa."

Back in Toronto, Zaneth meticulously arranged the letters between Phillips and Wise, according to date, and matched them with notes in red and green ink.

It took months for the bureaucratic wheels of extradition to get started. The papers requesting Mike Trotta's extradition were not ready till July. Meanwhile, the Italian government was proceeding slowly with the extradition of Flavio Masi, or so Ottawa thought. Zaneth was assigned to other cases. Then someone in External Affairs realized the government shouldn't have sent the request for the extradition to the Italian consul in Ottawa. A new request was filed through the British Embassy in Rome.

On October 19, the consul was notified that Flavio Masi had been arrested in Pescara, but the Italian government had ruled

Mike Trotta was legally an Italian citizen and not extraditable. Within a few days, all the necessary paperwork was ready in Ottawa.[34] There was a permit for Zaneth to carry a gun and handcuffs in Italy, and a letter of credit for $1,200. He sailed for Europe on October 31, in a first-class cabin on the *Empress of Scotland*. He landed in Cherbourg and spent the night in Paris, Zaneth took the train to Milan.

Zaneth's wife, Rita, had left him in 1928 and she was now living in Milan. Zaneth arrived in the city at 1:00 p.m. on November 8 and had a six-hour stop over. He then took the overnight train to Rome.

He spent the next three days trying to meet with the officials of the Italian departments of justice and the interior; booking passage to New York from Naples and clearing Masi's passage through the United States with the American consul. Then he left for Aquila, to sort out the extradition with the local attorney general. The attorney general repeated that Mike Trotta was not extraditable and he would be prosecuted in Italy if Canada provided the necessary evidence.

Zaneth went to the local prison, Citta Saint Angelo, where he finally met Flavio Masi, who handed over his passport and a border crossing permit issued by American immigration.

Zaneth booked passage on the Italian luxury liner, *Conte Biancamano*. Second class had been filled, and he "was compelled to travel first class." The Lloyd Sabuado line was, of course, somewhat reluctant to have a prisoner on board their ship, but Zaneth smoothed the waters by saying he would treat Masi as an ordinary passenger.

Zaneth arrived in Naples on November 20, found Masi in the cells of the harbor police and the next morning the prisoner was escorted to the liner. Masi was very talkative during the voyage, asking about Kingston Penitentiary, blaming Paul Clement and the consul for everything, claiming he believed Wise when Wise said that the permits were coming from a member of parliament. On the afternoon of November 30, the *Conte Biancamano* arrived in New York.

Zaneth followed the traditions of the Silent Force when he

faced the New York press: he kept quiet. "There were . . . a number of newspaper reporters who bombarded me with a number of questions which I evaded, but they seemed to be in possession of certain facts," he reported.[35] Zaneth and Masi boarded a train for Canada.

When the train reached the border early on December 1, Zaneth formally arrested Masi. They took the train to Hamilton, where he allowed Masi to go home and meet his wife and children before being taken to court.

A couple of days later, Masi's preliminary hearing opened in Hamilton. Luigi Maconi travelled from Windsor under RCMP guard (he had received threats from Detroit gangsters). Zaneth, "looking very little like Hollywood's version of the redcoat" as one reporter described him, testified about the investigation. Masi was committed for trial.

The case dragged on. Frank Wise's trial was set for early May 1929. After hearing the first witness, Wise pleaded guilty to uttering forged documents. On May 23, 1929, he was sentenced to thirty months. Masi's trial was postponed to September.

Zaneth, meanwhile, had been working on another immigration fraud. In Hamilton, Corporal R.E.R Webster, in charge of the local RCMP detachment, was assisting Zaneth. He had found early in the investigation that at least two more outfits were selling immigration permits. The most important, Webster reported, was the Mutual Steamship Agencies, run by two men, Joe Scime and Anthony Kapelle.

The RCMP raided the steamship agency and came up with new forgeries and a modus operandi similar to that of the Masi-Wise racket. Zaneth seized extensive records that showed that Kapelle had contacts in Niagara Falls, Buffalo, Manhattan, Brooklyn, Memphis, and Kansas City.

Kapelle had forged permits issued by the commissioner of immigration for the eastern division, he had also forged the signature of the local immigration inspector in Hamilton. Once the immigrants who used the permits arrived in Canada, they would be smuggled into the United States. If they arrived by steamship in New York, "in transit" to Canada, they simply disappeared into the United States.

Kapelle went to trial a few days after Masi's case was postponed, charged with both forgery and uttering forged documents. The jury disagreed, and rather than face a new trial, Kapelle pleaded guilty and was sentenced to eighteen months. The complete list of illegal aliens was handed over to U.S. immigration officers.

It appeared that the Italian mob was both a victim of the Wise-Masi racket and a copycat. Wise and Masi had conned mobsters like Mike Trotta, Mike Surace and Frank D'Agostino into buying phony permits. Other mobsters, involved in the Mafia-run alien smuggling rackets realized somewhere along the line that they could forge their own permits, some like Tony Kapelle, went ahead and did so.

Paul Clement had been a busy boy. He started out supplying the genuine exit visas for Masi and Wise, then began to supply Tony Kapelle in Hamilton and finally Romolo Bobba in New York City.

When Kapelle's lawyer was talking to Zaneth, he let it slip that Clement was in New York. In early June, Zaneth again went to Manhattan, where he and a NYPD homicide detective located Bobba. He was working at the Knickerbocker Art and Novelty Company in Brooklyn, a factory that mass produced small statues. The smuggler had apparently come down in the world and was living with his wife in a small apartment in Brooklyn. There was no sign of Paul Clement.

Zaneth returned to Toronto, where Superintendent G.L. Jennings, Commander of O Division, had an assignment: a new immigration racket was apparently being worked among Macedonians and Bulgarians in Toronto. The file on that case has been destroyed, but the RCMP annual report for 1931 reported that Zaneth quickly wrapped the case after determining that the forged documents originated in Europe.

The trial of Flavio Masi opened on March 18, 1930. The seals, dies and forged documents were introduced as evidence. Frank

GENUINE PERMITS

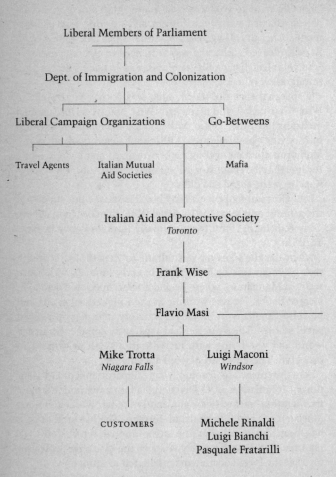

Liberal Members of Parliament

Dept. of Immigration and Colonization

Liberal Campaign Organizations   Go-Betweens

Travel Agents   Italian Mutual   Mafia
                   Aid Societies

Italian Aid and Protective Society
Toronto

Frank Wise

Flavio Masi

Mike Trotta   Luigi Maconi
Niagara Falls   *Windsor*

CUSTOMERS   Michele Rinaldi
                     Luigi Bianchi
                     Pasquale Fratarilli

FORGED PERMITS

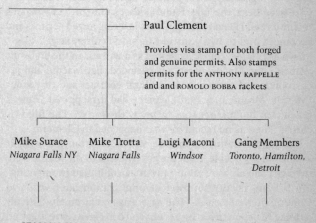

Paul Clement

Provides visa stamp for both forged
and genuine permits. Also stamps
permits for the ANTHONY KAPPELLE
and and ROMOLO BOBBA rackets

Mike Surace	Mike Trotta	Luigi Maconi	Gang Members
Niagara Falls NY	*Niagara Falls*	*Windsor*	*Toronto, Hamilton, Detroit*

ITALIAN FAMILIES, IMMIGRANTS AND OTHER CUSTOMERS

Wise was called from his cell at Kingston Penitentiary to testify. He said Masi had approached him with a list of Italians who wanted to come to Canada. When the supply of legitimate permits was exhausted, the forgeries began.

Wise testified that he had received two-thirds of the money and Masi one-third. The trial was then adjourned until Masi's lawyer, a Conservative member of parliament, was free from his Ottawa duties.

Two months later, while Zaneth was in Niagara Falls, he spotted Mike Trotta standing on a street corner and arrested him.

Trotta was charged and released on bail. Zaneth and the Crown concluded that the case against Trotta was weak but it was decided to keep him charged as he might be a good witness against Flavio Masi.

On September 22, after fifteen remands, the Crown withdrew the charges against Mike Trotta.

On November 27, the case against Flavio Masi resumed in Hamilton. After hearing the last witness, Luigi Maconi, Zaneth reported "his honor stated someone had failed to tell the truth." On December 1, the judge found at least some truth in Maconi's testimony and Flavio Masi guilty of uttering forged permits and sentenced him to two years in Kingston Penitentiary.

Two days later, Zaneth appeared as a witness in the civil suit against Luigi Maconi. The judge decided that Maconi and his customers had entered into an illegal contract and threw out the suit. Meanwhile, Paul Clement had disappeared. Zaneth noted that his mother was "crazy with worry." The file was closed. There is no record of what happened to Clement.

The Italian immigration case was a very tangled web; it seemed many people, from the government to the Mafia, were involved and all were taking advantage of Italian immigrants.

W.J. Egan, deputy minister of immigration later wrote to Commissioner Starnes: "The case was an extremely difficult one and Mr. Zaneth has by patient and consistent investigation unearthed the whole plot."

CHAPTER SIX

Operative No. 1 Undercover Against the Mob

IN 1922 THE OFFICER IN CHARGE of the Niagara Falls detachment of the RCMP wrote to the narcotics division of the Bureau of Prohibition in Pennsylvania about "suspected dealing in narcotics on a large scale" by an Italian immigrant in Canada named Rocco Perri. This was at the height of Prohibition, and Rocco Perri, the Hamilton-based "King of the Bootleggers," was one of the most prosperous and successful gangsters in the illicit booze business in North America. Perri's gang sent shipments of booze to the United States, and they often included a shipment of opium for processing. The drugs were then smuggled back into Canada and sold.

The RCMP knew about Rocco Perri. He "re-imported" good Canadian liquor and smuggled in raw alcohol, both violations of Canadian federal law. Rocco and his common-law wife, Bessie Starkman Perri, were major targets of a 1926 Royal Commission on Customs and Excise that examined bootlegging and smuggling. The early RCMP investigations into the Perri mob's involvement in drug trafficking focused on a number of underlings and on Bessie, Rocco's vivacious but ruthless partner-in-crime.

The drug scene in the mid-1920s was much smaller than it is today, and there was little public pressure for a fight against drugs. There was not enough manpower to go after the Perris themselves, but the Mounties had arrested and convicted several Perri gang members for drug trafficking in the early twenties. By 1926, the RCMP detachment in Hamilton had received highly credible intelligence information from U.S. sources that Rocco Perri was part of an international drug trafficking ring. The officer in charge of the RCMP in Windsor forwarded the new intelligence information to Superintendent Henry Newson who ordered Corporal R.E.R. Webster, in Hamilton, to launch a secret investigation into Perri's activities. Webster learned that there was much street information about Perri's involvement in the drug trade, but that the gang boss had carefully insulated himself from personal involvement. Webster concluded that any major operation against the Perri syndicate would be "too difficult to carry out."[36]

For the next three years, the RCMP watched Perri and his gang as their role in drug trafficking increased. Then, in the late twenties, there was a sudden influx of drugs in Ontario, and the RCMP perceived that there was a serious problem developing with drug addiction in Canada. Informers in the underworld reported that large amounts of drugs were being brought in and distributed by the Perri organization, which was beginning to look ahead to the post-Prohibition period. Under Bessie Perri's initiative, they were diversifying their criminal activities and significantly stepping up their importation and sale of narcotics.

In 1929, Frank Zaneth was assigned to investigate the Perri mob's drug activities. At the same time, Mounties in Windsor began their own undercover operation against two key Perri drug couriers in that city.

Zaneth started by recruiting a number of underworld people in Toronto, Hamilton and Windsor as his agents. The initial undercover agent in Toronto was Ernest Tomlinson, code named "E.T." Tomlinson was a former break-and-enter man, a pimp and an ex-con who was known in the Toronto underworld as a user and peddler of drugs. Tomlinson worked directly under Zaneth and Detective Hugh Mathewson, whom Zaneth was training for undercover work.

For the operation, Zaneth decided to play the role of a Quebec-based drug dealer looking to buy drugs in Toronto with the help of criminals such as Tomlinson, who introduced him around the city's underworld. Zaneth quickly targeted a group of men who hung around a well-known underworld gambling joint called the Marathon and Enosis Club in downtown Toronto just east of Yonge on Dundas Street. There, Zaneth was introduced to Tony Defalco, a twenty-three-year old Perri courier and to Antonio "Tony" Brassi, a middle-aged blind-pig operator from Stoney Creek, near Hamilton. Defalco and Brassi sold Tomlinson hundreds of cubes of morphine. (At the time, one ounce of morphine was 110 cubes.) To place the order, Defalco called in Tony Roma, a forty-year-old Italian who had lived in New Jersey and Philadelphia before coming to Toronto. It was Roma who produced the drugs and took payment from Tomlinson at the first buy on May 8.

Roma again appeared for the second buy, this time accompanied by Brassi and Defalco. Zaneth quickly determined that Roma was calling the shots in all of the transactions. In his Québécois character, Zaneth bought six ounces of cocaine and two ounces of morphine from Tony Roma on June 13 and another six ounces on June 20. Zaneth and Mathewson carefully marked all the money they gave the drug dealers so they could use it as evidence.

The undercover buys were not enough for the operation to be successful. Zaneth aimed to get at the source of the drug supply and at the leaders of the gang. He had decided that the initial RCMP intelligence information was correct, and that Rocco and Bessie Perri were the organizing geniuses behind a major drug ring operating in Toronto, Hamilton, Windsor, Peterborough, Montreal and the United States.

Through his dealings with Roma and E.T., Zaneth learned that the Perri mob's Toronto drugs and money were being kept at the home of Ned Italiano, a Hamilton native with close personal and business ties to Rocco Perri. Italiano had a house on Dundas Street in Toronto and was the go-between for Roma with Rocco and Bessie Perri. Italiano's family lived in Hamilton, and several of his relatives worked with Rocco in various criminal enterprises, including bootlegging.*

The RCMP brass was persuaded by a memo from Zaneth to take action directly against Rocco Perri. At the time, Zaneth and Mathewson were at a very delicate stage in the investigation in Toronto. Zaneth convinced Superintendent Jennings and the Commissioner that the only way to make a major dent in drug trafficking in Ontario was to infiltrate Perri's gang in Hamilton and to ensnare the Perris in the RCMP net. Zaneth's report led to a new undercover operation, one aimed directly at the Perris.

Zaneth's memo to Jennings was signed, "Operative No. 1". In the memo, Zaneth explained why he must go to Hamilton. His sources were telling him that the drugs were being distributed through Rocco Perri's first lieutenant, Frank Ross, a wealthy Hamilton-based bootlegger. Rocco Perri came originally from Plati, the same small town in Calabria that Tony Defalco, Ned Italiano and Tony Roma had come from. Speaking from his personal experience with the Italian mobs, Zaneth said, "These Calabrians generally stick together and do not associate with anybody else."

On three different occasions, when drugs were purchased from Defalco's gang, a part of a Hamilton newspaper had been used to wrap the drugs. Zaneth concluded the drugs came from Hamilton. On June 17, he began his frontal assault on Rocco and Bessie Perri. Accompanied by his supervisor in the RCMP Criminal Investigation Branch in Toronto, Staff Sergeant Herb Darling, Zaneth drove to Hamilton. Zaneth believed that a supply of drugs would be split in one place or the other and that some would be sent to Defalco. They were unable to watch Rocco's house at 166 Bay Street South "as there were people on the verandah apparently acting as a lookout." Zaneth and

---

* Alex Italiano was convicted in 1924 under the Ontario Temperance Act; Domenic Italiano, who was later convicted of a serious shooting on the streets of Hamilton, lived next door to and worked with Tony Papalia, another Perri bootlegger and scion of the Papalia Mafia family which continues today in criminal operations in Hamilton, Toronto and throughout Canada.

Darling watched Rocco Perri's garage and then Frank Ross's residence for five hours and then spent some time trying to locate the car holding the drugs. They had no luck. They returned to Toronto at 2:30 a.m.

The RCMP could not include the Hamilton end of the drug operation with their raids and arrests in Toronto. There wasn't enough evidence to arrest Rocco or Bessie Perri, Frank Ross or any other of the Perris' gang members in Hamilton.

Coordinated police raids were set for June 21. Drugs, money, a revolver and ammunition were found in a raid at Tony Roma's gambling joint, where Operative No. 1, still in his undercover role, was arrested with Tony Roma by RCMP Corporal Raymond Nelson.

When the Mounties raided Ned Italiano's house, they discovered a cache of drugs and most of the marked money.

Two hours into the raid, Bessie Perri arrived at Italiano's house. Police investigators quickly searched the bejewelled, beautifully dressed, petite Bessie, who had a soft voice and manner, which hid a sharp and tough interior. They discovered hundreds of dollars in cash on her person, though none of it was marked money. Bessie said she was just making a social call on Italiano and that she always carried money on her person. Hugh Mathewson knew why Bessie was there, but he didn't have enough evidence to charge her with anything.

Zaneth lost no time in starting his offensive against the Perri mob in Hamilton. A detailed, ten-page report from Operative No. 1 to Jennings outlined Zaneth's plan of action, explained the new developments and suggested a bold course for action. This was one of the few cases where the full, secret RCMP internal files on an ambitious operation are available. Zaneth's meticulously detailed reports provide a unique and astonishingly vivid picture of the sordid reality of the underworld at the time and a rare, inside glimpse into the secret world of RCMP undercover operations.

Zaneth had recruited another ex-convict as his main agent, a "rounder" closely connected with the Hamilton drug scene named James Curwood. Zaneth code named him "Informant

Q." Q was to help set up Zaneth's criminal connections in Hamilton. Operative No.1 was posing as Arthur Anderson, a Jewish mobster with underworld credentials visiting from Chicago.

Q told certain Hamilton underworld friends that he had a gangster friend coming from Chicago to make a drug buy. When he arrived in Hamilton by train from Brantford, Operative No. 1, as Anderson, was met by Q and Gordon Goins, a small-time black drug dealer. Mathewson was assigned to shadow Anderson. As they drove by taxi to the downtown King George Hotel, Zaneth, Goins, and Curwood exchanged gossip about mutual "friends" in the Chicago underworld. Anderson emphasized that he always carried a gun. At one point he took out and waved his "rod" in front of the frightened Goins. He was trying to impress the drug dealer and make sure that there was no attempt to rip him off. He told Goins that he was "not taking any chances" since he was carrying "five grand" in his pocket. He proceeded to flash the money in front of the pair.

When they got to the hotel room, Curwood brought in a case of beer and a bottle of good whiskey. After a few drinks, Goins told Anderson that he got his supply of drugs from local Italians named Frank and Tony Ross, Frank Romeo and Rocco Perri. Goins explained that the Ross brothers had been Perri's lieutenants in the bootlegging business, but were now running his drug business. Anderson asked to meet the brothers. Goins took Anderson and Curwood to a blind pig owned by Tony Ross:

I was requested by the Negro to remove my hat and allow the Italian to see my face. He then said to the Italian in the Italian language, "Here is the boss himself from Chicago. He wants to see stuff by tomorrow morning." The Italian, who looked somewhat frightened said to the Negro, "I have not got it now. What I was talking to you about was shirts." The Negro laughed and said, "Never mind, we will be back in the morning."

Anderson realized that Goins did not have the full confidence of the Italian mob.

After they left the blind pig, Anderson became hostile:

I adopted a careless attitude, without conveying the impression to him that I had understood what had been said in the house, and told him that I had come a long way to meet a bunch of suckers; that they had never seen thirty ounces of drugs . . . and that their limit was a two dollar deck, otherwise they would have been present to make the deal, but that I was confident that the big man he told me about was still out in the corner trying to sell his last deck.

Goins told Anderson that he would take him to "the big boss." Goins then drove to the home of Frank Romeo, where he asked where Perri was. Romeo chatted amicably enough with Goins, but said he didn't know where Perri was. Anderson gave Goins only a few more hours to produce the drugs. Goins, Curwood, and Anderson went back to the hotel at about 2:00 a.m.

Curwood questioned Goins's ability to produce the dope. Goins said the only reason he hadn't yet got the drugs was that the gang was scared of being held up by Anderson. Anderson replied that he would let them hold the gun if they would show him the drugs.

Goins left the hotel with Curwood to pick up the drugs. They returned at 3:30 a.m. with one John Flynn, who told Anderson that he was a drug addict who since 1923 had regularly purchased drugs from the Ross brothers and sometimes acted as their runner. He said he had been asked that very day by Frank Ross to get ready to sell six ounces of cocaine and ten ounces of morphine. Flynn promised to have the drugs for Anderson to examine the next morning.

On the following day Zaneth told Mathewson that he hoped that they could avoid telling the Hamilton city police about their new information, as they were aware that Rocco Perri was a dope dealer, yet they did nothing about it. He implied the Hamilton cops were on the take.

Curwood and Anderson went to meet with Flynn. When they arrived at the blind pig, Anderson was told to wait outside.

Flynn appeared with Goins about twenty minutes later. He seemed worried and told Anderson that the Ross brothers had "shut down their entire drug operation" because they were scared of Anderson. They still thought he was a ruthless Chicago gangster who had come to rip them off. Tony Ross was also suspicious that such a low-level rounder like Goins could have produced such a wealthy, well-connected gangster as Anderson.

Zaneth realized that he had placed too much confidence in Goins. Curwood had been wrong about Goins's ability to make a large drug buy:

> I then, before the informant and John Flynn, told the Negro that I was disgusted; that I had come a long way for nothing and asked him to get out of my sight, which he did in a hurry.
>
> On talking the matter over with John Flynn, who seems to be under the impression that he stands to make a couple of hundred dollars if the deal comes through, I learned that Tony Ross and Frank Ross have two separate caches, but that Romeo and Perri are the real bosses.
>
> He advised me to let the matter stand for a few hours, in the meantime he would consult with another runner known as "Spot" whom he thought would be able to convince the Ross brothers to come through with the goods.

Flynn chatted with Spot, who said he would see the Ross brothers and get them to sell the drugs. Zaneth returned to the hotel to wait, meanwhile Hugh Mathewson marked some money. He also alerted the RCMP in Toronto that there might be a raid, but nothing happened. That evening Zaneth learned from Curwood that the Ross brothers were still "shut down." Anderson told Curwood and Flynn he was going to Montreal to "buy a load" and dropped the name of the notorious Chicago gang boss George "Bugs" Moran to convince Flynn that he was a well-connected gang member.

A few days later, on July 6, Anderson returned to Hamilton and Curwood tried another contact, a bookie named Jim Crawford, who was close to Rocco Perri. Crawford approached the Ross brothers, but he, too, returned empty-handed. Anderson told Crawford he was in the market for thirty ounces and that if Crawford had a connection to contact Curwood. Anderson then "left for Chicago" — he went to Toronto.

In his report to his superiors, Zaneth said he thought no action should be taken for two months unless Crawford came through with the drugs. If Crawford set up a buy, Zaneth proposed to let it go through "without taking action." Inspector Denny LaNauze, acting commander of O Division while Jennings was on annual leave, agreed with Zaneth's suggestion.

Then Q came into Toronto to tell Zaneth that Tony and Frank Ross did not suspect Anderson was connected with the police. He said Perri decided no large sales of drugs were to be made until the court cases of his men were completed. Perri was wisely waiting until all the RCMP cards were played before exposing himself and his gang to further risks. He had followed this practice in bootlegging. In general, Rocco Perri demonstrated shrewd caution during many years of controlling criminal activity.

The Director of the Criminal Investigation Branch in Ottawa wrote on July 17 that headquarters thought the undercover operation should be put on hold. Ken Hossick, the deputy chief of the Narcotics Division of the Department of Pensions and National Health in Ottawa, was a former RCMP drug investigator and he advised the Commissioner to temporarily halt the operation.

By July 24, LaNauze suggested that the operation be expanded. He requested that Zaneth be given an expensive-looking new car with Illinois plates "to give color to the suggestion that Operative No. 1 is a drug runner from Chicago." He stressed the cleverness and thoroughness of the Perri mob in his report to Commissioner Starnes.

Three days later, Starnes formally authorized the purchase of a McLaughlin-Buick to be used only by Zaneth, and he ordered

Zaneth to drive to Chicago to get Illinois plates. Zaneth felt that the expensive car would convince the Perri gang that he was a well-connected Chicago racketeer. He believed he could "clean up" the Perri gang in less than a month.

Zaneth went to Hamilton to plan his Chicago trip and consult with Q. When he arrived, Curwood told him that a bootlegger named Jim Harris was waiting to see him. According to Curwood, Harris had been working with Rocco Perri since 1916. When the two met, Harris told Anderson that he had "the biggest connection in this country" for narcotics, but that he wanted to "satisfy himself" that Anderson was a "bona fide drug runner."

Harris then grilled Anderson about his "suspicious" activities. The Perri mob wondered why, if Anderson were so well connected, he had to buy the drugs in Montreal and Hamilton rather than in Chicago or Detroit. Anderson explained that he preferred to pay more money for the better quality drugs he could get in Canada. He added that if there was to be any cutting of the drugs, he would do it himself. Harris asked Anderson about his mob friends in Detroit and Chicago and demanded the names and addresses of two or three gangsters who could vouch for him. Anderson, taken aback, replied that he wouldn't give names because Harris was a stranger to him. He added that he would have to consult his criminal colleagues first to check whether they would mind having their names used as references. This satisfied Harris for the time being. Another meeting was set up for several weeks later, when Anderson would return to Hamilton from Chicago.

Harris and Anderson then had a few friendly drinks together, during which time Harris opened up a bit about Rocco Perri. He told Anderson that Perri would take no part in the first sale of drugs. But by the time of his second purchase Anderson would probably be dealing with Rocco Perri.

Anderson and Curwood then had a meeting at another bootlegger's joint. Curwood suggested that Anderson take him to Detroit. There, Curwood claimed, he could introduce Anderson to people who would be able to recommend him to the Perri mob. He mentioned a criminal brother in Ohio as well as a friend in Chicago who could be asked to vouch for Arthur Anderson "in case he is asked about his genuineness and power in the underworld."

Zaneth agreed and requested that his superiors allow him to drive with Curwood to Chicago via Detroit.

Anderson returned to Hamilton on August 1 to pick up Curwood en route to Detroit. But Curwood was nowhere to be found. Anderson waited all night at his house. Curwood arrived about 9:15 a.m. driving a car owned by Jim Harris. It turned out that Curwood had taken a job as a driver for the Perri syndicate.

This was quite a surprise. Informant Q was moonlighting, and he was involved in illegal operations with the very man they were targeting. Zaneth realized that Q's duplicity provided him with a perfect cover for introducing the RCMP into Perri's gang. But Zaneth was still wary of Curwood. He reported, "When I informed him that he would only receive his transportation back to Hamilton, and no other expenses, he advised me that all he had was one dollar and fifty cents and felt that he could not make the trip on that amount. Before I reached a definite decision I asked him who he had in mind in Detroit who could be safe in exposing himself. His answer was vague, and he thought that some of his relatives in Chatham, Ontario could vouch for me. This assertion was not satisfactory." So Zaneth decided not to take Curwood with him.

He drove alone to Chicago via Detroit and went directly to the Federal Building and the office of the Treasury Intelligence Service of the Internal Revenue Service, where he asked for Pat Roche, one of the top investigators in the unit. Roche, however, had recently left for a new job as chief investigator at the Cook County State's Attorney's office. Zaneth was introduced to Clarence L. Converse, a member of the unit that was just starting its tax case against Al Capone. On Roche's recommendation, Converse helped Zaneth get Illinois plates. (He circumvented the bureaucracy and corruption of the Chicago police.) He also introduced Zaneth to IRS informers and agents who would help him to develop his cover story for Arthur

Anderson and provide him with the references he needed from Chicago. One man Converse introduced Zaneth to was a Chicago bootlegger and IRS informer named Pat Horan, who promised to vouch for "Arthur Anderson" should any inquiries come to him. Horan ran a dance and bootleg booze joint called the Garage Cafe on East Thirtieth St., in Capone territory. He was in partnership with Sam Constantino, a well-known Chicago mobster who was later convicted of running an international theft and fencing racket. Horan was part of the effort to get Capone, and the cost of setting up the speakeasy — twelve thousand dollars — had been paid by the Secret Six, businessmen who were secretly supporting the feds. Horan introduced Zaneth to Constantino, who agreed to vouch for Anderson as a known racketeer. Later that evening, Horan and Constantino made it clear to everyone in their blind pig — including the many mobsters present — that Arthur Anderson was a trusted friend and criminal whom they had known for many years. Anderson returned to the Garage Cafe several more evenings to drink with his old friends.

After he received his fake Illinois plates from a source in the Chicago police (ironically, they had been taken from a stripped-down stolen car), Anderson called Q in Hamilton and told him to set up a meeting with Harris for August 7.

Anderson then drove to Hamilton and met with Curwood and Harris. He had every reason to believe his operation would be successful, but Harris was still suspicious of him. Harris and Anderson went for a drive to talk over the situation. Harris said that if he could establish that Anderson was "a bona fide drug-runner" then everything would be okay from his end. Anderson gave Harris the names and addresses of his two Chicago mob references, Pat Horan and Sam Constantino. Harris relaxed and mentioned that a shipment of drugs was due in from Windsor. After a few drinks, Harris told Anderson that the drug courier coming from Hamilton had recently been doing drug business for Perri in New York City, Germany and Switzerland. He also mentioned several times that Rocco Perri was the boss of the drug empire. Anderson told Harris that he would return to Hamilton in a few days, after he picked up some drugs in Montreal.

Harris maintained that he was serious about doing business with Anderson and said they should meet when Anderson was on his way back from Montreal. When asked for his Chicago address, Anderson immediately gave the home address of Clarence Converse. Anderson suspected that Harris was stalling until the Italiano case came up in court in September. But this only partially explained the Perri mob's reluctance to deal with him. Zaneth found out what the real problem was at his next meeting with Harris. Curwood was not there. It turned out that the Perri mob were very leery of Jim Curwood, who had a habit of getting drunk and talking. Harris warned Anderson about Curwood, saying he was untrustworthy and quite possibly "a police agent."

On orders from the Commissioner, Q was removed from the operation. Zaneth was on his own.

Later in August, Harris asked Anderson what had become of Jimmy Curwood. Anderson said he thought Curwood had gone to Montreal. Harris said he was sure that Curwood was a stool. Anderson agreed that the man was unreliable and should be avoided.

Anderson felt he had finally obtained the momentary confidence of Harris. At Harris's insistence, he and Anderson went to meet two of Harris's friends at a gas station. The two were drug peddlers, and on the drive back to Hamilton they discussed ways of avoiding detection from the police while smuggling drugs. The group went to Harris's house for drinks, where the discussion continued until four in the morning. Anderson felt he had finally persuaded Harris that he was legit. As Anderson was about to leave, Harris suggested he pick him up on his way from Montreal and drive him to Detroit. Zaneth hedged his bets, not knowing what headquarters would think of his chauffeuring a major drug dealer across the border. He told Harris he was not sure exactly when he would be driving through Detroit. Zaneth was sure that it would be useful to take Harris to

Detroit, and that he would then drive on to Chicago just in case Harris had him followed in order to confirm his credentials.

Superintendent Jennings readily agreed to Zaneth's request to be allowed to go to Chicago with Harris.

When Anderson was ready to leave, Harris unexpectedly decided not to go with him; instead, he wanted to send his friend Frank Poles, a cousin of Rocco Perri, and two other men and a woman. Harris told Anderson that if Poles and his colleagues were satisfied with him after their trip to Chicago, the drug deals would go ahead.

Anderson carefully prepared for this newest test of his gangster credentials. Poles and his drug dealer friends, who were driving their own car, a Buick sedan, were to meet up with Anderson at the ferry in Windsor. Anderson brought two club bags with him, one of which he checked into a hotel in Windsor before he met with Poles and his gang at the ferry. On the ferry, Poles asked Anderson how he was going to bring the drugs across the border without being detected. Anderson explained that he had a speedboat taking the drugs across and that his man in Detroit would pick them up.

On September 1, Anderson met up with Poles and his party in Detroit. They stopped off in Cicero, a Chicago suburb at the heart of Al Capone's territory, while Poles and his colleagues visited with local Italian mobsters there. Once in Chicago, the party insisted on being taken right away to Pat Horan's speak for drinks.

The drinks were an excuse, Anderson decided, and Poles wanted to see if the well-known racketeer was "really friendly" with Anderson. When they arrived at the door of the tough booze can, the black man guarding the door immediately came up to Anderson and said, "Hello Arthur, Pat wants to see you." Horan played his role well throughout the evening, and the group was given many bottles of bourbon whiskey and draft beer on the house. Later Poles and his party went to a hotel and Anderson went "home."

For the next couple of days, both parties pursued their own separate business. Zaneth spent two days with Converse and

Arthur Madden, who headed the IRS team that would nail Al Capone.[37]

On September 5, Anderson joined Poles and his group, and they drove to Hamilton where they were met by Jim Harris. Anderson returned to Toronto. He would meet with Harris later in the week.

In his analysis of the trip, Zaneth was "positive" that his travelling companions were "neither on vacation nor any important business." He theorized that "the sole purpose in mind was to trail me, watch my actions, and see just whom I would get in touch with." Zaneth felt that he had played his part carefully. The critical problem facing him with the Perri mob, Zaneth reckoned, was the constant questioning about his relationship with Curwood:

The only phase of the situation which I am afraid of is that they are very suspicious of Informant Q and that whilst in Chicago, and wherever we happened to stop, Mr. Poles would broach this subject most carefully, asking questions such as how long I had known the man ... and whether he ever worked for a man from Ottawa of the Mounted Police. I informed these people that I had no knowledge of Jim Curwood having ever worked for any Police Forces ... However, they again stressed the point that I should keep away from him as they felt positive that owing to what he said from time to time he was employed by the Police. I informed Mr. Poles that I had severed my connection with this man some time ago when I found he was not giving me any results, and that he is now in Montreal. I stated further that I hardly ever saw him, but that from time to time he had been able to give me a good deal, and that I had purchased from that man and got away with it ... These people are under the impression that I am Jewish, and do not understand the Italian language. Before leaving Hamilton I informed these people that unless they show results I will not bother with them any more, and that on my way back to Chicago next Wednesday [from Montreal] I shall expect a definite answer, as I am getting tired of driving such a long way and that I could easily have my stuff come to Windsor from Montreal, and from there have it transferred to Detroit, and get it from the latter mentioned city.

Anderson seemed finally to be on the verge of making the buy from the Perri mob. But in part the success of the operation depended on keeping Q out of the action. He was being "kept under surveillance" in Toronto by E.T., to keep him away from Hamilton. Q had become a major liability. Meanwhile, Anderson soldiered on, and on the evening of September 11 he finally hit pay dirt. After a quiet lunch and a drive with Harris in the country around Hamilton, a firm deal was in the works.

But Anderson had to pass one more test before the Perri gang would deal with him. On Wednesday Anderson met with Harris in Hamilton, where he was introduced to a Hamilton bookmaker and hotel owner, Jim Murphy, who was an associate of the Perri mob. That evening, Anderson was taken by Harris and Murphy to meet Mat Hayes, another Perri gang member and a bookie, to whom Anderson had been introduced very early on in the operation.

At about 11:30 p.m., Harris and his colleagues suggested that Anderson accompany them to a roadhouse just outside Hamilton. Anderson knew something big was happening. At the roadhouse they were met by the proprietor, one Tony Bone, who was told by Murphy that Anderson should "be given a room out of the way" any time he came by, as he did not like "to be observed by anyone."

Mat Hayes made a telephone call. About twenty minutes later a Marmon roadster pulled up to the roadhouse. Bessie Perri, the boss of the Perri drug trafficking gang, emerged from the sports car and made a grand entrance. She was immediately escorted by Bone to a private room. The three Perri men, Harris, Hayes and Murphy, then took Anderson to Mrs. Perri. This was to be the final test for Arthur Anderson of Chicago." Could he stand up to the cross-examination and scrutiny of the brains behind Rocco Perri's criminal empire? Bessie was the person who made most of the deals, corrupted many of the public officials on the Perri organization payroll, collected most of the money coming in to the Perri mob and met with many of their gangster allies in the States, and ran her criminal empire with an iron fist.

Bessie was introduced as "Mrs. Rocco Perri, the wife of the biggest man in Ontario." During the brief conversation, Bessie asked Anderson if he was Jewish. Anderson was taken aback, fearing that she would engage him in conversation in Hebrew, a language that he "was not very familiar with." Anderson replied yes, but, as he later reported, "Fortunately she did not speak the Jewish language to me." After having a drink with Anderson, Bessie Perri left the roadhouse.

Zaneth decided she must have approved of him; "otherwise she would have shown it right there and then, as she is just the type that would not hesitate to say what she thought." A relieved Anderson told Harris and his friends that he thought they were putting him "through a rather stiff process" and that he felt he was taking a big chance by letting "all these people give me the 'once-over,' not knowing who they were." Harris replied that they had to be careful as they were "the biggest dealers in the country" and that "they did not take any chances until they were absolutely satisfied they were dealing with the right party."

The next morning, September 12, Anderson met with Harris and Murphy at the Market Hotel. Both men assured Anderson that they felt certain by the following Wednesday, September 18, "they would be in a better position to talk business with me, knowing that the boss had seen me."

Anderson's last meeting with the gang before his scheduled testimony at the Italiano trial was scheduled for September 18. He drove with Harris and Murphy to Toronto's Ward district to deliver a parcel, which the pair handed over to a gentleman waiting outside an Italian restaurant. They returned to Hamilton, and Anderson made an effort to force the issue. He was asked to accompany the pair to the roadhouse. There Anderson was told that the drug gang had only one objection to a deal. Harris thought Jim Curwood might be about to testify against some gang members in Windsor. Anderson said that Curwood had nothing to do with him anymore and was not part of the deal in any shape or form.

A phone call was made, and within twenty minutes a courier arrived in their private room with about a half an ounce of pure morphine in cube form. The drug was exactly the type the RCMP seized at Italiano's house. Anderson was asked to examine the drug, and if he was satisfied, they would have the required amount available for him next week at twenty-five dollars an ounce. Anderson couldn't wait a week — the Italiano case would have already begun. He insisted he needed the drugs by the following day so he could provide them to his connection in Montreal. Harris promised he would do all he could to get the drugs by the next day. Anderson said he would meet them at noon at the Market Hotel. But at the meeting the next day, Harris reported that he couldn't consummate the deal as "the big boss was out of town." He wouldn't have an answer for Anderson until next week.

On Monday, September 23, the Italiano trial began. Zaneth testified briefly then boldly drove to Hamilton for his final meeting with the Perri gang. He guessed that no one at the trial would have had time to report to Hamilton if he had been spotted. This was Anderson's last chance to make the buy.

He arrived at Mat Hayes's residence to meet Harris, who was there with Jim Murphy and Hayes, but they seemed "cold and uninterested." Anderson concluded that "something was weighing heavily on their minds." Fearlessly, Anderson continued to press the men for the drugs, but there was to be no deal. They said they had lost their New York City drug connection, and that they would be in no position to negotiate with him for some time. *

Harris then confronted Anderson with damning new evidence

---

* That connection was likely Arnold Rothstein, the man who fixed the 1919 World Series. Rothstein was the biggest narcotics importer in the United States at the time. He had been shot and killed in New York in November, 1928, six months before Zaneth's investigation of the Perri gang began.

about Curwood. They had positive proof that he was "employed by the Mounted Police in Toronto." Anderson replied that Curwood had never done anything in his presence that would indicate he was a stool, but said he had dropped Curwood in Montreal "to shift for himself." It was clear to Zaneth that Curwood had in some way breached the security of the operation. In a report, attached to Zaneth's last memo on this undercover operation, Superintendent Jennings offered this analysis for the RCMP Commissioner:

> Since the arrest of the Italians in Toronto we have endeavored to have our Operative get nearer to the source of supply. It is quite apparent from this file that the leaders are very shrewd and have deliberately withheld introducing a new customer until they knew more about him. Up to the time that our Operative was called upon to give evidence he was not unduly suspected but after his appearance in court on Monday I am quite satisfied that those connected with the ring in Hamilton were posted as to his identity.

Jennings offered fulsome praise for Zaneth's work.

> At this stage I would like to comment upon the favorable work performed by Operative No. 1 in bringing the investigation to this stage and it is through no fault of his own that he is unable to bring same to a successful conclusion. He has taken great risks and has shown considerable initiative in following up this case.

Commissioner Starnes officially ordered the termination of the services of Q on September 30, 1929. With this, the Perri operation was shelved until, as Zaneth put it, "another good informer" came along.

On September 24, 1929, Hugh Mathewson testified that Bessie Perri visited the Italiano house during the police raid. According to police testimony, Rocco and Bessie visited the house while it was under police surveillance on at least three occasions.

The papers had a field day with his dramatic courtroom testimony. The Toronto *Telegram* offered the front-page headline, MRS. ROCCO PERRI DESCRIBED AS NARCOTIC TRAFFIC LEADER. Similar stories appeared in the Toronto *Globe*, The *Mail and Empire*, The Windsor *Star* and papers across the country.

Crown attorney Tom Phelan was able to convince the jury that Italiano's money had been used to buy the drugs. On September 27, Italiano and Defalco were sentenced to six months for possession of drugs. The messenger, Tony Brassi, who had testified that the drugs found at Italiano's home belonged to Roma, received three years in Kingston Penitentiary.

Tony Roma had jumped his bail, skipped the country and missed the trial. A warrant was issued for his arrest, and the bail was forfeited, but it turned out that the real estate used as surety for the bail had been greatly overvalued.

Zaneth shifted his emphasis away from trying to charge Rocco and Bessie Perri for drug trafficking to bringing Tony Roma to justice. Neither Bessie nor Rocco Perri was ever formally charged with drug trafficking.

CHAPTER SEVEN

Everywhere and Nowhere

FRANK ZANETH WAS RELENTLESS and resourceful as an investigator. His pursuit of Rocco Perri and his mob colleagues in the drug and bootlegging business in Canada bordered on obsessive, and he used every stratagem at his disposal to arrest and jail these high-profile criminals.

Zaneth cast a wide net to find Tony Roma, the vital missing link in the Italiano case. On September 23, "a personal friend" who knew Roma and his common-law wife, an Englishwoman named Helen Groves, told Zaneth that Roma was staying in a town near the border and was known to frequent a place that was a rendezvous for gunmen, gamblers, drugrunners and bootleggers. Roma had been crossing the U.S./Canadian border "frequently" with the assistance of friends with "fast cars and speedboats."

By September 30, Zaneth, armed with a formal bench warrant for Roma's arrest, started his search in St. Catharines. The trail led to South Thorold, near Welland, where he visited a source who ran a house of prostitution. Operative No. 1 posed as an investigator working for Roma's lawyer; he was trying to reach Roma to help him. Zaneth quickly found that his source had been correct, that Roma and Helen Groves had been in Thorold. They had moved to Buffalo a few days earlier. Zaneth spent a day in Buffalo's underworld, but Roma seemed one step ahead of him.

At Bridgeburg, across the Niagara River from Buffalo, a bootlegger was rumored to be housing Roma. Zaneth met a Bridge-burg lady who knew Roma and could identify him. She informed Zaneth where Roma might be found and said he was driving a green touring car. Zaneth watched the address until 3:00 a.m., but came up with nothing. Roma had eluded his net.

Zaneth and Herb Darling, meanwhile, were trying to develop a new informant, Pietro Licastro, a Calabrian building contractor who had money problems. He told the RCMP he could supply information about narcotics and said it was Perri who had "furnished Roma with sufficient funds to keep him going." He promised to bring more information but a few days later reported that it was understood among the Italians that "no mention is to be made of Tony Roma," and so he couldn't find out much. He later confirmed for Zaneth that Perri had coordinated the escape of Roma so the case against the rest of the drug traffickers would be weaker.

By November 25, Zaneth was onto a new source, a woman in Thorold, Mrs. Domenic Frada, who knew Roma and his wife well and was a close friend of the Perris. According to Zaneth's intelligence, she was set to receive a fur coat on behalf of Helen Groves. In February 1930, Zaneth received a hot tip from one of his informants in Toronto, that Tony Roma was hiding out in Connecticut or New Jersey. The informant gave Zaneth Roma's entire itinerary after he had left Ontario.

It turned out that Roma's son was running a bakery in Newark, the address of which could be ascertained through the Italian quarter in Meriden, Connecticut. Zaneth, with the help of local police, visited all the Italian gangster haunts in Meriden as well as in neighboring Bridgeport, where there was also a large Italian colony. It was an area that Zaneth knew well: the Zanetti family often spent part of the summer at the beaches at nearby Milford.

Zaneth then went to New York City where he made the rounds of "pool rooms, cafes, restaurants, gambling houses, and all places of ill repute" in the Italian ward, showing photographs of Roma wherever he went. Finally, Zaneth arrived in Newark, New Jersey, where with the help of local police he made considerable progress in his search. Zaneth located Roma's son's bakery. He soon found out that the young Roma was the sole owner of the place. He also discovered that five months earlier "the father joined him and assisted him in the delivery of the bread." Zaneth spent several weeks working with police searching for Roma in Newark, New York City and Connecticut. His quarry was always one step ahead of him, and once again Zaneth had to give up his search.

Then, on February 27, 1930, Zaneth developed significant new information from Mrs. Frada. It turned out that Tony Roma and his wife had a major fight in Mrs. Frada's kitchen on the day Tony Roma jumped bail and went to Buffalo. Here was Mrs. Frada's account of the heated dialogue as it appeared in Zaneth's RCMP report:

> MISS GROVES ("Mrs. Roma"): What a fine friend Rocco Perri turned out to be. After he asked you to stop doing business with Jimmy (Frank D'Agostino, Merritton) and buy from him, in time of trouble he refuses to help you.
> TONY ROMA: The reason why I stopped buying from Jimmy is because Perri gave it to us much cheaper. Rocco has too much money and cannot take a chance to show his hand in this thing.
> MRS. ROMA: At least he could have helped you financially to pull through your trial, whereas now you must leave the country.
> TONY ROMA: The reason why I am leaving is not the question of money but because I am wanted in Montreal on a murder charge and it will be better for the rest (meaning Italiano and Defalco) if I do go away.[38]

According to Mrs. Frada, Roma had hidden in a restaurant in Buffalo. Mrs. Frada offered to become a full-time agent if she was compensated for her expenses. She told Zaneth that she would have to "pay out a few dollars reward to gain the desired information." She then allowed Zaneth to go through a trunk the Romas had left behind, but all he found was lingerie. She also gave Zaneth a recent photograph of Roma and his son in

Newark. Soon there was word that Roma had been seen in Newark. On March 11, Superintendent Jennings immediately sent Zaneth to Newark to make the arrest. But it was another wild-goose chase. Similar spottings in Niagara Falls and Bridgeburg, Ontario also turned out to be false after Zaneth went to investigate. Truly, the wily, shadowy Tony Roma was everywhere and nowhere.

Finally, in late April, through informants in Ontario and the United States, Zaneth developed hard information on Roma's whereabouts: he was hiding out in the Italian quarter in Philadelphia, where he was being looked after by his brother. Zaneth immediately rushed to the city of brotherly love to investigate. Two Philadelphia police detectives were detailed to help Zaneth in his search for Roma. Zaneth also activated local contacts in the U.S. immigration, postal and narcotics services to help in the location and arrest of Roma. He began his search on Saturday, April 19, 1930 — in his second week in Philadelphia — by watching a restaurant near an apartment building at 751 South Seventh Street, in the Italian area, where a reliable source had seen Roma.

Zaneth spotted Helen Groves on the street and followed her to Roma's hideout. At one point during his surveillance, Zaneth saw Roma hiding behind the curtains. But it appeared that certain members of the local police force were on the take and Zaneth was unable to make an arrest. At one point, Roma, acting through a friendly Philadelphia policeman, offered Zaneth a bribe, which Zaneth indignantly refused. Zaneth was also threatened by Italian neighbors of Roma who told him that "Canada was much healthier than Philadelphia." Zaneth stubbornly told those who tried to bribe or threaten him that he was "simply doing his duty" and that "nothing in this world" would prevent him from executing his orders. When Zaneth finally arranged a raid on Roma's hideout, only Helen Groves was there to be picked up by U.S. Immigration agents. Tony Roma himself once again managed to escape Zaneth's grasp by skipping town as soon as he heard Zaneth was in the neighborhood. Roma was certainly a very devious, crafty professional criminal, with an uncanny ability to remain on the lam.

In a post mortem on the Philadelphia fiasco, Zaneth wrote a report explaining that two U.S. narcotics agents had gone to Camden, New Jersey on their own to find Roma, and that they had gone around town showing his photograph.

Commissioner Starnes sent copies of Zaneth's reports to Colonel Charles Sharman, the closest thing Canada had to a "drug czar." In 1927, Sharman became chief of the Narcotics Division of the Department of Pensions and National Health, which, along with the RCMP, investigated narcotics traffic in Canada.*

Sharman remarked in a memo to Commissioner Starnes that Zaneth "was the victim of very bad luck." Sharman went on to say that "it is a reasonable assumption that the arrest of Tony Roma was not effected by reason of the action of certain members of the United States Federal Narcotics Service." Sharman explained a bit about the internal problems within the Narcotics Division of the United States Bureau of Prohibition, beginning with Colonel Nutt, the head of the service. It had recently been discovered that Nutt's son was a drug addict directly supplied by the late mobster Arnold Rothstein. "Nutt is no longer connected with the Narcotic Service, while some eleven Federal narcotic officers in New York are, I understand, under indictment. Numerous transfers have also been authorized . . . One Representative of New York in Congress is pressing for a Congressional investigation into the Narcotic Service in New York City." Sharman added that Harry N. Anslinger, a member of the U.S. delegation to Ottawa in January on the rumrunning negotiations between Canada and the United States, had just been appointed chief of the narcotic service.**

---

* Sharman had been a member of the Royal North-West Mounted Police from 1898 until 1904, and had served in England, France and north Russia during the Great War. His job as Chief Clerk at the Department of Agriculture, interrupted by the war, lasted from 1904 until 1927, then he became head of the Narcotics Division. His appointment came as result of the 1925 Geneva Convention on narcotics, the real beginning of the international effort against drugs, sponsored by the League of Nations.

Sharman was to meet with Anslinger in Washington in a few weeks to discuss the Roma matter and other matters of ongoing cooperation between Canadian and American law-enforcement agencies. He said he would use Zaneth's bad experience in Philadelphia, when "I consider the occasion opportune," as an example of "poor cooperation."

Meanwhile Zaneth's colleague, Constable Andrew Veitch was sent down to Niagara Falls on August 10. Helen Groves was expected to arrive after her deportation from the United States. Zaneth was out of town, working on an undercover operation in Bobcaygeon in the lake district north of Lindsay. Jennings had Constable Veitch go down to Niagara Falls, Ontario to shadow Groves. Veitch followed Helen Groves to Toronto. In a note dated August 13, 1930, Jennings told the Commissioner that when Zaneth returned from Bobcaygeon, "I shall have him get in touch with Mrs. Frada, who may be able to furnish us with information as to this woman's movements whilst in Canada." Jennings dropped the full time surveillance of Groves as "she is apparently on the alert and any shadow operations will soon be discovered," but he took steps "to have all her mail covered in the hope that this may be of assistance."

That same day, Bessie Perri was killed by shotgun blasts in the garage of the Perri home on Bay Street South in Hamilton.*

** Anslinger was named assistant commissioner of Prohibition for the narcotics division. In 1930, President Herbert Hoover took the narcotics division out of the Bureau of Prohibition division and created the new Bureau of Narcotics, part of the U.S. Treasury Department, and named Anslinger U.S. Commissioner of Narcotics.

* On the evening of August 13, 1930, Rocco and Bessie Perri had left the home of Rocco's cousin, Mike Serge and driven home to 166 Bay Street South. Two hitmen with shotguns were waiting in the Perri garage. Rocco got out of the car and turned back to close the big garage doors. Bessie was just stepping toward the door that led to some stairs to the kitchen, when a blast from a shotgun crashed into the wall beside her. Seconds later she was struck in the back of the head and neck by a second shot and killed. As a third shot finished Bessie off, Rocco had panicked and ran from the garage.

By the time Zaneth returned to Toronto from Bobcaygeon, Bessie Perri had received the largest gang funeral in Canadian history. On Sept. 5,

Some months later, from sources close to Rocco Perri, including Mrs. Frada, Zaneth learned that Bessie had been murdered by hit men from Rochester, New York. Bessie Perri owed them money for narcotics. The night before her murder, Bessie had refused payment and turned three Rochester drug dealers out of her house.

Zaneth continued his search for Roma for several years. Then, in July 1935, the popular magazine *True Detective* ran a picture of Tony Roma in its Most Wanted section. The next summer he was spotted and arrested in the small town of Fowler, California. Mathewson was sent to Los Angeles for the extradition hearing in August, 1936. Roma was back in Toronto by October. The trial did not make any headlines — it took place in the middle of the abdication crisis in December, when King Edward VIII was about to give up his throne.

After an eight-year search, Zaneth finally got his man. The elusive dealer was convicted of three charges of selling morphine and cocaine and one count of possession. He was sentenced to two years in jail. After Roma got out he tried to re-enter the United States, but he was deported to Italy.

1930, a coroner's jury had come down with the usual verdict, murder by "person or persons unknown."

Some sources told the Ontario Provincial Police that "Perri's gang is strong for him." Later it was reported had Rocco and Bessie had made enemies, including Mike and Tony Trotta, Ned Italiano and other gang members.

CHAPTER EIGHT

Modus Operandi : The Life of Operative No. 1

Regt. No. 6743 Sgt. Zaneth F.W

There is nothing this man cannot "tackle." He is a lone worker and afraid of nothing. — From "Training Circular Memorandum No. 44"

FRANK ZANETH WAS A SUPERB DETECTIVE. Case reports show that he had a unique tenacity. He would hang on to a case, following up leads, when his colleagues were ready to give up and his superiors ready to close the investigation.

Zaneth was also an alert, highly intelligent and meticulous observer who had a keen eye for detail. As P.F. Lawson had reported in the *Searchlight* , he took careful notes in the small notebooks he would use all his professional career.

Zaneth was self-educated. He never spoke perfect English, never really lost his Italian accent, and his quick notes or personal letters were not always grammatically correct. Yet the language of his RCMP reports improved immensely over the years. He learned to provide reports carefully written in a formal but expressive style.

What kind of man was Zaneth? Younger Mounties — younger then, now in their eighties — saw him through the filter of strict RCMP discipline and hierarchy. To most, he was a rather distant figure, especially after he became a commissioned officer.

Jim Lemieux, who later became deputy commissioner, got to know Zaneth quite well during the mid-Thirties. Lemieux said:

Mr. Zaneth always had some kind of special duties, that very few people knew anything about . . . He was known as a crackerjack detective, he really knew his Criminal Code . . . we were most of the time referring to him as a BTO, a big time operator. He was a . . . strict disciplinarian, but if we needed any advice, he was always quite willing to help us. Zaneth had the ability to surround himself with the best and he had no tolerance for inefficiency.

I always considered him a model policeman . . . He would have fitted in — even in this day and age, when some of the old time police wouldn't. He was a very hard worker, working sixteen, eighteen hours a day.

By the 1940s, Zaneth's exploits were a legend within the RCMP. Retired Mountie John Stevenson remembered one story he heard in 1940. "Zaneth was attacked by a very savage dog. He never batted an eye. He had a revolver, he could have shot it, but he wrestled if off. I think he was a very cool bird; that would startle many men. He never turned a hair. It's just a barrack room story, but it was very impressive. I'm sure the other fellows would take it seriously. I never heard anything but good about Zaneth. Everyone admired him."[39]

Another Mountie who served under Zaneth's command in the early 1940s was B.D. Peck, who later retired as a Staff Sergeant Major.

"Zaneth had an accent, a pleasant one," Peck remembered. "He was a jovial man, not at all a disciplinarian, although I know later he was very strict as far as administration was concerned. He was a damned good detective and a good all round policeman. He could go from administration to being a detective and go from one to the other, which some couldn't do."

Like most Mounties of the era, Peck was surprised at Zaneth's height. "He was a smaller man, and most of them, like myself, were taller, bigger men. I came on in '33 and in '32 was the takeover of the five provinces. He was in before that time, and in undercover, height didn't matter." Another veteran, Jack Chester, agreed. "You sort of looked at him when you first saw him and wondered how he ever got into the Force. They were very strict in those days, five feet eight inches was the minimum.

The late Commissioner Len Higgitt remembered his surprise, as a rookie in the mid-1930s, at being inspected by a very short inspector. Some of the recruits at first thought the inspection was a joke. Zaneth's height fooled a lot of people over the years, most of them crooks.

There are a few hints of Zaneth's life outside the RCMP.

Jim Lemieux was a wrestling fan. Zaneth was a wrestling fanatic. Lemieux recalled:

> The younger members of the Force knew very little about his personal life. I knew a little more because I used to go to the wrestling matches with him.
> [This was quite strange.] He was wise to the ways of the world, and as far as he was concerned, all sports were rigged, except, believe it or not, wrestling. There was a wrestling show every week. I went with him many times when I was a young man. He believed that wrestling was on the up-and-up. Professional wrestling was the only thing he used to get all whet up about. I went many times with him [to the Montreal Forum] . . . I do think wrestling was more on the up-and-up then than it is now, and as far as he was concerned it was the real thing. He did go to the training camps of many of the wrestlers. He was quite friendly with some of them, that's possibly why he thought it was on the up-and-up. *

Little is known about Zaneth's marriage. His wife, Rita, had joined him in Quebec City in 1923 after an apparent six-year

---

* Zaneth's nephew, Bill Rivers, also remembers Frank defending wrestling. "He'd always defend them as athletes, and my mother and father would never buy it, especially my father: it's a show, he would say."

separation. When Zaneth was transferred, they sold their furniture and moved to Toronto on March 26, 1926. In July, Zaneth was officially posted to Niagara Falls, where they lived on River Road. But there were problems with the marriage. Sometime in 1927, Rita returned alone to Italy and settled in Lacchinarella, Milan. In about 1933, Rita Scevola was committed to a mental hospital in Milan. Until the Second World War interrupted communications six years later, Zaneth sent money to pay for the care for his wife.

The Italian families of Springfield would often spend their vacations on beaches around Milford, Connecticut. Bill Rivers, Frank's nephew, recalls that when he was very young, Frank would playfully pick him up and toss him in the surf. "I thought he was strong, but then I was a young kid. I suspect he was. He was short, that's true, but big to me."

Zaneth would take the Montrealer train south to Springfield on his family visits. Rivers remembers him dressing conservatively, in a three piece suit. Once he brought his red serge with him to show the kids. He went upstairs, changed into the scarlet uniform, wore it for about an hour then changed into a sports shirt and slacks.

After 1927, Zaneth put most of his energy into his work as a police detective. Len Higgitt, observed, "His life's work was going after the mob."

Zaneth's dedication did not endear him to everyone. John Marrett, who worked with Zaneth after he retired, says, "Frank was not a very popular person within the RCMP, particularly with some of the brass — people whom he knew when he was serving in the ranks . . . He was just absolutely straight forward and dead honest. The man had very unusual standards of behavior and was not necessarily the most diplomatic person. Frank was a very direct individual. He would express his views and his findings without hesitation. You knew exactly where you were with the man, which is the kind of person I like."

In the first twenty-one years of his career as a Mountie, Zaneth seldom wore his uniform. In the forged-immigration permit case, the Crown ordered Zaneth to follow the standard procedure of the day and appear at the trial in his red serge uniform. There was one problem. In a memo, Zaneth reminded Superintendent Jennings, "my red serge was issued to me in 1917, and although I have preserved same very carefully . . . I am of the opinion it will not be very presentable in a Court of Justice as it is not a good fit now and is also faded."

Commissioner Starnes responded;

> After giving this matter further consideration, I have decided that it would be better not to have Sgt. Zaneth in uniform and he may therefore give his evidence in this case in plain clothes.
>
> I am now of the opinion that if Zaneth appeared in uniform, it would advertise him too much and jeopardize his usefulness for work undercover.

As a non-commissioned officer, Zaneth never did get a new uniform. There is just one known photograph of Frank Zaneth in uniform in his early days on the force, a formal portrait taken when he was promoted to sergeant in 1920.

Zaneth was always a smart dresser, on or off duty. According to Higgitt, Zaneth always wore a trench coat and fedora.

Jim Lemieux remembered, "He had a beautiful raccoon coat that everybody was envious about . . . He had his uniforms made to order by a special tailor in Montreal, who I went to later on.

When he was undercover, Zaneth would dress to fit his role, for example, the pinstripe of the gangster, complete with flashy tie and pearl-gray hat.

Zaneth would most often begin a case not with a switch to the undercover world, but with surveillance. He would carefully watch his suspects and noting their movements, where they ate and slept, before going undercover.

In the late summer of 1928, the British Home Office requested Canadian assistance in a case. They believed someone was apparently involved smuggling narcotics to North America inside Dutch bulbs. The suspect was a young Dutchman named William Huybers who was in Halifax "on business." After a preliminary investigation by the local RCMP, Operative No. 1 was activated and Zaneth took the train to Halifax. After a briefing, he began watching the Green Lantern Ice Cream Parlor where Huybers would often met his girlfriend, a young woman named Joyce Bradford. Although he had a car, Zaneth first looked for Huybers' coupe on foot.

> About 11:10 I noticed two young ladies, one of whom answered the description of Miss Joyce Bradford, emerging from the Green Lantern Ice Cream Parlor, accompanied by a young man, who I took to be William Huybers. They immediately drove south . . . In order to determine whether Huybers was going direct to his residence . . . and also to establish the fact that the man I had seen was Huybers . . . I hired a taxi and, on the pretext of being a visitor to the Exhibition, I requested to be driven around town . . . I was successful in noticing the car in question parked in front of 247 Tower Road . . . .

Joyce Bradford lived at 247 Tower Road.
Zaneth spent the next couple of days trying to follow Huybers around Halifax. At one point, he almost lost him:

> Owing to heavy traffic . . . I was unable to follow him, for he is a very fast driver and seems to know just how to get around, whereas I, in a strange City, with a huge car, I am somewhat handicapped. However, I have been able to give his companion a good look and he appears to be an under-world character, about 40 years old, 5'10" tall, clean shaven, weighs about 170 lbs. Wears a blue suit and a bowler hat . . .
>
> About 2.25 p.m. he proceeded down town and parked on Barrington St., opposite the Keith Building. He remained in his car approximately ten minutes when I noticed him entering the building in question. Twenty minutes after-

wards he emerged on the street accompanied by a man who was wearing very heavy glasses — dressed in a rather dirty looking Palm Beach suit. They both proceeded down Sackville St. I shadowed them on foot to the National Drug and Chemical Co. of Canada where they both entered and remained forty minutes."

The man in the dirty suit turned out to be an eye doctor.
Zaneth tracked William Huybers for the next couple of days, and once followed him into a movie theater hoping to sit next to him and strike up a conversation. He noted Huybers "seems very well supplied with funds and his sole interest in Halifax seems to be, so far, Miss Joyce Bradford."
Zaneth was wary of following Huybers around much longer.

As long as I am not in a position to make his acquaintance in the proper manner, it is rather risky to follow him too often, either on foot or by car, as it is evident that Huybers has been in Halifax long enough to be able to pick up a strange car and a strange face, and being implicated in such a nefarious game, naturally, he is alert all the time. He must have seen me a dozen times already and although there is no indication he suspects me, yet it is very difficult to determine what runs in his mind, as he seems very bright, intelligent and cautious, and keeps to himself all the time.

Zaneth kept up the surveillance; he watched Huybers as he visited a steamship office and a lawyer's office. About an half hour after he left the lawyers office, Huybers' coupe was parked outside the Green Lantern. Zaneth decided to go inside.

Upon entering this place, I found Mr. Huybers reading and explaining a letter which was written in Dutch, and bore the postmark of Copenhagen, to Miss Bradford, who was sitting with him at the Soda Fountain.
I could only see the Postal Mark of this letter, but I could not see the address from my point of view and I did not dare

show curiosity in case of suspicion. It was, however, evident that Miss Bradford was displeased over something for I heard her say in a very angry voice, "I don't see why they don't get a move on then and what is the cause of the delay?" Mr. Huybers good naturedly was endeavoring to keep her from attracting attention. I do not know what Miss Bradford was referring to, but I would not be at all surprised to learn that this girl is well posted on this man's movements.

That afternoon Zaneth managed to get a room at a local boardinghouse, and meet some fellow roomers, including a young woman who was a friend of Joyce Bradford's.

Through this lady, who seems to be a live wire and the life of the party, so they tell me, I am in hope to be able to meet the man in question.

When Zaneth was ready, when his surveillance was complete, or could be handed over to other RCMP officers, he went undercover. He would play any part or profession to gain access to a target. In Halifax, Operative No. 1 was ready to finally meet Huybers and his girlfriend. He became a CNR clerk on vacation. Operative No. 1 had already met Joyce's girlfriend at the boardinghouse; a few nights later, the girlfriend asked him to drive her to the Halifax Tower where they would meet Joyce and William and have some drinks from a bottle at the top of the tower. (Joyce and her friends liked to party.) From then on, Zaneth's reports would call his female companions "my alleged friends." Meanwhile, Operative No. 1 was still carefully shadowing Huybers. It was a display of confidence and ability not often seen today, where the undercover and surveillance teams are separate. Time and time again, Zaneth would switch easily from his cover character to that of police officer, apparently with little fear that he would be found out and apparently successfully.

Zaneth followed Huybers as once again he visited his lawyer's office in downtown Halifax, then watched as he met a man, apparently an American, for lunch at the Green Lantern. The American left and drove south in a Studebaker.

About 7:30 p.m. both Huybers and Miss Bradford came to the residence of one my alleged friends to attend a party, and there Huybers displayed a bank roll of twenties and fifty dollar bills, which in my estimates would amount to at least five thousand dollars. The party, which turned out to be rather wild, broke up at 3:50 a.m. Huybers and Miss Bradford proceeded to their respective residences.

Zaneth continued the surveillance, getting close to Huybers at the nightly parties. At the same, as he always did in his reports, he informed his superiors of his estimation of Huybers' character.

I might point out that Huybers is very reserved. Although very sociable in a way, yet never drinks to access [sic] and never discusses his past, present or future, nor the motive of his presence in the city. He is very well supplied with money, well dressed and spends freely.

My ladie [sic] acquaintances informed me, during a casual conversation, that Huybers is a rum runner, drug smuggler, Diamond smuggler etc. but that he is too clever to implicate himself and has a number of men working for him.

One night Operative No. 1 drove Joyce Bradford home at 2 a.m. "much the worse for liquor." The next day, the morning newspapers that announced that Joyce was sailing for Europe. Operative No. 1 and his "alleged friend 'C'" said goodbye as Joyce and William boarded the *S.S. Devonian*.

I must point out that Huybers has behaved most peculiar throughout my short acquaintance with him, He is very shrewd and very clever, close mouthed and evidently trustworthy. Even though he did not explain his stay in Canada, yet, he understood that my alleged lady friends had informed me of his activities, which seems to make him proud of being able to get away with it . . .

Only on one occasion since I met have him, have I seen him display a large bank roll. It is, however, possible that he has made all the necessary arrangements to have the bulbs (drugs) cleared, transferred etc. with some one here in Halifax. I know approximately who are his friends and I presume that they must be the ones to be kept in mind; however, I am awaiting your instructions for I have to carry on as usual with my alleged friends in order not to arouse suspicion.

(Sgd.) Operative No. 1

The brass decided to keep Zaneth in Halifax until the next scheduled shipment of Dutch bulbs arrived. The RCMP and Department of Agriculture inspectors in Halifax and Montreal were checking and X-raying all shipments of Dutch bulbs entering Canada. They discovered plots to smuggle bulbs into the United States, which was restricting the entry of bulbs from Europe, and decided not to do anything about it. Meanwhile, Inspector G.F. Fletcher, who commanded the Maritime Provinces District, was getting worried about costs. As usual, Zaneth had more than usual expenses. Fletcher reported:

The expenses in this case are rather heavy: Including the payment for the hire of the car, I have already advanced $660 to Operative No. 1 and I know that he has only about $20.00 of this amount left . . . The manner in which he is necessarily carrying out his investigation is expensive, but I do not see how it can be avoided. He is obtaining his information by entertaining three women at parties, and those parties cost money . . .

The *New Amsterdam* arrived but there were no bulbs on board. Zaneth was recalled to Toronto and the Dutch bulb case collapsed. The British discovered that inserting any material into a bulb would destroy it. It was all an expensive rumor. After a little more investigation, Halifax RCMP concluded that Huybers was nothing more than a bootlegger, selling booze to the Boston mob.

There is a record of a couple of typical days in the life of Operative No. 1, when he was tracking Romolo Bobba, the alien smuggler, and searching for Paul Clement in New York City. The record is an example of Zaneth's tenacity and imagination.

Early in the morning of his arrival, Zaneth went straight from the train station to call on a special agent in the narcotics division of the Prohibition Bureau, a man he had worked with on a previous case. The agent told Zaneth to go to Ellis Island. There he met an immigration inspector, who agreed to help him search for Paul Clement at the New York address obtained from the Clement family in Ottawa. Zaneth and the officer took a cab to James Street, "which is very short, and is inhabited by Italians and Greeks of the lowest class." A check showed there was no 84 James Street. Around the corner was a public school on Oak Street. Zaneth and the immigration officer went into the school to talk to the principal.

> During the conversation this lady informed me that about 8:30 AM. (thirty minutes before I arrived in New York) a man called her up by telephone and requested to speak to Mr. Clement. When she informed him that there was no man there by that name, he asked if that was not 84 James Street. She informed him that there was no such number and wanted to know who was speaking. This man, according to this lady, stated he was an Officer of the Immigration Department and immediately concluded the conversation.

Zaneth decided "Someone was aware of the fact that I was proceeding to New York to look Clement up and had tried to tip him off."

Zaneth and the immigration officer then went to the Village to check out Romolo Bobba's house on Barrow Street. No one was home. Zaneth decided to watch the place on his own.

> About 9:30 I noticed a man, who I suspected was Bobba . . . accompanied by a woman proceed to Tenth Street where he hired a taxi. I then did likewise ["Follow that cab!"] and

followed him to "Casa Lopes," a Night Club on Broadway and Fiftieth Street. Being under the impression that they might go there to join Clement or that Clement might join them, I also entered this Club where I took up a point of observation.

About 1:30 a.m. after Bobba had spent freely eating, drinking and dancing, he proceeded to Montmarte, 205 West 50th Street, also a night club, where he remained until 3:30 a.m. when he returned home . . .

The next afternoon, armed with a letter of introduction from Starnes, Zaneth went to the headquarters of the New York Police Department, where the homicide squad assigned a detective to help him. The two investigators canvassed James Street, James Slip Street and Jane Street. Jane Street was in the Village, a few blocks from Barrow. Again nothing; 84 Jane Street was being renovated. No one had lived there for three months. They checked the post office. Four letters had been waiting for Paul Clement at general delivery for more than two weeks. Letter carriers in the neighborhood had never heard of him. Zaneth was convinced that the family in Ottawa was lying to Staff Sergeant Ramsay when they insisted that Paul Clement was living at 84 James Street. He decided it was time to return to Canada.

One of Zaneth's skills was the recruitment of informants. There were two kinds of informants. The first were the people the RCMP called "agents," small-time crooks, and rounders, who supplied information to RCMP "operatives" and who set up bootleg or drug deals. The second were those who gave information to RCMP operatives for reasons of their own.

One such man was Joe Scime, of Hamilton, who had been Zaneth's source inside the Mutual Steamship Agencies in the immigration case — he informed on his partner, Tony Kapelle — and in the Rocco Perri case. In January 1931, Zaneth described how he manipulated Scime as he recruited him to keep his eye on the drug trade in Hamilton.

I have known Mr. Joseph Scime since 1927 and he has been engaged in Steamship Agencies, Real Estate etc . . . I learned that his business is very poor (real estate) and he finds it very difficult to earn the mere necessities of life. Mr. J. Scime is married and has a number of children. Some time ago this man asked me to make a special effort with a view of securing a position with CN Express and it was with this in mind that I approached him on this occasion.

Joseph Scime is acquainted with Frank Ross, Tony Ross, Rocco Perri and others. I informed him that I was not successful in securing him a position and suggested that in as much he was up against it, he could turn over to me certain information and in doing so, he would be able to earn a few dollars.

When I noticed that my suggestion was accepted with pleasure, I informed him that my chief concern was narcotics, and it was up to him to turn over the desired information. At this point, I refrained from mentioning any names to him and arranged to meet him the next day.

I returned to Joseph Scime's office . . . where I resumed the conversation. On arrival he informed me that during the night he had thought matters over and decided to give me information provided that I would keep his name a secret all the time, and would not use him on the surface in any way.

I do not expect very much from Joseph Scime, but if this man is sincere and he is in need of a position he will turn over valuable information, but at no time will I volunteer any data which he might convey to the Ross brothers, and disclose our hand.

Another way of getting information was interrogation. Constable Andrew Veitch worked with Zaneth in Toronto in the late 1920s. Veitch recalled:

Zaneth told us how to get information out of people, particularly. I found that most interesting, getting a confession out of people. There are many ways. If I'm talking to someone about something that he's done, there's something that's going to flow back to me that he's lying. One of the things is the way he answers questions, the way he jumps to a certain point you bring up . . . You cross examine them on one of the things you saw made the person shock a little inside. You keep working on that angle . . .

You get so many fellows that deny the damn thing and get mad . . . you feel they might claw you to pieces. Now, some in the police can let themselves get out of control, get mad themselves. [Zaneth told us] keep cool, in a quiet voice and you see their picture . . .

So the word detective is well placed, where you're detecting every little thing, every movement in their face, their expression when you touch some certain subject, it registers with you and makes you feel the bugger knows more than he's saying. You get some people are very clever that way too, Zaneth was like that. There are so many angles to that, it's impossible to definitely convey. It's an art . . .

In his reports, Zaneth exhibited a rather dry sense of humor about manipulating others, especially those who were only slightly shady. Once he called a woman into town from vacation by pretending to be a friend of her boss. In his days in Calgary, he reported:

In connection with the petition which is being compiled at Calgary during Fair week to be presented to the Dominion Government asking for reinstatement of Postal Employees, I have been watching the movement and find that the signatures on the list are not original signatures of individuals as many persons are signing in some cases several times. For instance while at the Labor Temple on the 3rd instant, at the request of [Name Deleted] I signed the name of "Harry Blask" on her list. Later, Mrs. Corse asked me to sign her list and when I told had already signed [Name Deleted]'s list she replied, "Oh, sign again to help the boys out." As I could not sign "Harry Blask" I signed "James Jones" on Mrs. Corse's list.[40]

Another job Zaneth did for the RCMP was translation. In 1926, Joe Sottile, a mob boss in Niagara Falls, New York, allowed a load of alcohol to enter the market in upstate New York and Ontario. It was 93.9 percent wood alcohol and it killed a total of forty-five people.

Rocco Perri, Sottile's ally in Hamilton, helped Sottile flee to Montreal where the American gangster was granted Canadian naturalization, although he was not eligible. He paid $3,200 to Montreal MP Samuel W. Jacobs, the Liberal who had beaten Communist Michael Buhay in Cartier riding. Sottile went underground in Halifax. Then informants tipped the Ontario Provincial Police on Sottile's whereabouts. The RCMP in Halifax began a secret investigation to try and locate the gangster.

Sottile was getting letters, mostly written in Italian, through a Halifax restaurant. The Mounties were intercepting and photographing the letters. The officer then commanding Maritime Provinces District, Denny LaNauze, trusted no one in the Halifax. So the photographs of Sottile's mail were sent by special delivery to Zaneth in Toronto for translation. The letters gave Sottile cryptic news of his escape plan. Zaneth noted that one "is very badly written and I found it most difficult to gather any sense from it," while another "although written by an educated man, certain paragraphs are camouflaged and only the receiver is capable of understanding it fully." Later letters addressed the gang boss as "Don Peppe" and "Dear Godfather." Sottile was being helped by the Mafia network that smuggled illegal immigrants into North America. Now they were using the process in reverse. In November 1926, Sottile sailed from Montreal. He was one step ahead of LaNauze and the Mounties and got safely in Sicily. While Zaneth was often sympathetic to the needs of prisoners like Flavio Masi:

On arrival in Hamilton I found Mrs. Flavio Masi waiting at the station. This lady begged me to allow her husband to go home for a few minutes to see the children who were waiting for him. Being too early to take him to court and not wishing to take him to the Police Station for a few hours, I decided to allow him to go home, where we remained for about 20 minutes.

Other people, from gangsters to the Bronfman brothers, got no sympathy from Zaneth. In his reports Zaneth was open about his feelings: he hoped the nefarious offenders would get what they deserved.

Younger officers remember Zaneth as a teacher as well as a leader. Zaneth once asked for Veitch's help on a smuggling investigation in New York and Long Island. The job was to follow a sleeping-car conductor suspected of bringing drugs or alcohol into Canada from the United States.

Veitch was to go to the man's house in Jamaica, Queens, then trail him to Grand Central Station. "The job was to get on the train without getting detected," Veitch said. "I was a pretty young chap. I will always remember Zaneth came down with me the first time." Zaneth took Veitch into the bowels of Grand Central Station to help him sneak onto the train.

Frank had a lot of guts, he covered that ground first, he went on that car and was making up all kinds of excuses . . . and we had a good look around.

One of my difficult jobs was to find out if a certain bag was in one of the cars. I knew what his [the suspect's] baggage looked like, so my job was to see if he was on every train. We had to get on the train without him knowing who we were . . .

I always remember I had an excuse made up, about who I was, you don't tell them who you are . . . there was nobody there and the club bag wasn't there, so I figured he wasn't there. All of a sudden, who should walk in but this guy and one of the men from the station.

So I said I had a friend and I was to meet him and he didn't show up and I was just wondering if he was on and what his bag was like. It's funny being caught there, they might think you're in there to steal something, but he said take a look around.

The case turned out to be a wild goose chase, one of many every policeman goes through. No charges were ever laid.

"In those days Zaneth was a boss, and you don't really discuss things. I copied a lot of his good points . . . I thought he had what I could use," Veitch concluded.

In 1930, Zaneth was given command of an operation, the search for a bootlegger near Bobcaygeon, Ontario that combined his strengths in undercover operations and the traditional northern RCMP bushcraft. It may be the only time Zaneth paddled a canoe on duty.

For years, O Division, which covered western Ontario, had received tips that there was a bootlegging operation somewhere near Bobcaygeon, a small town on Sturgeon Lake north of Lindsay. There was a giant still that produced large amounts of whiskey which was sold around Canada and smuggled into the thirsty United States. The moonshiner was a man named Bruce Freeburn. According to the RCMP annual report, "for several years [he] distilled whisky illegally, evading all efforts to arrest him; searches of his premises were without result; the occasional discovery and seizure of his stills caused him no serious inconvenience." In March, 1930, Jennings ordered a preliminary investigation and used the results to set up an undercover operation for Operative No. 1.

No records have survived of the Bobcaygeon case, which was one of Zaneth's biggest undercover operations. The RCMP annual reports for 1930 and 1931 give some information. Jennings reported:

On August 8, [Operative No. 1] playing the role of a racketeer, appeared at Bobcaygeon. He soon gained the confidence of Bruce Freeburn and his family, and it was not long before a business proposition was broached whereby Bruce Freeburn was to sell a large quantity of bootleg whisky to his racketeering friend as a preliminary to a larger buy, if satisfactory arrangements could be made.

Zaneth "managed so well that the moonshiners showed him the still in operation." He also learned that the Freeburns had a back-up still. Then, without telling the Mounties, the Ontario Provincial Police raided the first still and arrested Freeburn. The OPP were unable to make a case, and Freeburn began supplying his customers from the second still. The second still became the new RCMP target. Jennings reported:

> A special detail, with the aid of a motor-boat and camping outfit, was selected to occupy a point of vantage on the island known as Boyd's Island under cover of night. The still was located and the party placed in a strategic position. This was on September 11. At noon of September 12, the party closed in and effected the arrest of Creighton Freeburn (son of Bruce Freeburn) and Sam Hill, who had come to run the still and, after disposing of the prisoners, waited further developments. Around 9 p.m. the same date, Bruce Freeburn approached Boyd's Island in a motor-boat, accompanied by Delbert Freeburn (another son). Leaving the boat, Bruce Freeburn walked to the still, where he was apprehended. Delbert Freeburn temporarily escaped capture by jumping into the lake and swimming away. He was, however, later arrested at his home.

The two sons and Sam Hill were convicted but the case against Bruce Freeburn was dismissed.

In the late summer of 1931, Zaneth and the RCMP decided it was time to try again to crack Bruce Freeburn's moonshining operation. Young men began appearing at cottages for late summer vacations. "The operations of Detective Sergeant Zaneth and the constables who assisted him covered a large area," recorded the 1931 Annual Report, "extending from Lindsay to Coe Hill, and were conducted in the intricate region of lakes and islands adjacent to Bobcaygeon." Zaneth set up a secret camp in the woods near the main still, while surveillance teams kept an eye on the moonshiners. Here is a brief surviving quote from the annual report.

> We took up a post of observation, across the street from Freeburn's home, and from 9:30 until midnight, a dozen cars, bearing American license plates, were observed to call

there, and someone from the rear of the house would come forward to meet them and make delivery of what I presumed to be bottles of illicit spirits."

A second reads:

Mr. [Name deleted]'s cottage is situated approximately six miles from Havelock, Ont. in the bush. Upon our arrival, it was observed that about ten young couples, averaging from fourteen to eighteen years of age, were lying around it, all under the influence of liquor.

The report also quotes:

At 1 a.m. we left the camp on foot, carrying all the blankets, tent and provisions, arriving in the vicinity of the still at 5:45 a.m. Not knowing at what time the still was worked or if it was being watched by Freeburn, after concealing our efforts in the bush we returned to the cottage. At about 5:45 p.m. we proceeded by car, to the site of our old camp, where we left the car in the bush and continued on foot to where our provisions were now hidden. Having ascertained that there was no one around the still, we entered one of the shacks, where we remained for the night . . . it was with great difficulty that we managed to reach the shacks from the road, a distance of about a quarter of a mile, as Freeburn had marked the trail, by scattering twigs and branches on it, so as to be able determine whether anyone had visited the still.

On October 17, 1931, Bruce Freeburn and Sam Hill were caught operating the still and were arrested. Within hours, nine local bootleggers were also arrested.

Freeburn was convicted and sentenced to ten months in prison and was fined $1,500. Sam Hill was sentenced to three months and a fine of $200. The nine bootleggers were also convicted.

There were other cases, most routine. One was a long-running investigation of a Chinese drug smuggler named Lee Wong, where the Crown attorney reported "Sergeant Zaneth is partic-ularly efficient." As well, Zaneth worked with American authorities in New York charged with breaking up the mob control of the fur industry in the city; he also checked out reports that morphine was being smuggled into Canada in shipments of sultanas and figs.

In the summer of 1931, Cortlandt Starnes told the newly elected prime minister, R.B. Bennett, that he wanted to retire. Bennett's choice for a successor was Major General James MacBrien, until recently Chief of Staff for the Department of National Defence. MacBrien, who had been a Mountie briefly in his early career before serving in the military, was working in the civil aviation industry. He was reluctant to take the job, believing it should go to someone from inside the force. Most of the senior officers, however, were near retirement age and Bennett persuaded MacBrien to accept the job. From the day the new commissioner took office on August 1, 1931 the force began to expand and modernize. Men who had left during the twenties were encouraged to re-enlist. In 1932, the RCMP would take over provincial policing in Alberta, Manitoba, New Bruns-wick, Nova Scotia and Prince Edward Island. (The RCMP had begun similar duties in Saskatchewan in 1928). Over the next few years, MacBrien would also modernize the fingerprint section, encourage the establishment of a crime lab and modus operandi section, begin a weapons registry and improved liaison with American law enforcement agencies.

In the late fall of 1931, the RCMP planned to promote Zaneth to staff sergeant and transfer him to Montreal. On December 5, he re-enlisted and on January 1, 1932, he took up new duties in Montreal.

CHAPTER NINE

Zaneth and the First
« French Connection »

THE MOST NOTORIOUS drug and gambling kingpin in Montreal's underworld in the early 1930s was a debonair Romanian Jew named Harry Davis. Montreal was a city where all of the rackets flourished. There were dope dens, brothels, gambling houses, blind pigs and roadhouses. In the 1920s, a public inquiry had discovered that corruption of officials and police by organized crime was pervasive. Harry Davis was at the top of this world.[41] The tall, slender, elegantly dressed Davis had started his criminal career as a messenger for the underworld when he was a newspaper boy during the first decade of the century. As an adult, the street-smart Davis graduated to more lucrative criminal operations — bank robberies, prostitution, gambling, fencing, extortions and narcotics trafficking. In 1924 he was charged and later convicted of narcotics trafficking.

Davis had connections in Europe and powerful allies in the New York City underworld, among them Louis "Lepke" Buchalter, a partner with Davis in drug trafficking. Buchalter had strong ties with the Italian Mafia gangs of New York, Lepke exerted considerable control over the taxi-cab, chicken, shoe, laundry, and restaurant industries in New York City. Through extortion of unions and the businesses, Buchalter was thought to be making more than $10 million a year in the thirties.*

---

* In the late thirties Buchalter later ran a notorious execution-for-hire outfit with Albert Anastasia which the sensational press of the day dubbed Murder Inc.

Lepke Buchalter and Harry Davis had a partner in the international drug business: Pincus Brecher. Brecher had curly black hair and a scar on his left cheek, stood about five foot seven and was of medium build. He had been in his early twenties when he emigrated from Romania just after the turn of the century. He settled in the Bronx, in New York City, and became a prominent silk merchant. He also became closely connected with Buchalter and his mob in the fencing of stolen goods and the smuggling of silk and drugs, but unlike Buchalter, the secretive Brecher tried to keep in the background of his criminal empire.

In 1932, the Dominion Preventive Service, a division of Canadian Customs, had been disbanded, largely because of systematic corruption in its ranks. Among other duties, the Preventive Service had investigated smuggling activities and other organized attempts to avoid paying customs and excise duties. The RCMP had taken over these duties.

In mid-February, Zaneth was assigned to special duties in Ottawa. He was told to take charge of an inquiry, begun earlier by the Dominion Preventive Service as an examination of silk smuggling into Canada. It had turned into a probe of one of the largest, most sophisticated international drug-trafficking networks until that time.

The worldwide investigation involved close liaison with European police forces as well as with the new U.S. Bureau of Narcotics under its dynamic head, the first U.S. Commissioner of Narcotics, Harry Anslinger. Anslinger was determined to cut the flow of illegal drugs into the United States, and the growing use of cocaine, opium, morphine, heroin and marijuana. He had sent a senior Bureau of Narcotics official to New York City expressly to target the American and European ends of a number of drug rings about which the bureau had intelligence. Anslinger also set up what he later called a "secret panel," which included prominent law-enforcement officials from the United States, Europe and Canada. Canada was represented by Colonel Charles Sharman, chief of the Narcotics Division at the Department of Pensions and National Health.

The gangs were finding new routes to bring drugs to North America. Europe was replacing China as a source of narcotics. In New York, the Bureau of Narcotics targeted the retail end of the operation, where the ringleaders organized the flow; French police dealt with the European end, where the drugs were purchased and processed. The Canadian investigators under Sharman included Zaneth and Superintendent Freddie Mead, commander of C Division. They targeted the Montreal part of the network, where the drugs were often imported and distributed.

Zaneth's assignment now was to find and interrogate scores of witnesses in Canada, the United States and Europe with a view to doing what customs had failed to do: to build a solid case against the Canadian leadership of the new international drug syndicate.

In the 1920s, it was still legal for giant European pharmaceutical companies to manufacture large amounts of morphine and heroin. They imported opium from China under license, for manufacture of "limited quantities" of medicinal heroin and morphine, but then looked the other way when purchasers arrived at their doors. One gangster named Jacob Pollakowitz bought his morphine from Hoffman–La Roche; he was supplying Buchalter and Brecher in New York.

Behind Pollakowitz was the biggest dope dealer in Europe, a Paris-based Greek named Elias Eliopoulis, nicknamed "Elie" and also known as "the Baron." Elie bought raw opium in China, sold it at a discount to the pharmaceutical companies, then arranged for drug smuggling and trafficking throughout Europe and North America. Elie was so confident and audacious that he had made an arrangement with one of the highest officials of the Paris police: if his men didn't sell dope on the streets of France, they would be left alone. Although he left the Elie gang in peace in France, Elie's police contact passed his information on to the U.S. State Department which created an extensive file on Elie. In one conversation, Elie said that a man named "Paull" was his best customer. Paull was a favorite alias of Jacob Pollakowitz. Pollakowitz's associates, who included

Jacob Bloom, Charles Wimmer and Lepke's men, Joe and Sam Bernstein, along with scores of middlemen, worked directly for New York and Montreal gangsters in handling the flow of drugs from Europe to New York City and Montreal.

The method was simple. The drugs were concealed in trunks and other baggage, en route to the United States and Canada on board some of the finest passenger liners of the day — the *Ile de France*, the *S.S. Majestic*, the *S.S. Montcalm* — always the fashionable ships. The gang employed couriers and middlemen who operated in Europe and the Far East with false Canadian and U.S. passports and an assortment of aliases. When necessary, they corrupted customs officers and other officials in Canada, the United States and Europe. In Montreal and New York, the gang employed hundreds of pushers to distribute and sell the drugs on the streets.

The first break in the case came in 1930, when the smuggling network filled a trunk with opium and tried to smuggle it into New York City via a luxury passenger liner as part of the baggage of a prominent English diplomat. The lord picked up his luggage personally and disowned the extra trunk. Customs officials opened it and found the drugs. Days later, morphine was found on a second ship. Customs arrested Charles Wimmer and Joe Bernstein. Bloom was taken off a ship at Southampton and returned to the United States; Pollakowitz escaped to Europe.

The unravelling and identifying of the leadership of the international drug empire began in Montreal in June 1931, when well-known silk smuggler Charlie Feigenbaum decided to become a stool pigeon. Feigenbaum, known locally as the King of the North because he controlled slot machines in the Laurentians and North Montreal, was a short, fat racketeer who had been in partnership with a great many unsavory characters in a number of dubious enterprises including bookmaking and gambling operations in the wide-open, decadent Québec of the twenties. He had started out in the clothing business and was primarily engaged in illegal silk and perfume smuggling, but he was also the manager of the notorious White House Inn in Lachine, the largest and most popular gambling club in Quebec.

The inn was owned by Harry Davis in partnership with Montreal gambling czar Max Shapiro and two other underworld figures.

Feigenbaum (aka "Fat Charlie") was involved in so many criminal ventures with so many notorious characters that he slipped effortlessly into the narcotics rackets without even knowing it. In his silk smuggling racket, Feigenbaum had been systematically bribing customs officers for years. He started with the drug syndicate by providing Davis and Brecher with a proven and secure route for getting trunks into Canada without inspection. He soon became a middleman for the higher echelons of the drug ring. He provided false Canadian passports and arranged other tactical support for the drug-smuggling network. For Feigenbaum, smuggling narcotics was a natural and lucrative extension of his silk and perfume smuggling activities.

In December 1930, his luck ran out. One of the corrupt customs officers on his payroll became remorseful and told his story to his superiors. By 1931, Feigenbaum was in St. Vincent De Paul Penitentiary contemplating his five-year sentence. He was now seeking revenge against Davis and Brecher for not providing him with financial or legal support. In June 1931 he gave a detailed statement to Detective Isaiah Savard of the Preventive Service, and with other customs investigators Savard spent the better part of the next year independently checking out the facts of the charges and assembling witnesses. But for all this work, the Customs investigators felt they could not make a case against Brecher or Davis. The file was passed on to Sharman.

In February 1933, Sharman briefed Zaneth, then handed over the whole investigation to the Montreal office of the RCMP for prosecution. Zaneth was to go after the mob kingpins. He would be in charge of building an airtight case against the leadership of the drug-trafficking network.

First Zaneth pored over Charlie Feigenbaum's statement. He wanted to piece together enough hard facts that could be proved in a court of law that the principal conspirators in Canada and the United States could be brought to justice for conspiracy to import morphine, cocaine, heroin and opium into Canada. Zaneth quickly decided to go after the gang's leader, Montreal rackets boss Harry Davis, and to attempt to ensnare the mastermind of the mob, the elusive and powerful New York City millionaire gangster Pincus Brecher. The frustrated Americans had jailed a number of the middlemen and couriers in the trafficking network, but considered Brecher untouchable due to New York's corrupt judicial system.

How was Zaneth was going to get the goods on these big-time criminals? His first job was to develop an air tight case of conspiracy against the leader of the Canadian end of this vast and sophisticated international operation. This was the first of the modern conspiracy cases. Zaneth was a pioneer. Later, in an article for the *RCMP Quarterly* in 1937, Zaneth explained the philosophy behind his approach:

> The offenses of organized crime are difficult to detect and are still harder to unfold — so deeply entrenched are the perpetrators. This being so, the law-enforcing bodies must resort to weapons that are in some measure strong enough to stem the wave of lawlessness. It should be remembered that criminals of today, especially the type we have to deal with; i.e., those particularly interested in the evasion of the revenue laws, have the resources to enable them to equip themselves. They remain in the background directing operations from a place of safety, and when an arrest is made it is invariably one of their many employees who takes the responsibility . . . It often occurs that there is very little or no evidence to justify a charge under the Act against "Higher-ups", but, the old adage "There's many a slip 'twixt cup and lip" applies. In almost all transactions evidence in some form is left, — telephone calls, telegrams, letters, entries in a note book or a note on a scratch pad, deposits in the bank, or withdrawals on or about the day of the transaction. With luck, a painstaking investigator can glean all the evidence necessary.

Like many a modern investigator, Zaneth's understanding of

"conspiracy" was fairly broad and he help to set a precedent in criminal investigations by the RCMP:

> The crime of conspiracy is completely committed . . . the moment two or more have agreed that they will do, at once or at some future time, certain things. It is not necessary in order to complete the offense that any one thing should be done beyond the agreement. The conspirators may repent and stop, or may have no opportunity, or may be prevented, or may fail. Nevertheless the crime is complete; it was completed when they agreed.

To develop the conspiracy charge in the Harry Davis case, Zaneth interviewed fifty-six witnesses, including couriers, corrupt customs officers, convicted drug dealers, the wives of some of the principals, bank and hotel clerks, and police and Customs investigators. By far the most important witness was Charlie Feigenbaum and Zaneth spent many days going over details with his main informer. Feibenbaum had told the police about the structure of the gang, told how the drugs were obtained and described the elaborate strategy used to smuggle the drugs into North America.

Feigenbaum had met Pincus Brecher in March 1930. Harry Davis and his business contacts in New York City had told him that the wealthy New Yorker would help him make quite a bit of money. Another meeting took place in July 1930, when Pincus Brecher and his secret partner in the drug rackets, Lepke Buchalter, came to Montreal, where they met with Harry Davis and Charlie Feigenbaum at their gambling joint, the White House Inn. Feigenbaum did not know he would be helping the narcotics flow; he was told only that he would be facilitating the illegal importation of shipments of trunks from Europe. He was told the trunks contained Swiss watches.

Feigenbaum's first job was to help Jacob Pollakowitz, Jacob Bloom and Joe Bernstein get false Canadian passports for the couriers. Next, Feigenbaum arranged with his Customs contacts for the safe entry into Montreal of some numbered trunks. He did this by bribing customs officials, as he had always done.

At the end of July, Brecher introduced Feigenbaum to Charles Haims, a bootlegger-turned-watch-smuggler, and again asked Feigenbaum if he could arrange things with Canadian Customs. Feigenbaum said he knew an officer who would let in a few cases of goods for some money, which Brecher provided. If Feigenbaum was successful at getting the trunks smuggled into Montreal, he would receive a percentage of Haims's profits on the goods. Brecher explained that another associate, Irving Stein, would soon be shipping two trunks containing the Swiss watches as well as some French perfume.

The first shipment arrived in Quebec on board the *S.S. Montclair* on August 15, 1930; Pincus Brecher, Lepke Buchalter and several of their New York City gangster colleagues (including Jacob Pollakowitz's wife) were in Montreal to check up on its passage. But there was a problem: the customs officer on duty wasn't on the take, and he wouldn't allow the trunks in without inspecting them. Brecher and Davis suggested that the trunks be sent on to New York City — that way they would remain in bond and Customs would not have to examine them. While the trunks were waiting for a train to New York, the men came up with a way to retrieve the drugs.

Feigenbaum arranged for one of his corrupt Customs officers, Joe Lapalme, to handle the paperwork for the shipment from Montreal to New York City. Lapalme was paid $6,000, and quietly released the trunks to Charlie Feigenbaum's brother, Max. The trunks were trucked to Max's house in Montreal. Davis picked up the trunks and removed the narcotics, then returned the trunks to Max's home, where they were filled with old clothes. The trunks were returned to the customs warehouse and sent down to New York City. This was the trial run, and Feigenbaum had passed the test.

Brecher, Davis and Buchalter asked Feigenbaum to become a partner in the importation of merchandise from Europe. They wanted Feigenbaum to go to Paris, where he would meet with Pollakowitz and prepare the next few shipments to Montreal. Feigenbaum and Brecher went to New York City and the next day Feigenbaum sailed on the *S.S. Bremen* for France. He met with Pollakowitz, and they devised a system of identifying trunks so Feigenbaum's customs officers would recognize which to let through uninspected. Feigenbaum spent five days arranging a complex numbering system for the trunks that would be coming in over the next few months on several different passenger liners. Then he met Brecher in New York and the two went on to Montreal where they met with Harry Davis to discuss how to get money to Pollakowitz in Paris.

Feigenbaum gave Zaneth the key to the conspiracy case against Davis and Brecher when he said that Harry Davis's drug-trafficking network had been the source of drugs seized by Detective Sergeant L.J. Black in an undercover operation in Montreal. In October 1930, two street-level drug dealers, Sam Arcadi and Harry Tucker, were arrested in the process of selling a kilo of morphine to Sergeant Black and an international undercover team. After the arrest, Harry Davis had confided to Feigenbaum that he had sold Arcadi and Tucker the drugs because the cubes of morphine were too large to be sold in New York City. Brecher was annoyed with Davis for disposing of the morphine in Montreal, and publicly chastised him. Zaneth and his team were able to independently corroborate Feigenbaum's account of the conversation with Davis by examining the seized cubes. Zaneth could now tie the multi-million-dollar drug shipments coming into New York City via Montreal to a specific street level sale busted by the RCMP, because they already had the physical evidence.

On the morning of April 7, 1933 the attorney general of Quebec signed a preferred indictment against Davis on nine counts of conspiracy to traffic in narcotics. A special prosecutor, Gustave Monette, had obtained a warrant for Davis's arrest from the Chief Justice of Quebec. Zaneth, accompanied by two other Mounties, went to the Berkeley Hotel in downtown Montreal to arrest Davis in his room. But Davis was nowhere to be found. Zaneth and his men kept the hotel under surveillance all night but to no avail. Working with five other RCMP officers, Zaneth searched the Montreal underworld for two days without success.

On the afternoon of April 9, Davis's lawyer, Joseph Cohen, called and asked Zaneth why the RCMP was looking for his client. Zaneth refused to divulge the nature of the charges, but persuaded the lawyer that it would be best if Davis gave himself up. Cohen went to see Zaneth and offered to produce Davis "if the charges were minor." Zaneth told Cohen that he personally did not care whether Davis "remained under cover or not," as Zaneth felt that he would eventually apprehend him.

On the morning of April 11, 1933, Harry Davis appeared at the court house. Zaneth and Monette, the special prosecutor, immediately brought him before a judge who read out the charges against him: nine counts of conspiracy to traffic more than eight hundred kilograms of opium, morphine and heroin, worth millions of dollars on the street, between January 1 and December 31, 1930; and corruption of public officials. The charge mentioned Jacob Pollakowitz and Pincus Brecher, who were indicted in New York a few weeks later, along with several other members of the gang. Bail was set at $100,000, an astronomical sum in those days; Davis was carted off to Bordeaux Jail.

The trial of Harry Davis opened on October 1, 1933, and lasted five days. The Crown had fifty-six witnesses ready, but called only seventeen to the stand, including the stool pigeon "Fat" Charlie Feigenbaum and the drug dealer Sam Arcadi, both of whom had been kept for some months in protective custody by the RCMP.

The "French connection" route was proved during the trial. The drugs brought up the St. Lawrence on European steamships had long ago disappeared on the streets of Montreal and New York. But in New York there was a trunk full of morphine, in the haul seized after a trunk of opium was disowned by the English diplomat and seized by U.S. Customs in 1930. The morphine was proved to be identical to the drugs seized from Sam Arcadi and Harry Tucker. The morphine had been manufactured by Hoffman – La Roche and shipped in the company's metal tins.

The jury took less than an hour to declare the accused guilty.

On October 20, 1933, as he sentenced Davis to fourteen years in jail and ten lashes,* Mr. Justice Greenshields was eloquent about the reasons for such a stiff punishment:

> The traffic in deadly narcotics must be stopped. Hopeless as it may seem, there is one way at least to aid in the process, and that is, and I know of no other, to put you and the pestilential vultures of your class beyond the reach of the drug; to put them where the helpless public cannot be corrupted or even tempted by your nefarious trade and traffic.

Davis's conviction caused a stir in the underworld. Never before had such an important crime boss in Canada been charged, convicted and sent to jail for such a lengthy time. By the severe sentence Greenshields hoped to tell all drug dealers of the penalty that awaited them. The judge commended the work of Zaneth and the Mounties, and strongly urged the government of Canada to proceed with the extradition of Pincus Brecher from New York City, where he had been freed on narcotics charges because the offenses for which he had been charged had occurred in Canada.

While Zaneth was in New York City working on corroborating the facts of the case, Col. Sharman had attended a meeting in Ottawa with the minister of justice, the minister of pensions and national health, the assistant deputy minister of justice and other bureaucrats. He had specifically been instructed to "take no further action" on the possible extradition of Pincus Brecher. The politicians and senior bureaucrats felt that it wasn't worth the money to try to nail Brecher. Sharman asked that the order be passed on to Zaneth.

It is clear from the secret RCMP memos that Zaneth ignored these orders in his zeal to get Brecher. By now Zaneth was a master of getting around the concerns of the bureaucracy. He

---

* It was common in the early part of the century to add the lash or strap to the punishment for serious offenses. The usual method was to give half the lashes at the beginning of the sentence and the remainder at the end of the prison term.

reported from New York City that the prosecutor felt "deep regret" for not being in a position to prosecute Brecher there, but that they all considered Brecher "one of the most daring and ruthless" underworld bosses in New York. Zaneth also reported that the authorities in the United States felt "rather surprised to learn that he would not be extradited [as] there was sufficient evidence to justify Court proceedings against him in Canada."

In mid-May, 1933, Sharman came to Montreal to meet with Monette and Zaneth to discuss the investigation of Harry Davis. Sharman agreed that Canada should attempt to extradite Brecher; he noted that "this [was] an exceptionally important international narcotics gang and both the French and the Americans [had] certainly done their share." But he thought Brecher would fight the extradition with everything within his power; Sharman's department did not have the funds to fight back. It was decided that the attempt to extradite Brecher would have to wait until after the conviction of Harry Davis. Then the narcotics branch would be in another fiscal year. Canada, it seems, could not afford to take on two major drug kingpins in major legal battles at the same time.

After the conviction and sentencing of Harry Davis in October 1933, Zaneth began working full time on the extradition of Pincus Brecher. He assembled all the principal witnesses so they could be brought to Montreal or New York City to testify at the extradition hearings. The Canadian government proceeded cautiously, not wanting to tip Brecher off. A warrant was issued on March 26, 1934, and the request for the arrest of Brecher was delivered to the British consulate in New York by coded telegram. Later that day, Brecher was arrested by the Bureau of Narcotics and taken to jail at the Tombs to await an extradition hearing on charges of conspiracy and drug trafficking in Canada. Police informers reported the arrest caused a major shock in the underworlds of New York and Montreal.

At a special hearing in Montreal on March 27, 1934 called to take extradition depositions, key witnesses were questioned by Canadian government lawyers and by Brecher's lawyers from

New York City. Those on the stand included drug dealer Sam Arcadi, stool pigeon Charlie Feigenbaum, "Fat" Charlie's brother, Max, some former customs officials and many other bit players. The hearings then moved to New York City.

Brecher's lawyers, two of whom had been U.S. attorneys in the city area, used every procedural and legal wrangle they could to prevent the hearing from taking place. They accused Canadian government officials of trying to "railroad" Brecher into Canada. On April 27, Colonel Sharman himself testified at the extradition hearing in New York City, and on May 1, Zaneth went to New York to help the government's lawyers in the extradition proceedings.

Zaneth was in court to see Pincus Brecher take the stand. The fifty-seven-year-old Brecher testified that he had serious heart problems and that he was not getting proper medical treatment in jail. He claimed he was not up to the physical strain of being held in jail, and he was especially unfit for the long, arduous trip to Canada. His arguments carried little weight with the extradition commissioner. On June 21, 1934, he ordered that Brecher be held for trial in Montreal on all five counts of conspiracy to traffic in narcotics. Brecher's lawyers appealed the decision, and it wasn't until July 5 that the official warrant for Brecher's extradition to Canada was issued. The RCMP escort, under the command of Zaneth's colleague, Corporal Jean Raymond, fearing a rescue attempt, secretly took the prisoner from his cell at the Tombs to Grand Central Station and then by train to Montreal, where the group arrived unscathed on July 18. In spite of all his influence and status, Brecher, the mastermind of the drug gang, was ensconced in the Bordeaux Jail.

In December 1933, two months after Davis was sentenced, Charlie Feigenbaum had been released on parole. He knew he was a marked man, for he had betrayed the trust of his former criminal colleagues. But Feigenbaum dropped his police protection and went about his criminal business as usual.

On the evening of August 21, he was preparing to take a holiday in the Laurentians. He was outside the home of his sister-in-law at Mont-Royal and Esplanade, handing a package to his eighteen-year-old son. He hadn't noticed the Hudson with Illinois plates parked across the street. It contained three men. One got out of the car, casually crossed the street, leaned on Charlie's car and emptied his revolver into Feigenbaum's stomach, then nonchalantly walked back to the Hudson. Feigenbaum died in front of a number of witnesses, one of them his horrified son.

Montreal's homicide squad and the RCMP drug squad were at the murder scene within minutes. Eyewitnesses gave conflicting descriptions of the murderer and the driver of the get-away car. An intensive investigation by all police forces in the Montreal area was inconclusive. The RCMP learned the identity of the Canadian who had driven a second getaway car, and they learned that two hit men had been brought in from New York to execute Charlie for a fee of $250 each and expenses. But there was not enough evidence to bring anyone to trial. Many people had had a motive for removing Charlie.

The Brecher trial began in Montreal on a morning in late September. The cold-blooded killing of Charlie Feigenbaum cast a chill over the proceedings. The testimony of the late Mr. Feigenbaum, which just a few months earlier had been so crucial to the conviction of Harry Davis, was disallowed as evidence. Called as a Crown witness in the case, Harry Davis refused to talk, but only "stuck out his chin and clamped his jaws," according to a newspaper account. The execution of Feigenbaum had obviously sent a potent message to potential stool pigeons in the underworld. But Zaneth had done his homework, and he presented the court with two hundred thirty-three exhibits — thousands of documents, including telegrams, bank drafts, hotel and ships' registers, and records of long-distance phone calls — and he had more than fifty witnesses to prove the charges. Only forty-two of the witnesses were called to testify, and only sixty of Zaneth's exhibits were submitted in evidence during the five-day trial. Monette and Zaneth felt that they had more than enough evidence to convict Brecher of conspiracy even with Feigenbaum's death, which the judge said occurred at "an inconvenient time." As Mr. Justice L.J. Loranger pointed out in his address to the jury, "Direct evidence is almost never obtainable and is not necessary" in conspiracy cases, as "conspiracies are not formed in public." He told the jury to rely on the credibility of circumstantial evidence.

On September 28, 1934, after just forty-five minutes of deliberations, the jury found Pincus Brecher guilty on all the counts of conspiracy to traffic in narcotics and corruption of public officials. Justice Loranger praised Zaneth and the RCMP for "their splendid work." Brecher, hitherto untouchable king of the drug ring, faced a lengthy prison sentence in Canada. His face went white when the verdict was announced. He smiled and bowed to the judge in a gesture of acceptance, then pretended a sudden illness and demanded to be taken to the prison hospital. Less than a half an hour after he was convicted, as he was being led to the prison infirmary on the second storey gallery at the Bordeaux Jail, Pincus Brecher broke away from his guards and jumped head first over the rails. Five minutes later prison doctors pronounced him dead of a fractured skull. Brecher had not waited for sentencing or appeals.

Newspapers across Canada and the United States had a field day with the story. The New York *Mirror*, in a lengthy, exclusive feature article by Ernest Jerome Hopkins entitled HOW CANADA GOT THE DRUG KING WHO LAUGHED published on December 1, 1934, credited Zaneth and the Mounties with achieving what could not be achieved in the United States. In Hopkins' view, Canada's criminal justice system was far more tenacious, effective and severe than that of the United States:

> It was the whole Canadian justice system, from police to jailors, and prosecutors, and judges, and behind it all the awful dignity of British law and majesty of the deeply symbolic King. To an American accustomed to the general sloppiness and slot machine chanciness of American justice from the pinch to the prison, the Canadian machinery of criminal justice is doubly impressive.

While this is certainly exaggerated, it is true that in the 1930s, at least, the Canadian justice system had a very good record compared to that of the United States, particularly in the drug trafficking area. This is confirmed by the outspoken Harry Anslinger himself, the longtime U.S. Commissioner of Narcotics. Amongst the thousands of documents in the Anslinger Papers at the Pattee Library at Pennsylvania State University is a 1930s memo entitled simply, "Canada." In it Anslinger suggested that Canadian courts dealt more firmly with narcotic smugglers.

In December 1934, the U.S. Bureau of Narcotics began a nation-wide round-up of drug dealers, addicts and drug king-pins. On December 8, 1934, five hundred and sixty people were arrested from coast to coast in what the *New York Times* called a "drastic clean-up." It was one of the first of many all-out wars on drug trafficking in the United States.

The end of the Brecher — Davis drug syndicate eventually led to the targeting by American narcotics officials of the senior partner of the gang — Louis "Lepke" Buchalter, the shadowy figure behind Pincus Brecher. Buchalter continued in the rackets for many years and increased his power in the drug business. In 1937, he was indicted by a New York grand jury after the Bureau of Narcotics proved he had imported a shipment of heroin worth ten million dollars. Buchalter avoided arrest and went into hiding, then had the main witnesses against him murdered. That was a mistake. The murders sparked one of the first joint-forces operations against organized crime in the United States. The heat was on, from the Bureau of Narcotics, from J. Edgar Hoover's FBI, from the New York City and State Police. Gangland members sent the word to Lepke, "Give up." He surrendered to columnist Walter Winchell and was sentenced to fourteen years in jail for drug trafficking. But by this time, the press had begun to tell the story of Murder Inc., and Lepke became a deadly legend in the United States. Through brute force, which included beatings and savage murders, Buchalter had become the most feared gangster in New York. Finally the other mob bosses decided he had to be stopped. One of his colleagues testified against him in the murder of a candy-store owner, a man who had witnessed another of Lepke's killings. "Lepke" Buchalter was sentenced to death and executed in 1944.

Harry Davis was not much more fortunate. He served more than ten years in jail for drug trafficking. Shortly after his release, he was shot to death in the streets of Montreal by one of his criminal associates.

On April 1, 1934, as Detective Staff Sergeant Frank Zaneth was preparing for the final court battle in New York City for the extradition of Pincus Brecher to Montreal, he was promoted to Detective Inspector in charge of special criminal investigations. He was the first member of the RCMP to be appointed to the newly created rank.* In both Canada and the United States the convictions of Harry Davis and Pincus Brecher had become a public relations coup for the RCMP. Zaneth had helped to prove once again that the RCMP did indeed get its man.

---

* In its story about the promotion on May 4, 1934, the Ottawa *Citizen* stated that Zaneth's persistent efforts resulted in the disbanding of the "Montreal branch" of a "one million dollar plus dope drug ring with international ramification," and the story fully credits Zaneth with the conviction of Harry Davis, the kingpin of local dopesters, and the bringing to justice of Pincus Brecher, the brains of the organization.

▲

The Zanetti family, perhaps before their arrival in Springfield, Mass. Frank is the small boy on the right. *(Rivers Family Collection)*

◄

Ambrose and Christina Zanetti *(Rivers Family Collection)*

Frank Zaneth
(Rivers Family Collection)

▶

Superintendent Frank Zaneth
visiting the now-controversial
St. Joseph's Training School in
Alfred, Ontario, in 1947 *(RCMP
2285)*

▼

Frank and Edith Zaneth outside their home in
New Glasgow, Québec
(Rivers Family Collection)

The house in New Glasgow
(Rivers Family Collection)

Here He Is

Harry Blask/James Laplante.
A photograph taken of Frank Zaneth undercover in
the labour movement. It was published in the *B.C.
Federationist* along with David Rees's exposé.
(B.C. Federationist/University of British Columbia)

PINCUS BRECHER

WASHINGTON, December 1, 19__
CONFIDENTIAL LIST No. 180

Nationality:- American (naturalized)
Place of birth:- Chones, Austria (Now Rumania).
Date of birth:- Februar, 11, 1883.
Residence:- 2740 Holland Avenue, Bronx, New York City.
Height:- 5 feet, 7 inches.
Hair:- Mixed gray and black
Eyes:- Brown
Distinguishing features:- Scar on left cheek

SIGNATURE:-

Pincus Brecher

Photograph taken about 1924.

In a recent investigation in Canada it was disclosed that PINCUS BRECHER had played a very prominent part in the smuggling of narcotics into Canada and from there into the United States.

It appears that BRECHER has been a leader in an extensive narcotic ring, which included Jacob Polakewitz, Joseph and Sam Bernstein, Harry Davis, Hyman Holtz, Irving Stein, Charles and Max Feigenbaum and Oscar Rosensweig, the latter alleged to be a brother-in-law of BRECHER.

BRECHER is at present residing in New York and is believed to be in communication with associates in Canada.

U.S. Bureau of Narcotics Confidential List entry of Pincus Brecher
(National Archives of Canada C 133471)

The Drugs. A U.S. Customs photograph of the tin boxes of European manufactured morphine seized from steamships in New York in 1930. Zaneth proved that the Brecher/Davis gang used identical tin boxes to smuggle morphine into North America through Montreal after the New York pipeline was closed.
(U.S. National Archives)

The smugglers' trunks: the Brecher/Davis gang used these trunks to smuggle morphine into Canada.
(National Archives of Canada C 133768, C 133470)

Flavio Masi: this picture was
attached to his extradition papers.
*(National Archives of Canada
C 133472)*

Mug shot of Tony Roma
(U. S. National Archives)

Mug shot of Rocco Perri
(Archives of Ontario)

Annie Newman, in her fur coat, entering
court in Windsor in 1940
(Windsor Star)

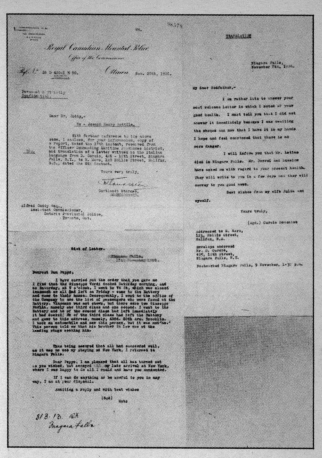

"Dear Godfather" letter to Joe Sittile, translated by Frank Zaneth
(Archives of Ontario)

RCMP "C" Division, Montreal 1944.
(left to right) Insp. J. R. Lemieux, Insp. McKay Brady, Supt. Brunet,
Commissioner S.T. Wood, Insp. Frank Zaneth, Insp. C.W. Harvison,
Insp. Poudrette *(RCMP)*

C.I.B. Officers' Special Instructional Course – October 30th to November 4th, 1950.

Front Row, L. to R. – Insp. N.W. Churchill, Insp. D.J. McCombie, A/Comm'r. L.H. Nicholson, A/Comm'r. F.W. Zaneth, Supt. J.R. Lemieux, Insp. M.F.A. Lindsay.

Middle Row, L. to R. – Sub-Insp. W.G. Fraser, Supt. N. Courtois, Insp. W.H. Williams, Supt. E.H. Pentose, Supt. J. Howe.

Top Row, L. to R. – Insp. R.W. Wonnacott, Sub-Insp. J.A. Henry, Sub-Insp. J.A. Young, Insp. E.A. Penrook, Insp. S.F. Kurow, Supt. G.B. McClellan.

CIB Officers Special Instructional Course, 1950
(RCMP 1164)

The main entrance to the Rosedale Mine, near Drumheller, in 1914
(E.S. Toshach/Glenbow Museum NA-2389-42)

View of Drumheller, Alberta, in 1916. The Canadian Northern station
and freight shed are in the foreground.
(E.S. Toshach. Glenbow Museum NA-2389-25)

The corner of Yonge St. and Charles St. in Toronto, in the late 1920s, looking north to Bloor Street. RCMP Headquarters was above the old Edwardian post office on the northeast corner, in the right of the photograph. *(City of Toronto Archives Salmon 218)*

The 1929 McLaughlin Buick was special – the Silver Anniversary edition of the automobile. There were several luxury styles of the car – seen in this General Motors artist's conception. *(Courtesy Bill McLaughlin)*

CHAPTER TEN

Zaneth and the
Bronfman Conspiracy

GET THE HIGHER-UPS.

That was the order Commissioner James MacBrien had given Zaneth when he was posted to Montreal in January, 1932. The first assignment was drugs. The second, and perhaps more important to the force, was bootlegging. Before he was elected, the Conservative Prime Minister, R.B. Bennett, had promised a full scale investigation of the liquor industry.

The government, the RCMP and Frank Zaneth knew who was behind the major bootlegging rackets — the Bronfman brothers of Montreal, led by the irascible Sam Bronfman. He was Zaneth's new target.

The Bronfman business had a "respectable" side — the Bronfmans imported quality European liquor to the French island of St. Pierre and then smuggled it into the United States. Zaneth decided to build his case against them on old-fashioned moonshining. The Bronfmans were shipping millions of gallons of raw alcohol to Newfoundland then selling it to smaller rumrunners who smuggled it into Canada.

Quebec was the one part of North America that had never had Prohibition. Wine and spirits were sold in government stores; beer was available in grocery stores and taverns. It was possible to buy a glass of beer or wine with a meal in a restaurant, an act that was illegal in neighboring provinces of Ontario and New Brunswick.

Yet rumrunning was flourishing in Quebec. Many rural districts had voted dry in "local option" referendums. Bootleggers landed gallons of alcohol by night along the shores of the St. Lawrence. Most of it was grain alcohol from Poland and other European sources. It was used in Quebec to make *whisky blanc*, raw alcohol and water, slightly sweetened and flavored.

Zaneth's men had already arrested, charged and convicted many of the small-time Québécois smugglers.

When the Mounted Police had taken over the Preventive Service in 1932, they had acquired a small navy which became the RCMP Marine Section. The Mounties had patrol boats watching for rumrunners along the Gulf of St. Lawrence and the coasts of New Brunswick and Nova Scotia. In 1932, the mounted police had taken over provincial policing in New Brunswick, which had had government liquor stores since 1927, Nova Scotia, which had adopted government stores in 1930 and Prince Edward Island, which was still dry.

As a detective inspector, Frank Zaneth had the authority to coordinate an investigation that would cover four provinces — Quebec, Nova Scotia, New Brunswick and Prince Edward Island — and two foreign countries, Newfoundland and the United States. France had made it clear early in the days of rumrunning that investigators were not welcome on the profitable island of St. Pierre.

In Montreal, Mead and Zaneth set up special squads. One was headed by now Detective Corporal Clifford Harvison. He had grumbled when only the small-fry smugglers were arrested. Now, under Zaneth's command, Harvison was placed in charge of four constables who would concentrate on liquor and bootlegging in the Montreal area. The squad operated from an apartment safe house away from the mounted police barracks on Sherbrooke Street West.

Zaneth concentrated on Sam Bronfman and his brothers, the men who ran North America's biggest and most profitable liquor empire, Distillers Corporation – Seagrams Limited. In 1934, the Bronfmans had been known for their premium Seagrams brands, sold legally in government stores across the country. But on the prairies in the early 1920s, the Bronfmans were alcohol blenders based in Yorkton, Saskatchewan, mixing alcohol with real whiskey and other additives for the American market. Some of the booze also reached customers on the dry Canadian side.

The brothers, Abe, Harry, Sam and Allan, had gone into the hotel business, prospering in the prairie boom before the First World War. In the first years of Canadian prohibition, Sam Bronfman and his brother-in-law, Barney Aaron, moved to Montreal and went into the "mail-order" business. (It was perfectly legal, under federal law, for a customer in a dry province to order his stock by mail from Quebec.) The business quickly became a profitable one. Abe Bronfman stayed in the west and opened a warehouse that supplied the prairies from Kenora, Ontario, near the Manitoba border.

When the government outlawed the mail-order business under the War Measures Act in 1917, the Bronfmans went home to Saskatchewan, got a license and went into the wholesale drug business in Yorkton selling "medicinal" alcohol. It was legal.

When the war ended, the Bronfmans were blending their own Scotch, rye and bourbon in ten one-thousand-gallon vats. They used a mixture of overproof ethyl alcohol, real aged rye whiskey or Scotch, depending on the end product, water and coloring. The mix was aged for a couple of days, then bottled and labelled with close imitations of well-known European brands. Within two years the Bronfmans had millions of dollars in their account with the Bank of Montreal. When the Bank of Montreal absorbed the Bank of North America, it gave Harry Bronfman, who was then running the business, unlimited credit. The government was happy to take its cut in excise taxes.

The family soon had warehouses — called "boozoriums" — along the border, and a registered common-carrier transport company that rented cars to American bootleggers. Then trouble began. Loads were hijacked. Other bootleggers filed lawsuits, a Bronfman brother-in-law was murdered in 1922. There were accusations of bribery, and there was growing pressure from the Saskatchewan government, which eventually put the

Bronfmans out of business in the prairies.

Harry Bronfman went to Kentucky, bought a distillery and shipped it to Ville La Salle, just outside Montreal. It opened on March 31, 1925. Sam, meanwhile, was in Scotland making a deal with Distillers Company Limited (DCL) — American Prohibition agents called it the "British Whiskey Trust" — which owned such famous brands as Johnnie Walker, Black & White, Vat 69, White Horse, Haig and Tanqueray. DCL had been supplying the Bronfmans with raw grain whiskey since 1920. Sam proposed to the blue-blood owners that they become his Canadian partners. Six months later, DCL bought fifty percent of the Bronfman business and granted the brothers the Canadian license for DCL products. With Prohibition still on in the United States, it was also the de facto American license. The Canadian company was called Distillers Corporation Limited. In 1927, the British DCL took control of the old Seagrams distillery in Waterloo, Ontario. The two Canadian firms were owned by a holding company called Distillers Corporation – Seagrams Limited. By this time, Sam Bronfman ran the show.

In 1926, revelations about corruption in the Quebec branch of Canada Customs led to the Royal Commission on Customs and Excise. It was one of North America's first public inquiries into organized crime. The commission's final report had a long section on "the Bronfman interests," listing the companies they had run in Saskatchewan and two based in the Maritimes, Atlas Shipping and the Atlantic Import Company.*

The commissioners recommended that Harry Bronfman be charged with attempting to bribe a prairie customs officer. A few years later, in Saskatchewan, the Conservative government put pressure on Ottawa for Harry Bronfman's arrest on the bribery charge. In reality, the Tories were more interested in trying to uncover connections between their Liberal opponents

---

* One recommendation included in the commission report was that the government sue all brewers and distillers for back taxes. Ottawa demanded $40,051 from Distillers Corporation Limited and $79,918 from Joseph E. Seagrams and Sons.

and the Bronfmans. In November, 1929, two RCMP officers arrested Harry Bronfman in Montreal, refused him permission to call a lawyer or his family and put him on a train to Regina. The newspapers, never sympathetic to the Bronfmans, called it a kidnapping. Represented by the best lawyers money could buy, Harry Bronfman was acquitted.*

Zaneth had to start where the Royal Commission had left off seven years before. On July 17, 1934, Frank Zaneth sailed from Halifax on the *S.S. Nova Scotian* bound for St. John's, Newfoundland.

He arrived on Friday, July 20, and went right to work. First he met with the Commissioner for Customs, Postal and Finance to learn everything about a firm called Eastern Trading Company. It was a paper chase. He began to trace imports and exports of Polish grain alcohol and to make copies of all the import and export entries of Eastern Trading. The customs staff agreed to do the work, on overtime, if they were paid by the RCMP.

Eastern Trading had been incorporated in 1927; its officers were two St. John's lawyers and their law student. The company had apparently shut down in 1933.

A check of hotels showed that no one named Bronfman had ever registered in St. John's.

Zaneth tracked down a woman who had been the stenographer at Eastern Trading:

[She] was spending her vacation in the country, and under the pretext of being a friend of her friends in Montreal, I induced her to come into St. John's. There being no other mode of transportation, I found it necessary to send a taxi for her.

On arrival, I opened conversation by mentioning names of people I knew she was acquainted with, finally leading up to the business of the Eastern Trading Co. Ltd. During the conversation, I found this woman very sharp and seeing

---

* One of the lawyers was Alfred J. Andrews of Winnipeg, the former strike prosecutor.

I could not carry on my scheme any longer, I disclosed my
identity. She then expressed her annoyance for having been
brought back to the City on the expectation that she would
talk about the business of her ex employers.

However, she was rather late, as she had already furnished
me with essential information . . . insofar as the auditing
of the books, payment of wages, etc. and the name of the
bank in which Eastern Trading Co. Ltd. did business with,
were concerned. In all she painted a very good picture of
this firm's activities and definitely connected the
Bronfmans.

On Saturday, Zaneth tried to find out who audited Eastern
Trading's books and what happened to the books when the
company closed, but, as he noted, "the inhabitants there were
already aware of my presence and are not willing to give any
information." He spent that evening in the customs office,
making a preliminary examination of the customs papers.

On Monday morning, Zaneth found he had another problem.
Newfoundland would not let him take the customs forms out
of the country. He had to buy blank forms, hire a typewriter
and stenographer and show the steno how to copy the forms.
Export entries often read "to the high seas" but they named the
boats. The RCMP could trace the vessels from Quebec, Nova
Scotia and New Brunswick, and find their captains.

By Tuesday, July 23, Zaneth had recruited an informant who
named a taxi driver who had worked for Eastern Trading. The
cabby told Zaneth he would answer questions only if his lawyer
was present. That evening, Zaneth got the information he
needed. The taxi driver had told his friend — Zaneth's informant — the name of the man who ran Eastern Trading in St.
John's. It was Franklyn Blair. Zaneth had searched Blair's home
in Montreal, in the fall of 1933, as part of the earlier investigation, but he had found nothing. The informant told him that
Blair had handed the company's books to a St. John's auditor.
Zaneth was able to check the customs records and discovered
that a box, presumably containing the books, had been sent to

a Montreal customs broker.

Zaneth's informant said the Bank of Montreal branch in St. John's handled Eastern Trading's accounts. It was part of the Bronfman modus operandi, to use the services of the bank that backed the family. Zaneth asked the Bank of Montreal head office to give him permission to examine Eastern's accounts in the St. John's branch. The bank refused because it feared legal action for "breach of trust."

The St. John's police chief put Zaneth in touch "unofficially" with a friend who worked for the accounting firm that audited Eastern Trading's books. The accountant told Zaneth that Eastern Trading purchased large quantities of spirits from Europe and paid by bank drafts. He told Zaneth that Eastern Trading's St. John's account never exceeded $5,000. After expenses were paid, the account was always refreshed from Montreal to the limit of $5,000. The auditing firm's reports were mailed to a company called Canadian General Distributors, at a Montreal box number.

There was one last bureaucratic foul-up. Zaneth needed a specimen signature from a collector of customs who was on extended sick leave. On the morning of Saturday, August 4, Zaneth took a taxi fifteen miles out of St. John's, got the signature, went back to St. John's, got that signature certified then went to the dock in time to board the *Fort St. George* as it sailed.

Halifax was the next link in the chain. The Bronfman company in the city was called Atlas Shipping. It had originally been named the Domestic Dominion and Foreign Company, but within a month of its incorporation in 1925, the name was changed to Atlas Shipping. The company directors were Barnatt Aaron, Sam Bronfman's brother-in-law, merchant; F.W. Carline, merchant; and a stenographer. Zaneth noted "that this office was located in the heart of the Bootlegger's district."

F.W. Carline was dead and his widow, Evelyn, had succeeded him. She was described to Zaneth by a local Mountie as "very shrewd, well posted in the bootlegging racket and difficult to handle."

Zaneth decided to work on a young woman who had once worked for Evelyn Carline. The young woman now worked in an insurance office. Zaneth called her, claiming once again to be a friend of the Bronfmans.

Having registered at the Nova Scotian Hotel, I decided to move into the "Lord Nelson Hotel," and registered under an assumed name. The matter was too important to take any chances, as I did not wish my identity disclosed.

I . . . requested her to have dinner with me. She was informed of my friendship with the Bronfmans and she immediately asked me if I knew Mr. Carline ■ ■ ■ She was informed I knew the gentlemen, but I had not had the pleasure to meet Evelyn Carline. She then informed me that I did not miss very much, as the woman was no good.

During the conversation, I gathered that although these women were friends, there was no love lost between them, and that with a little coaxing, I might be able to get some information. She went onto explain that two years ago Evelyn Carline, let her out of employment, and took charge of all the activities of the Atlas Shipping Co.

She further stated that the Bronfmans paid this woman $150.00 per month, and that a number of rum-running boats were owned, controlled and operated by the Bronfmans, the expenses of which were paid from the Bank account of the Atlas Shipping Co., which account was maintained by Evelyn Carline.

Zaneth met the young woman for lunch the next day and again she was very chatty. She had no idea what had happened to the records of Atlas Shipping, but she remembered that each week, a statement on goods imported, goods exported and the cash paid was sent to Montreal.

During the first two years, she said, all the liquor was smuggled out of Halifax. Later the Bronfmans made a deal with the Department of National Revenue. They would pay duty on liquor imported at Halifax, ship it to Windsor and export it to the United States. At least two boxcars a week went by the Canadian National Railway to Windsor, addressed to phony names, then the booze was smuggled across to Detroit.

Liquor arriving from Europe was unloaded and put in a bonded warehouse, and Atlas provided customs with the two copies of the required B-13 export permit. She could not explain why Atlas was permitted to ship spirits into the then still dry province of Ontario.

Zaneth proposed that the young woman drop in on Evelyn Carline to try to find out where the Atlas records were kept. He warned her not to ask too many questions and to allow Evelyn Carline to do the talking.

The young woman met Evelyn on the afternoon of Wednesday, August 8, and that night she told Zaneth what she had found out. It seemed that Carline was running Atlas Shipping out of her home and was trying to sell three large boats, apparently owned by the Bronfmans, that were tied up in Dartmouth.

Zaneth obtained a warrant, got a corporal and a constable from the local detachment and raided Carline's house on Spring Garden Road.

This woman became very nervous and commenced to shed tears . . . When Evelyn Carline found we were determined to search every nook and corner of her home, she expressed an ardent desire to render whatever assistance she could. It was obvious, however, that she was not sincere, and was endeavoring either to camouflage the issue or place herself in good with the authorities.

In the front part of the house, Zaneth found a typewriter; there was an unfinished letter addressed to the Bronfmans in the machine. He requested Evelyn Carline to finish it, which she did.

The Mounties found a large number of documents in a cupboard. In his report on the search, Zaneth rather gleefully noted, "It is sufficient to say that enough incriminating evidence was found to show nefarious activities of the Bronfmans since

1926." The documents included detailed expense accounts for eight rumrunning schooners. What appeared more interesting was that the rumrunners had their own shortwave radio station. Codes used to communicate with the rumrunning schooners and were changed very frequently (as one letter said, "so that the rats will not get on to us"). One of the code books, Zaneth reported, was "binded by a lead cover, which would sink if thrown over-board, in case of arrest on the High-Seas."

He also seized a note "instructing Evelyn Carline to destroy everything." It looked like the note was written some months before the raid. When Zaneth showed it to Evelyn Carline, she became very agitated and her only comment was, "I wish I had."

Zaneth found and seized more than two hundred documents in Carline's home, documents that showed a widow was running one of the biggest rumrunning operations of the Prohibition era.

By August 16, Zaneth was back in Montreal, working to produce a conspiracy case in his usual meticulous fashion. His preliminary report included long lists — for example, a list of all the liquor imported to Newfoundland by Eastern Trading. Zaneth wryly noted that as soon as the Bronfmans got wind that the RCMP were investigating smuggling, Eastern Trading went out of business. All the company's merchandise was transferred to the island of St. Pierre, to another Bronfman company, Northern Trading. Zaneth concluded that liquor exported from St. Pierre went to the States and alcohol exported from St. John's went to Canada.

Zaneth planned three key raids in Montreal: the Peel Street offices of Distillers Corporation – Seagrams Limited and the home of Franklyn Blair on Pratt Avenue were to be hit first, followed by the Bank of Montreal branch at St. Catherine and Drummond.

On August 20, precisely at 11:15, Zaneth and Corporal Jim Churchman arrived at the office of Distillers Corporation–Seagrams Limited along with two constables. Harvison raided the Blair home.

At the Distillers offices, the Bronfmans were away, and an

office manager was in charge. Zaneth, Churchman and their men began a search of the executive offices. They seized documents, put them in cardboard boxes and took them to a paddy wagon parked on Peel Street.

After an hour, Zaneth got a call at the Distillers' offices. Harvison wanted help at the Blair home.

Franklyn Blair was in Newfoundland; his wife Mary and seventeen-year-old daughter, Phyllis, were at home. Harvison had found a receipt for a safety-deposit box. The corporal had asked Mary Blair for the key. She had refused to tell him where it was.

Zaneth arrived, was briefed by Harvison and asked Mary Blair about the receipt. Again she said she wouldn't hand anything over. Zaneth ordered Harvison to continue the search, then told Mrs. Blair that, if they had to, the Mounted Police would get a court order to open the box.

What happened next was later disputed. Harvison had found some old trunks in the basement and took Zaneth down with Mrs. Blair to see them.

Zaneth would later say there were a few trunks in the basement. He said he asked Mary Blair about them; she told him they were old, they belonged to her sister and she did not have the key.

"Not wishing to destroy the lock of these trunks, I informed her that I would take her word for it," Zaneth said in his report.

Mary Blair's recollection in later testimony was very different.

"They went down in the basement and opened some old trunks and they were greatly pleased to find an old code book that was forty years old and belonged to my brother."

She said Zaneth told her. "If you and Mr. Blair tell everything you know you won't have to worry, but if you don't, you may be picked up and suffer for it."

Mary Blair, already upset, remembered that as a threat.

After ten minutes, Zaneth went back downtown to Peel Street. When the office closed at 5:30, armed, uniformed Mounties guarded the doors. Another shift of uniformed Mounted Police guarded the offices overnight.

The search of the vaults continued the next day. Accountants from Price Waterhouse, Distillers' auditing firm, showed up to watch the seizures. So did Lazarus Phillips, the Bronfmans' lawyer and a leading member of Montreal's Jewish establishment, who had close ties to the Liberal party. Phillips met with Zaneth and asked for a copy of the search warrant. Phillips then went to see Mead, who refused to give him any information, except to say that the Mounted Police were preparing a charge of conspiracy against the officers of Eastern Trading, Atlas Shipping, Canadian Investment (another Bronfman company) and Northern Trading.

But Zaneth soon discovered that key documents were missing. The books of Atlas Shipping didn't exist.

When Zaneth went to the Bronfmans' branch of the Bank of Montreal at St. Catherine and Drummond, he found a gold mine. The bank had kept a series of letters that showed, step by step, how the Bank of Montreal had taken in millions of dollars from bootleggers over the years. All the money had been sent to Montreal in phony names, and the money had gone into the Bronfman accounts. Top officials of the Bank of Montreal had no qualms about taking in the bootleggers' millions, but the bank's rules had to be stretched. The money-depositing scheme was created to fit into the procedures laid down by the bank. As well, the Bronfmans were selling liquor through a series of companies and agents, none of them directly connected with Distillers Corporation–Seagrams Limited. This pioneering scheme would eventually have a name — money laundering.

The documents in the bank described a growing empire that reached from Montreal to Tahiti, Belize and Bermuda. Zaneth and the special Crown prosecutors had to find the answer to one question, were the Bronfmans doing anything illegal or were they just very smart businessmen?

On August 22, Mary Blair, of her own free will, opened the safety-deposit box and handed the contents to Harvison.

Zaneth spent the next few weeks going through all the documents he had seized and concluded that Evelyn Carline was a pivotal figure. It was Carline who ran the bootlegging operation out of Halifax, dispatching ships and taking in money from "the boys" in New York.

On October 1, Zaneth went back in Halifax, and summoned Evelyn Carline to the Halifax barracks to be questioned under the harsh provisions of the Customs Act.*

Zaneth questioned Carline on the morning of Tuesday, October 2. Her lawyer, R.S. McInnes, was present. Zaneth found that she was "averse to answering questions," and he believed that "she had been primed by her Counsel and perhaps threatened by the Bronfmans if she talked too much."

The next day Carline was even more belligerent, and questioning was postponed for a week.

Zaneth checked the Bank of Montreal branch in Halifax and discovered that F.W. Carline had opened the Atlas bank account in 1926, when it was legal to export liquor to the United States. When the Canada Export Act was passed and it became illegal to export liquor to the United States, a new account was established in the name of "Evelyn Carline in Trust." The money from the account was used to charter boats, to pay for supplies and to employ a customs broker to look after the extensive legal side of the business.

The bank records in Halifax showed that large amounts of money were transferred from New York City to the Carline trust account, and that money was transferred from the Bank of Montreal, Drummond and St. Catherine branch. This indicated to Zaneth that the Bronfmans had transferred money to Evelyn Carline and that payments for liquor sold to New York bootleggers were collected in New York and the money transferred to Halifax.

---

* Senior RCMP officers, like Superintendent Mead, were granted special powers to hold inquiries under Section 134-A of the Customs Act. These special powers allowed the RCMP to force witnesses to testify in private. People who refused to cooperate could be jailed. Many lawyers thought these special powers were a dangerous intrusion on civil liberties, especially when a junior constable or corporal used knowledge of Section 134-A to threaten suspects.

Zaneth spent time narrowing down the list of bootlegging boats, those that were working between St. Pierre and New York, and those that were smuggling liquor into Canada. On the Halifax waterfront it was common knowledge that the Bronfmans either had owned or had chartered all the boats from Halifax that discharged their cargo at Rum Row just off Long Island, N.Y.

On October 4, R.S. McInnes, Evelyn Carline's lawyer requested a meeting with Inspector Len Nicholson, then in charge of the Halifax Criminal Investigation Branch. The lawyer had a list of complaints about Zaneth's questioning of his client.

McInnes had been the lawyer for Atlas Shipping and told Nicholson he could supply any information that the RCMP wanted. Nicholson quickly concluded McInnes was more concerned with the Bronfmans than with his client. Nicholson had known McInnes for sometime; the lawyer was a prominent member of the Conservative party. With a Conservative government in power in Ottawa, McInnes had been given the usual patronage, a job as prosecutor for Customs and Excise cases in the Halifax area.

Nicholson also knew the Bronfman brothers had a license to build a distillery in Illinois; the lawyer was afraid that the U.S. government would cancel the license if it got proof of the Bronfmans' Prohibition activities.

According to Nicholson, McInnes suggested that Zaneth was "collecting evidence for the United States government" and might blackmail the Bronfmans. "He would be in a position to go to the Bronfman organization and demand $10,000.00 for the evidence in his hands, threatening, if his terms were not met, to deliver this evidence to the United States authorities." Nicholson ordered McInnes out of the office and recommended to Ottawa that he be fired as a special Crown prosecutor.

Meanwhile in Montreal, Zaneth went to the offices of Distillers Corporation–Seagrams Limited to look for missing documents and ledgers. One day, Sam Bronfman was in the building. He called Zaneth into his office and asked Zaneth if he was interested in ledgers. Zaneth replied that he was.

Sam Bronfman handed Zaneth a ledger and said, "take this and come back in half an hour."

Zaneth opened the ledger. It was full of cash.

Zaneth kept the ledger and told Bronfman he would send it and the money to Ottawa. He had one problem in laying a charge of attempted bribery: the conversation was private. There had been no witnesses.*

By Saturday, October 19, 1934, Zaneth was ready. He met with the two special crown prosecutors, James Crankshaw and Jean Penverne, and handed them a summary of the Bronfman Conspiracy case.

Atlas Shipping was the mother company to three firms; Eastern Trading Company, which operated out of St. John's, Nfld., Northern Trading, which operated out of St. Pierre, and Southern Trading, which operated out of Hamilton, Bermuda.**

Zaneth reported the trail began with the account at the Bank of Montreal branch at Drummond and St. Catherine Streets, Montreal. Atlas legally bought liquor from the Bronfmans' distillery. Atlas also purchased alcohol and liquor in Europe and shipped it to the Eastern Trading, Northern Trading and Southern Trading companies. The Bronfmans controlled the operations. Money collected by Frank Blair from Canadian bootleggers found its way into the account of Atlas Shipping.

Shipments of liquor were never directly consigned to Atlas Shipping. But one of the letters in the Bank of Montreal file showed that in 1932, Atlas had $1,400,000 worth of booze on hand on the islands of St. Pierre and Newfoundland, in the

---

* After he retired, Zaneth told his friend John Marrett that there had been about one million dollars in the ledger. Zaneth said he sent the ledger and money to Ottawa and requested permission to lay charges against Sam Bronfman but that he never heard of the ledger again. The available documents from the Bronfman case file make no mention of this incident.

** Zaneth's investigation did not concentrate on the Southern Trading Company, which was concerned with smuggling liquor into the United States.

British Honduras (now Belize), and in Nassau, in the Bahamas.

Frank Blair and other employees had established Eastern Trading in St. John's in 1926 — soon after the Bronfmans had moved to Montreal. Eastern Trading supplied its customers with raw alcohol from 1926 until 1933, when the RCMP began investigations in the Gulf of St. Lawrence. Then the company was shut down.

Beginning in the earliest days of Prohibition in the United States, the French island of St. Pierre was an important harbor for bootleggers. Young, tough and farsighted New York gangsters, like Frank Costello, had recognized the importance of the islands's French sovereignty. By 1924, the gangsters were transferring first European and later good Canadian liquor from St. Pierre to boats that offloaded their wares on the high seas at Rum Row, just off Long Island and New Jersey.

The Bronfmans were established on St. Pierre by 1928. They used a company called Northern Export Company, owned by Atlas Shipping, to import European liquor for sale on the high seas. In 1930, the Canada Export Act made it illegal for Canadians to export their products to countries that had prohibited the sale of alcohol. St. Pierre became even more important for Canadian distillers: it was legal to export to St. Pierre. The island was used to launder Canadian liquor.

In 1931, the Bronfmans and other Canadian distillers briefly formed what was called "the Pool." (Investigators in the United States called it the Canadian liquor cartel.) Atlas Shipping owned 70 percent of a new company, Northern Trading Company, and the other 30 percent was owned by other members of the pool. The pool didn't last long, as there were too many disagreements, and after the formal dissolution, one member, Great West Wine Company, owned by Hyman Ripstein, remained, with 22.5 percent of the stock of Northern Trading.

The books of Northern Trading were supposed to be in the Peel Street offices, but the RCMP found only an empty looseleaf binder. The books of Brintcan Investments, the Bronfman holding company, showed a total annual net profit at Northern Trading of $1,497,600.27 for the years 1929 to 1931. Where did that money come from? At the Bank of Montreal, Zaneth found a letter from Atlas Shipping notifying the bank that the company was doing business as Northern Export. According to his reports, he found "huge sales by the Distillers Corporation–Seagrams, through the Atlas Shipping, to the Northern Export or Trading Companies." In addition, there were large shiploads of liquor imported from Europe. All of the liquor was bound for the American market.

The Bronfmans set up a company, Canadian General Distributors, as a laundering vehicle for both liquor and cash. Zaneth questioned officials from the Peel Street offices and found "Letterheads of this company were used at times by various officials of other companies . . ." The name Canadian General appeared again and again in the sales slips of the Eastern Trading Company. Eastern sold to Canadian General Distributors then Canadian General sold to the ultimate purchaser. Every purchase and sale was a step in the laundering chain.

Zaneth tried to trace cargoes and money through the Bronfman's insurers. He tried to find out from his sources if the insurance contracts contained clauses that covered cargoes coming down the St. Lawrence. Such clauses would prove that the Bronfmans knew the liquor was being reimported to Canada, and that they had a hand in the smuggling as well.

Zaneth's chief target was Sam Bronfman, the man who ran Distillers Corporation–Seagrams Limited. His brother, Abe Bronfman, ran the day to day activities of the companies, hired the agents for Atlas Shipping in the United States and handled sales. Barney Aaron, the brother-in-law, and Allan Bronfman, another brother, worked with Abe in running the most lucrative of the Bronfman companies, Northern Trading. By 1934, Harry Bronfman was described in an RCMP report as the "technical man, more interested in the operations of distilleries."

Together the five men owned the family holding company. The name was based on their original cable address, Bronfman Interests Canada. Through Brintcan, the Bronfmans controlled Distillers Corporation.

Zaneth had discovered the five men owned a maze of companies — Brintcan Investments, the Investment Co. of Canada, Atlas Shipping, Canadian General Distributors and Northern Trading Co. — all used as a cover for bootlegging and he noted "the profits realized . . . were not shared with the shareholders of the Distillers Corporation."

Zaneth also foresaw a problem that always troubled him: separating the guilty from the innocent. Zaneth's investigation did not concentrate on the Southern Trading Company, which was concerned with smuggling liquor into the United States.

> The ramification of Bronfman interests is so extensive, their operations so complicated that it is almost impossible to be able to know where a line should be drawn in order to bring into this conspiracy the shareholders of the Distillers Corporation Ltd. with a view to preparing a clear cut case and avoid the punishment of innocent parties.

Zaneth focused on two men. One was Franklyn Blair, who ran operations in St. John's and St. Pierre. The other was David Costley, the secretary-treasurer of Brintcan. Costley had been a manager at the Bank of Montreal in Regina and had gone to work for the Bronfmans in the mid-1920s. He handled the books for Northern Export and, in later years, was a director of Eastern Trading. Zaneth kept finding the initials D.C. on checks. Costley also had the power of attorney for a company called Joseph White Reg'd. That, Zaneth discovered, was the key shell company in the laundering scheme.

Zaneth and his men had searched Costley's house and found only a few documents. One was a letter from an American company, addressed to "Atlas Shipping. Attention: Abe Bronfman." It disputed the commission paid on a shipment that ended up in Philadelphia. The letter also referred to three rumrunning schooners, one called the *Yvonne Joanne*. *

---

* U.S. Coast Guard records show the *Yvonne Joanne*, loaded 1,400 cases of liquor on December 15, 1933, nine days after Prohibition officially ended in the United States, smuggling did not stop. The Coast Guard also

The laundering trail began after the Canada Export Act had become law. The Bronfmans told Evelyn Carline to open the trust account in Halifax. Money from that account was used to purchase or charter rum boats. The supplies for the boats and the liquor they shipped came from Northern Trading Company and its Caribbean counterpart Southern Trading. Most of the deposits to the trust account came from the United States and then were transferred into the account of Atlas Shipping.

By checking the books of Distillers Corporation, Zaneth was able to track money from Atlas Shipping. In 1930, three million dollars went from Atlas to Distillers.

In a second arm of the laundering scheme, the various "agencies" that sold Bronfman liquor in the United States deposited millions of dollars in the account of Atlas Shipping in the Bank of Montreal branch at St. Catherine and Drummond. In 1930, more than one million dollars was deposited in cash. And then there were checks, as Zaneth commented, "The [deposit] slip, in the majority of cases, gives only the brief information 'Clark' or 'Gold' or, in one case, 'Boys $50,000.'"

Millions of dollars were deposited in two names, "John Norton" and "Joseph White." Dudley Oliver, the bank's branch manager, told Zaneth they were "trade names." He said Atlas's bookkeeper purchased bank drafts with checks they received from the buyers in the United States. The drafts were then deposited into the Atlas account. As Zaneth explained, "This system eliminated the necessity of endorsing the checks or of showing the amount of each check on a deposit slip and made the tracing of these payments almost impossible."

In December, 1930, the Bank of Montreal brass began to worry about their "unusual" arrangements with the Bronfmans. They itemized their concerns in a careful letter that described the account of a "liquor exporting concern whose product finds a

---

suspected the *Yvonne Joanne* of smuggling drugs from the Bahamas into the United States.

Later Costleys wife was interviewed by author Peter C. Newman and said her husband had burned some papers in the basement before the raid. *Bronfman Dynasty* p. 129n.

market in the U.S.A." and described how the bank's unnamed clients had devised the scheme to "prevent their name or the name of this bank being connected with remittances from United States sources."

According to the bank's memos, a bootlegger in the United States often paid for his booze by telegraphing money. The telegram was usually worded: "Notify and pay $—— to John Norton by order of Jones."

If the Bank of Montreal received a telegraphic transfer to "John Norton," the money was automatically deposited in the account of the bank's unnamed "customer" — Atlas Shipping.

Bankers' drafts were untraceable, the Bank of Montreal noted, because "the endorsement is of no consequence as the *purchaser* of the draft is not known to the issuing Bank." So bootleggers mailed the drafts to Atlas Shipping, in care of the Distillers Corporation office. The drafts were taken to the bank and endorsed in the phony name.

Checks gave the bank a problem — so it broke its rules. "We do not stamp them 'Deposited to the credit of John Norton' in accordance with our usual customs. This stamped endorsement is omitted so that payment cannot be traced to our customers," the memo said.

After a while, the bank lawyers decided there was a problem with the checks. They began meetings with lawyers from Jacobs, Phillips & Serber, the firm that represented the Bronfmans.* Years of negotiations resulted in a file of letters between the lawyers and the bank. The letters outlined how to launder money within the rules of the Canadian banking system.

The bank first wanted someone to take personal responsibility — an employee of Atlas would be the payee and the Bronfman brothers would accept full responsibility for Atlas

---

* Phillips was Lazarus Phillips, Sam Bronfman's friend, and Canada's top tax lawyer at the time. Jacobs was Sam Jacobs, the MP who had beaten Michael Buhay in 1921 in Cartier riding, the same MP who had the clout to get the American gangster Joe Sottile Canadian citizenship.

Shipping and guarantee its account. The Bronfmans flatly refused.

The system they eventually approved involved setting up a "duly registered entity." The "entity" would endorse the checks, but would not have an actual bank account. All transfers, checks and drafts would pass through the Atlas Shipping account, which Brintcan Investments would guarantee.[42] The Bank of Montreal already had the guarantee for Brintcan from the Bronfmans.

On July 2, 1932, Dudley Oliver, the branch manager, wrote to his boss to clarify the way the branch would handle the checks, so that the endorsement of Atlas Shipping never appeared on the actual checks:

> We issue a draft in payment of said checks, payable to "J. Norton," endorsed in that way (John Norton) and by the Atlas Shipping Company. The checks are endorsed by an initial such as "A.B." [Abe Bronfman] or "D.C." [David Costley], these initials constituting the endorsement of the Atlas Shipping Company Ltd. . . . in accordance with a Waiver of Endorsement executed by that Company "1st October, 1931" and lodged with the bank.

The Bronfmans accepted the idea. On July 30, 1932, in the City of Montreal, they registered a general trading company called Joseph White Reg'd. Louis Groper, a young man related by marriage to the Bronfmans, was the president, but he had no duties beyond signing the papers that registered the company. He then gave Power of Attorney to the Bronfmans. David Costley had one of the powers of attorney. The next day, an office boy opened the account at the bank.

The last letter in the file was dated May 7, 1934. It was from the General Manager of the Bank of Montreal to Oliver and ordered him not to turn over the guarantees to the Bronfmans "until a reasonable time has elapsed to ensure that no claims will be made." In other words, the Bronfmans were aware of the investigation, and were hoping to destroy the paper trail.

The Bank of Montreal was worrying about a bum check in the account of its biggest customer.

From the figures available, Zaneth found that Atlas Shipping had made eight million dollars in 1930 and almost five million dollars had passed through Joseph White Reg'd. to Atlas Shipping Company in 1933.

Zaneth knew he would have a stronger case for court if he tied the Bronfmans to the raw alcohol sold along the lower St. Lawrence. He based his case on the "small fry":

In the fall of 1928, Alfred Levesque, a notorious bootlegger of Edmonston, N.B., and Notre Dame du Lac, Que . . . called at the offices of the Bronfmans in Montreal and arranged the purchase of 5,000 gallons of alcohol. Levesque was advised that Ulric Tremblay, Captain and owner of the Barge *Tremblay*, would transport the alcohol for Levesque but that Tremblay could not enter the Port of St. Pierre as his clearance papers covered the transportation of coal from Sydney, N.S. to Quebec.[43]

One hundred dollars were paid to the Captain of a scow who conveyed the 5,000 gallons to a point a few miles off St. Pierre where it was transferred to the Barge *Tremblay* to be landed by that vessel at Rivière du Loup.

Three months later, Levesque again interviewed Abe Bronfman in Montreal and arranged for the purchase of 8,000 gallons from St. Pierre; afterwards, on examining this shipment at Riviere du Loup, Levesque found that approximately 1,000 gallons were rusty and not fit for sale. He returned to Montreal and in the presence of [Franklyn] Blair, complained to Abe Bronfman. After learning the location of the liquor cache, Bronfman promised to send a man from his distillery to help in clearing the alcohol.

Abe Bronfman failed to keep his promise and Levesque called on him . . . On this occasion Abe told him that the alcohol could be cleaned by passing it through a loaf of bread. Then, [when] Levesque expressed his annoyance at this advice, Abe promised him that the loss would be made good on future shipments. No adjustment was ever made.

Zaneth also reported that two "notorious bootleggers" from eastern Quebec visited the Distillers Corporation offices and purchased three thousand gallons of alcohol. The alcohol was delivered to the vessel *Gracie MacKay*. The *Gracie MacKay* offloaded five hundred gallons to a speedboat in the Gulf of St. Lawrence. The speedboat was seized by the RCMP.

By late November, Zaneth had a list of people to be charged in the case. Mead wanted everything ready to go in two weeks. Mead was hoping that, once the charges were laid, the RCMP could get a preferred indictment from Quebec's Attorney General. The indictment would eliminate the need for a preliminary hearing.

On December 11, the RCMP announced that 61 people were wanted, including the four Bronfman brothers. It was hot news, a "gigantic-roundup" of the "biggest liquor smuggling ring on record" with the total conspiracy worth five million dollars. It was called the biggest case in RCMP history.

There were five charges:

- Illegal possession of liquor smuggled into Canada, a violation of the Criminal Code and the Excise Act.
- Keeping and selling alcohol unlawfully imported into Canada without paying Customs duties worth five million dollars, a violation of both the Criminal Code and the Customs Act.
- Defrauding the Canadian government of customs and duties worth five million dollars.
- Smuggling five million dollars worth of liquor into Canada.
- Conspiracy to smuggle liquor into the United States, a violation of the Canada Export Act.

The RCMP were treating the small fry just as they were treating the Bronfmans. The Maritime conspirators were being "invited" to Montreal. If they agreed to surrender, the government would give them return fares for the preliminary hearing

"THEY ALWAYS GET THEIR MAN"

The Halifax Herald was quick to give Zaneth the credit in the Bronfman conspiracy case. The newspaper called him "the man who sprang the trap which sent a score or so of Communists either into Canadian penitentiaries or unwillingly to Europe a few years ago." It ran this special editorial cartoon of a Mountie, standing on a beach, with the tunic printed in red ink.

and the trial. There was some trouble in Halifax, where Member of Parliament W.G. Ernst accused Zaneth and other Mounties of using "third degree methods" — police brutality — to break down suspects.

At nine o'clock on the morning of Monday, December 18, Sam Bronfman and his brother Allan appeared at the RCMP barracks on Sherbrooke Street, where Zaneth served them with warrants. The two were then photographed and fingerprinted. Half an hour later, Abe and Harry Bronfman, Barney Aaron, David Costley and Frank Blair appeared. They were arrested by a corporal. Then eleven Nova Scotia suspects surrendered to Zaneth. The men were led out of the headquarters to three waiting cars. Harry attempted to cover his face to hide from photographers, but Sam stopped him. The four Bronfman brothers were each granted $100,000 bail; bail for Costley, Aaron and Blair was $1,500; and for the Nova Scotians it was $900 each.

Mead and Zaneth met with reporters to deny the charges of brutality.

"We can safely say that not one of the 61 persons, with the exception of Mrs. Carline was questioned in connection with the case," Mead said. "When our men did question Mrs. Carline, however, it was in the presence of counsel and I am sure that she was not forced or tricked into divulging information."

The Bronfmans had a team of defense lawyers that included their old friend Lazarus Phillips and the leading Montreal advocate Aimé Geoffrion, considered the best criminal lawyer in the city. Geoffrion was an old friend of Premier Alexandre Taschereau. The Quebec attorney general refused to issue a preferred indictment.

The preliminary hearing opened on Friday, January 11, 1935, before Judge Jules Desmarais. Eve Carline (as the press called her) and fifty other accused occupied the public benches on one side of the court. At the Crown's table were the two prosecutors, James Crankshaw and Jean Penverne, and Zaneth, Harvison and Churchman. A scarlet-clad Mountie guarded the exhibits.

Almost immediately all the Maritime defendants, including Eve Carline, were permitted to go home. Penverne said they would begin with the evidence against "the Montreal group," the Bronfman brothers and their advisers. Argument began immediately over each of the documents Zaneth and his men had uncovered. The arguments went on for days.

All the documents related to "smuggling actions," Crankshaw told the judge.

"We deny that," replied the chief defense counsel, Aimé Geoffrion.

On January 14, Geoffrion rose to object to the fact the RCMP had used the draconian Section 134-A of the Customs Act, to question H.G. Norman, a Price Waterhouse auditor who had checked the books of Distillers Corporation–Seagrams Limited. Geoffrion said the RCMP had had the idea too late of hiring an accountant and were now trying to force the Bronfmans' accountant to give evidence. Crankshaw replied that to force Norman to answer questions under the Customs Act would save time, and then bluntly told Judge Desmarais, "Your lordship has no power to prevent the police from examining a man under 134-A."

Then a new problem developed in the Crown's case. The Canada Export Act had never before been tested. The provisions outlawing the export of alcohol to countries with Prohibition had no penalties. The Crown was relying on a section of the Criminal Code that provided a year in jail for anyone breaking any Act of Parliament. Lazarus Phillips, for the Bronfmans, raised the question of government complicity. Ottawa was collecting nine dollars in excise tax for each barrel of whiskey that was sold for consumption in Canada but that was instead smuggled into the United States.

After a long day of arguments, Desmarais reserved judgment until sometime in February.

Penverne and Crankshaw wanted stronger evidence that Atlas Shipping was smuggling liquor to the United States. Zaneth was sent to New York "for the purpose of lining up two or three U.S.A. officers who actually made seizures of Bronfman liquor and to check up on fines paid by the crews on Bronfman vessels for infractions of the American anti-smuggling laws."

In New York, Zaneth checked first with U.S. Customs and then the following week with the U.S. Coast Guard. He saw the intelligence files on smugglers' boats he knew were working out of St. John's and Halifax. He also asked for the log books and trailing logs for Coast Guard cutters and destroyers. The ships were on the lookout for what they called "blacks" — a ship running at night without lights. One log contained a report of the USCG Destroyer *George E. Badger* , which had tracked the black *Isabel H.* on January 6, 1932.

The *Isabel H.* was a notorious smuggler, from Yarmouth, Nova Scotia, last seized by the Coast Guard on February 1, 1930, before the passage of the Canada Export Act. The 1930 reports showed that the owners of the *Isabel H.* were three local Yarmouth fishermen, but the money for building of the ship came from "Canadian Distributors" of Montreal. Canadian Distributors was described by the business research firm R.G. Dun & Company as "an unregistered name used by the Bronfman family."[44]

Zaneth also saw the logs on the *Audrey B*, a schooner out of LaHave, Nova Scotia. On Christmas Day, 1930, the Coast Guard spotted an "off shore rum cruiser, heavily loaded" off Long Island, and gave chase. The cutter fired three blank rounds at the black which made smoke and tried to flee. The cutter then fired three live rounds. All hit. The *Audrey B* hove to and surrendered.

The schooner had cleared from St. Pierre for Nassau on December 10, 1930 with 2,800 sacks of liquor on board. When the Coast Guard seized the *Audrey B* she had already disposed of 663 sacks.

Zaneth returned to Montreal with the intelligence files and trailing logs for eleven key vessels, but on February 4, Judge Desmarais dismissed Count 5, the charge of conspiracy to smuggle alcohol in the United States. He accepted the arguments that violating the Export Act was not an indictable offense and if it was not a indictable offense, there could be no criminal conspiracy.

According to secret dispatches from the U.S. Consul, Wesley

Frost, to the State Department, the Bronfmans were trying political influence: "Street rumor at Montreal is to the effect that the Bronfman brothers went to Ottawa a few weeks ago and offered to contribute one million dollars each to the campaign funds of the Liberal and Conservative parties if the prosecution is dropped." A few weeks later Frost reported:

The Dominion authorities at Ottawa are just now rather irritated by the tactics which have been pursued by the Bronfmans and their attorneys, which include political and financial pressure . . . If the Canadian elections in the late spring or early summer should result in the return of a Liberal government to power, the Hon. S.W. Jacobs, MP KC, who is one of the leading attorneys for the Bronfmans (although not appearing in court), will be very influential in Ottawa, and might be able to secure adoption there an adverse policy toward any requests made by the American government for the evidence in question.

The Crown turned to proving its charge that liquor was reimported into Canada. In the afternoon, Captain Alfred Levesque was called from his penitentiary cell to identify Abe Bronfman and Frank Blair as the men who sold him eight thousand gallons of alcohol. Levesque and other bootleggers were on the stand for the next three days of the hearing. Levesque said he between 1929 and 1933 he bought fifteen cargoes of alcohol from the Bronfmans through Frank Blair of Eastern Trading at St. John's. He paid by check or telegraphic transfer.

For two days, Penverne and Crankshaw took Levesque through his transactions with Eastern Trading. There were coded telegrams arranging sales and arguing over prices and financing charges. The liquor was dropped off on small boats between Quebec City and Cap Chat.

"Were the excise duties paid?" Penverne asked.

"Not by me," Levesque replied.

The next question before the court was the admissibility of documents found in the Blairs' safety-deposit box. The defense developed it into an argument over accusations of police brutality.

Phillipe Brais, the lawyer representing the Blairs, approached Zaneth and Harvison with an affidavit accusing Harvison of using "third degree" methods against Mary and Phyllis Blair.

Mary Blair claimed in the affidavit that Harvison threatened to have her arrested and have her fined and to use an axe to open her safety deposit box. She also claimed that Zaneth referred to officials of the Newfoundland government as "a bunch of bootleggers," and that he would "get the Bronfmans at any cost."

Zaneth was becoming frustrated with long, drawn-out legal arguments, and it showed just a bit in his reaction to the affidavit:

The affidavit . . . accuses me of having said to Mary Blair that Peter Cashin, Minister of Finance and Customs, was a bootlegger, that he had been bootlegging with the Honorable Sir Richard Squires, late Prime Minister of Newfoundland . . .

Furthermore, this affidavit asserts that I have asked where Franklyn Blair was at the moment and that if he would come to me and make a clean breast of all his activities he would go scot free, but that I would certainly like to get the Bronfmans.

I have a very vivid recollection of what took place during the few minutes I was in the Blair residence, which was during the raid . . . I can frankly say that Mary and Phyllis Blair were treated with every courtesy and the raid was conducted in a very orderly manner. There were a few trunks in the basement and in answer to my request Mary Blair informed she was not in possession of keys; that they belonged to [her sister] and that there was nothing but personal effects therein.

Not wishing to destroy the lock of those trunks I informed her I would take her word for it and certainly did not make the statements attributed to me.

Harvison called the Blairs' statements "a gross exaggeration."

Desmarais heard arguments on the affidavit on March 1, 1935. Mary Blair told Brais that she was very nervous after the "interrogation" by Zaneth and Harvison. She could not get in touch with her lawyer; she was afraid to sleep at home or to go out for fear of being interfered with by the police and she finally opened the safety-deposit box when Harvison said if she didn't, he would break it open with an axe.

Phyllis Blair, who was seventeen, confirmed her mother's testimony. Zaneth was called and denied making any threats. Then, Harvison was called.

"Did Zaneth threaten her that she would be placed under arrest, if she did not hand over the key?" Crankshaw asked.

"He did not," Harvison replied, "He was not in the house more than ten minutes and half that time we were in the basement. He asked about some of the trunks there and Mrs. Blair said they belonged to her sister and contained personal effects and Inspector Zaneth gave instructions not to touch them."

On Saturday, March 2, Zaneth met with a special agent of the United States Internal Revenue Service. Inspector G.F. Fletcher in temporary command at C Division, was present at the secret meeting, along with Wesley Frost, the U.S. Consul in Montreal. The IRS was starting a case against the Bronfmans for U.S. income tax evasion. The Consul reported that "confidentially" the police expressed a willingness to hand over evidence to the United States if possible.[45]

On Monday, March 4, Desmarais admitted the documents seized from the Blairs' safety-deposit box, ruling that the police had acted within their rights. By Tuesday, March 26, Penverne had introduced the last piece of evidence, a bank record that showed that a bootlegger named Luke Levesque had transferred five thousand dollars to Abe Bronfman in Montreal. Penverne was planning to ask the judge for a committal against the Bronfman brothers, Aaron, Blair, David Costley and Evelyn Carline; the Crown would proceed against the accused from the Maritimes in their own provinces.

Arguments began on April 8. Toward the end of the day, the judge pointed out that it was not sufficient to show a company had done something wrong in order to convict the shareholders. The shareholders might not know what the company was doing, Desmarais said.

Desmarais had made a point. The next morning, the Crown abandoned the first two counts against the men and withdrew all the charges against Evelyn Carline. Crankshaw admitted the Crown could not prove the charges of possession, harboring or concealing alcohol, but argued that he had proved the counts of conspiracy to defraud the government of excise and customs duties. The final proof was that the Bronfmans got all the profits.

The defense lawyers spent four days in reply. Geoffrion said that once Abe Bronfman sold the liquor to Alfred Levesque he had no further interest in it, and therefore there was no conspiracy. Why not charge every distiller in Canada? He pointed out that until 1930, liquor was exported with the knowledge and connivance of the Canadian government and that exports were still made with the knowledge of the government.

On June 14, Desmarais threw out the remaining charges, saying all of them should have been withdrawn once the Crown's case fell apart. He said the Bronfmans should not have been charged when the Canadian government encouraged the sale of liquor to the United States:

> The Crown claims that the accused opened agencies in Newfoundland and St. Pierre et Miquelon that were useless for any purpose other than smuggling and that sales made there to Canadians constituted proof of illegal conspiracy ... The agencies sold liquor to all who could buy and these acts were legal in the countries in which they operated. They were not obliged to verify the destination of the goods they sold ... Once sold, the goods were the property of the buyers and the accused could exercise no further control over their disposal."

Zaneth took a step beyond the grumbling of a normal policeman's disagreement with a judge's dismissal of a case. In a long memo, he mounted his own arguments to Commissioner MacBrien. After outlining the facts of the case, as he saw them, Zaneth tore apart Judge Desmarais' decision.

> In the Bronfman case, the evidence was very explicit. We proved an "agreement," "common design" and "common means." The agreement was proved in producing Levesque who purchased alcoholic spirits from Franklyn Blair. The "common design" was proven by the fact the spirits, purchased at a very low price, were to be smuggled into Canada, thus defrauding the Government of Excise duty. The "common means" was amply proven that the Bronfmans were the vendors, Levesque the purchaser and his employees the smugglers, thus completing the agreement . . .
>   Again, I might say that, in my humble opinion, this Magistrate overlooked the most important point in the whole case. The Bronfmans who are conducting a licensed distillery in Montreal, could have supplied alcohol to the bootleggers here, provided the Excise tax was paid, but this was not done. They created companies outside of Canada for one purpose only and that was to sell alcohol to bootleggers, thus defrauding the Canadian government of its revenues.
>   It was not their Montreal products they sold but pure alcohol to Canadians who were not licensed to make such purchases.

The RCMP did not trust Judge Desmarais. On June 15, the day after the judgment, they raided his safety-deposit box — and again found nothing.

As the case in Montreal faltered, Zaneth turned his attention to the "Maritime Ring." On March 29, 1935, he was in Halifax consulting with Nicholson. A number of the co-conspirators were persuaded to turn King's evidence, then Zaneth handed the case over to Nicholson.

On September 25, 1935, eleven skippers and crew members

from Nova Scotia were convicted. Another six from Nova Scotia and Prince Edward Island were convicted on February 29, 1936. Jail sentences ranged from one month to one day, with fines from three thousand dollars to five hundred dollars. Their lawyer called them the "small fry" in a "wheel-type liquor ring." The Halifax prosecutor noted, "It was the unanimous opinion of all concerned, including the Magistrates and all Counsel, whether for the prosecution or the defense, that it was the most perfect piece of police work any of them had ever seen."

Zaneth did not agree. He was always a private person, but hints are found in his reports about the Bronfmans' "nefarious activities." After he retired, Zaneth told his friend John Marrett that he had wanted to "get" the Bronfmans and the dismissal of the case was one of his greatest frustrations.

CHAPTER ELEVEN

Zaneth and the Communists (II)

LATE ON THE AFTERNOON of Tuesday, August 11, 1931, Zaneth, who was still stationed in Toronto at the time, and eight other Mounted Police officers were told to accompany Superintendent Jennings and report to the Queen's Park office of Ontario Provincial Police Commissioner Victor Williams. At the office they met more OPP officers and City of Toronto police constables.

"Gentlemen," Williams said. "We are going to strike a death blow to the Communist party — we hope. We are going to arrest the leaders, we are going to search their Dominion headquarters as well as the homes of the men and we are going to seize every document which will link the members with the party and the party with Russia.

"These arrests and these raids will be all made at seven o'clock. They are to take place simultaneously — to the second if possible."

The warrants were ready, prepared in the Ontario Attorney General's office. It would be the first time Section 98 of the Criminal Code of Canada, passed in 1919, would be used. Section 98 banned any organization that had the purpose of bringing government, industrial or economic change by force. It also banned supporting such an unlawful association in any way.

Zaneth was ordered to raid the home of the well-known party secretary Tim Buck. Nobody was in the house, so Zaneth and the two men with him (according to Buck) "unceremoniously pried the front door open, ripping the lock off." In the front room was a piano with sheet music for some popular numbers and a table with a child's exercise book. There were portraits of Lenin and Stalin in the living room. Outside, according to the Toronto *Star*, "mild mannered and startled rabbits chewed grass while watching the activities of the police."

Zaneth turned the place inside out and soon found what he was looking for, large files of correspondence including "letters from the biggest names in Communism," pamphlets and books, one of them a biography of Trotsky. As well, there was a ribbon from the national nominating convention of the American Workers' (Communist) Party in 1928. There were two gold medals bearing inscriptions in Russian and the hammer and sickle. Everything was packed in the car and taken to Queen's Park.

Tim Buck was arrested by the OPP at Communist Party Headquarters on Adelaide Street East. He was released on bail a few days later. The door of his home was swinging in the breeze.

"That wanton destruction," Buck said years later, "was described afterwards as 'a thorough search for evidence.'"

A few weeks after he wrapped the case of the Bobcaygeon bootleggers, on November 3, Zaneth was called to one of the large courtrooms at Toronto's City Hall, to appear as a witness at the trial of Tim Buck, charged with being a member and an officer of an unlawful association and with seditious conspiracy. Zaneth's task was to identify the records he had seized during the raid.

The documents included Buck's membership book in the Communist Party, letterhead from the Communist Party of Canada and the minutes of the political bureau of the Communist Party of Canada. Zaneth had to identify letters from Tom Ewen, considered by the police Number Two in the Party, to Buck. Tim Buck was defending himself, but he let the two lawyers representing the other party members, Hugh MacDonald and Onie Brown, challenge each of the exhibits as it was introduced. The presiding judge, Justice William Henry Wright, overruled the objections and admitted each of the documents.

With Zaneth in the courtroom was Sergeant John Leopold, who had infiltrated the Communist Party. Like Zaneth, Leopold had come to Canada from Austria-Hungary as a homesteader, settling in the Peace River country of Alberta. He had joined the RCMP a few months after Zaneth in 1918, recruited like Zaneth, because of his ability in languages and because he didn't look like a Mountie. In 1920, soon after Harry Blask had been uncovered, Leopold, using the name Jack Esselwein, had started attending left-wing meetings in Regina. When the Communist Party was founded in 1921, Leopold had become a member. For seven years, he rose in the ranks of the Communist Party, attending meetings and party conventions. He was arrested after organizing a demonstration to protest against the execution in Massachusetts of the condemned anarchists Nicola Sacco and Bartolomeo Vanzetti. In 1928, a drunken ex-Mountie let it slip that Esselwein was an undercover officer. Leopold was expelled from the party. As they had with Zaneth, the RCMP made Leopold a regular police officer; he was sent to Whitehorse.

On November 13, 1931, after Leopold's testimony, the defendants were found guilty. The following day, Buck, Ewen and five other defendants were sentenced to five years, one defendant received a two year sentence.

As years went on, many people began to look beyond the fear of Communist activity in the Depression to the danger of Section 98 of the Criminal Code which allowed the government to ban organizations. The newly formed social democratic party, the Cooperative Commonwealth Federation (CCF), farmers' groups, organized labor and some newspapers campaigned for its elimination. After the Liberals regained power, MacKenzie King repealed Section 98.

In 1936, Spain was plunged into civil war. Right-wing officers attempted a coup against the leftist Republican government. That started a war that quickly became the battleground between the two totalitarian ideologies of the 1930s. Fascist

Germany and Italy supported the rebels; the Soviet Union under Stalin backed the Republican side. Tim Buck, out of jail, was one of the first Canadians to visit Spain during the early crisis. In Canada, backing for the Republican cause came not only from the Communists; there was support from the CCF, which distressed J.S. Woodsworth's pacifist followers and the liberal community.

Slowly, young men began to find their way to Spain, first independently and then in groups organized in Toronto and Montreal. Many of the Canadians were already left-leaning, disillusioned by the rule of the ineffective and arrogant Conservative government that did not know how to fight the Depression. Some just wanted adventure; others were fighting Fascism. One estimate is that about sixty per cent of the twelve hundred Canadians who served in Spain were affiliated with the Communist party or sympathetic.

Volunteers went to where they were screened — no RCMP informers or Trotskyists wanted. From there, they sailed via Canadian Pacific or went to New York to join the Americans who sailed as part of the Abraham Lincoln Brigade. In Paris, the volunteers met at a trade union office and soon after they were smuggled over the Pyrenees into Spain.

In February, 1937, the government of William Lyon Mackenzie King introduced a new and updated Foreign Enlistment Act to the House of Commons. It forbade any Canadian from accepting engagement in any foreign army. It also made it a criminal offense to give passage or assistance to "any illegally enlisted person." Recruiting went underground.

In July 1937, the Canadians who were serving in their own units within the Abraham Lincoln Brigade or with British volunteers, formed the Mackenzie-Papineau Battalion. It was named for William Lyon Mackenzie one of the leaders of the 1835 Upper Canada Rebellion (and the grandfather of the prime minister, Mackenzie King) and Louis Joseph Papineau, leader of the Lower Canada rebellion.

In 1938, Zaneth went undercover. His target was once more the Communist Party of Canada. Phillipe Brais, the lawyer who had defended the Blair family in the Bronfman case three years earlier, was a Liberal. Now that King was back in power, Brais was a special Crown prosecutor. Zaneth, Mead and Brais were trying to make a case against the Communist Party for recruiting men for the Mackenzie-Papineau Battalion. The father of one young recruit had complained to the RCMP in Montreal. Now, Zaneth and Brais were putting together what Mead considered "an excellent case of conspiracy" against the Communist Party.

Zaneth began in New York, making "guarded inquiries" at steamship companies about Canadians who had sailed from New York as third-class passengers with the Cunard White Star Line. Cunard was very helpful. Zaneth reported, "I might say that the Cunard representatives are . . . quite willing to assist in every way, and although I did not disclose the nature of my inquiries, I felt that the official to whom I was talking, knew what I had in mind."

The first part of the investigation was bureaucratic. Clerks in Ottawa checked passport applications. On February 28, the deputy minister of justice approved the RCMP request to proceed under the conspiracy sections of the Criminal Code against the Communist Party. Brais was "anxious to show the Courts a system covering the whole of Canada . . . The idea, at present, is to place three or four local persons on trial; then as the case develops, consideration can be given to further action."

RCMP commands across Canada were alerted that Zaneth would be visiting and should have "access to all files dealing with the recruiting of volunteers for Spain." Handling the Ottawa side of the case was Inspector Charles Rivett-Carnac, in charge of what was then called the Liaison and Intelligence Section. Rivett-Carnac supplied to Zaneth lists of men who had enlisted prior to the passage of the Foreign Enlistment Act in April 1937. He also noted that recruiting for Spanish service was being held up "for an undisclosed reason."

Zaneth was worried that there had been a leak and promised to let Rivett-Carnac know "when I may be forced to take certain action":

An effort is being made with the view to determine the reason why recruiting has ceased . . . it seems to be only a matter of policy. It is not because they are aware of the fact that the Government is investigating, but because orders from Russia are that no volunteers are to be sent into Spain until further instructions.

At the end of February 1938, Zaneth left Montreal for Ottawa to meet with Rivett-Carnac and Deputy Commissioner Stuart T. Wood. He picked up files and photographs — he also had a bureaucratic chore to take care of — he asked permission to forgo receipts and travel undercover "as the writer's name is well known."

Zaneth left for Toronto on March 4 on his way to Winnipeg. Commissioner Sir James MacBrien died the next day and was succeeded by Wood.

Rivett-Carnac was able to send photographs of men the RCMP suspected were Mac-Paps to Zaneth in Winnipeg. The only hints were newspaper reports that quoted letters home that said a man was in Spain. By the time Zaneth arrived in Regina, he was planning a simultaneous raids in Montreal, Toronto, Winnipeg, Regina, Saskatoon, Moose Jaw and Weyburn, all home towns of Mac-Pacs. Zaneth was finding himself a little overworked, in a handwritten, personal note to Rivett-Carnac, he reported:

You will note that reports have been scarce. There are a number of reasons. One is that I am putting all my time to the investigation in order that I may move on to the next place; Two, that there is so much data that I feel unable to do justice in one report here and there and prefer to wait until I return and, three, I am not taking any risk at this stage of allowing my identity and purpose of my visit to these different Divisions to be known by too many. One never knows . . .

In each Division, I am collecting the names of the parties directly responsible for the recruiting, the names of those that assisted them, the name of the party who sponsored the Passport application wholesale and the names of those volunteers who went through preliminary proceedings but for one reason did not go to Spain and the names of those who actually went but are now back in Canada and might talk . . .

There is no doubt that we will be able to establish beyond a shadow of a doubt that the CP is solely responsible for the breach of the Act in question. In each center the same modus operandi was employed, all connecting with Toronto.

Once the system has been shown in Court all the leading lights of the CP are equally and criminally responsible. The criminal act of one of the members is the criminal act of all, and all could be charged, tried and punished. In other words, this crime was not committed by a group of individuals but by the Communist Party.

The assistant commissioner in charge of F Division in Regina had reservations. Zaneth had suggested that men who had already returned from the fighting in Spain should be brought in to RCMP detachments for questioning. This, the Regina officer believed, would be "tantamount to arrest and that legal action might ensue."

Phillipe Brais planned to have the case tried in Montreal. All the search warrants would be issued there. The case would be tried there. It would, in effect, be a replay of the Winnipeg General Strike cases, when A.J. Andrews, from Winnipeg, seized evidence across Canada. Brais wanted to prove a nation-wide Communist conspiracy to send men to Spain. He placed a long distance call to Zaneth in Edmonton just as Zaneth was about to leave for Vancouver. Brais told him the new plan. Instead of moving the raids forward, however, the Brais plan stopped them. Zaneth had been working on the assumption that the warrants would be issued locally, a much simpler procedure.

After Zaneth took the train to Vancouver, W.F.W. Hancock,

the acting assistant commissioner commanding K Division in Edmonton, sent an urgent message to Commissioner Wood, warning that the raids could have major political repercussions in Alberta and reverse "the good feeling" between the Social Credit government of Premier William "Bible Bill" Aberhart and the RCMP. Hancock argued that while the federal government did have the power to order the searches for incriminating evidence against the Communist Party, any charges laid in Alberta would be the legal responsibility of the attorney general of very independent-minded Alberta. Hancock thought the action would put him in a conflict of interest because the contract between Alberta and the RCMP stated "in matters of the Criminal Code, the Officer Commanding took his orders from the attorney general" and not RCMP headquarters in Ottawa.

Hancock believed that many of the searches would not be successful and so he recommended that "every effort should be put forward to safeguard the interests of the Force."

On March 23, Rivett-Carnac prepared a memo for the Commissioner. He was also having some doubts about Zaneth's idea of raiding the Communists. Rivett-Carnac said, "It is also considered that the Government should be advised before wholesale searches are made and their reaction obtained." Later that day, Wood wrote a two page letter to the Minister of Justice, Ernest Lapointe outlining the case up until then and the political problems involved.

Zaneth arrived in Vancouver to find the warrants were to be issued in Montreal. That meant postponing the raids for a week to ten days. In a personal note to Rivett-Carnac, he also added a comment, indicative of his personal views: "I have perused with some interest and amusement the translation of 'The Voice of Labour.' It is hoped that some day in the near future some of these people will live to regret having expressed themselves so openly."

Zaneth had hoped that once the raids were complete he could head east from Vancouver, collecting evidence as he reached each RCMP Division headquarters, then coordinate the case in

Montreal. He wrote: "This gigantic conspiracy is shrouded with fraud, deceit, falsehoods and other illegal means and only the CPC as a whole was engaged."

In Zaneth's view, there appeared to be two purposes to the recruiting. One was to send idealistic cannon fodder to the Republican side in Spain. About seventy-five per cent of the men who went to Spain were on government relief before they left for Europe on "a pleasure trip." A number of notaries across the country had sponsored passport applications for volunteers "who were total strangers to them." The recruits were helped along the way, given tickets and passports, met in Cherbourg or Le Havre and then taken to Spain.

Zaneth saw a more sinister plot, as well.

It was also learned that when a volunteer was brought to one of these recruiting offices and it was found that his standing with the CP was not as desired, he was asked to secure his birth certificate in order that his passport might be obtained. Once this certificate was secured and turned over to the man in charge, the would-be volunteer was invariably told that the Department of External Affairs had refused to issue him with a passport and was asked to leave the birth certificate with them as it had no further value. This would indicate that the birth certificate was later used for the purpose of securing a passport either for a volunteer whose radical tendencies were well known or for a well trusted member of the CP who was not in a position to secure a Canadian passport himself to travel to Europe . . .

Having questioned a number of people . . . the writer was forced to the conclusion that this conspiracy goes further than the mere breach of the Foreign Enlistment Act. It has been brought to light that when a Canadian volunteer, travelling on a Canadian passport, arrives in Paris, France, his passport is taken away from him, not only to make him lose his identity, but to facilitate the travelling from one country to another of well trusted members of the Communist Party, whether Russian, French, Spanish, German or Italian. These passports are never returned to the party to whom they were originally issued.

The Canadian passport, the favorite of the drug dealers in Louis "Lepke" Buchalter's gang, was also becoming the best cover for Soviet and other spies, as future cases would prove.

Zaneth's brief makes it clear that the RCMP had little trust in the Social Credit Government in Alberta:

> In Alberta . . . in view of the fact the Provincial Government is receiving moral and some financial assistance from the CP, if the Federal Government were to execute searches in that Province and prosecution entered against Members of the CP the cry of "Persecution" "Fascist" and "Padlock Law" would be their slogan and would do more harm than good.
>
> Furthermore, the Social Credit Government will seize the opportunity of accusing the Federal Government with interference in the administration of the Criminal Law in the Province of Alberta. This, they are prone to do in every occasion.

Zaneth concluded that although the suggestion to consult with local attorneys general was logical, any meeting would mean that secrecy would be breached.

Then, on April 12, 1938, Lapointe, the minister of justice, stopped the investigation and ordered that no further be action taken under the Foreign Enlistment Act.

The case was a political maze from beginning to end, and the documents prove that political considerations do motivate RCMP decisions. It also shows that Canada had progressed somewhat in the nineteen years since the Winnipeg General Strike trials. Section 98 of the Criminal Code had been repealed. The powers and politics of the provinces checked the possibility of a nationwide roundup, coordinated by one prosecutor in Montreal. The natural caution of the Liberal government of Mackenzie King was different from the anti-Communism of the Conservative governments of Sir Robert Borden and R.B. Bennett. (Although the King government and the RCMP did back the union busting efforts of Ontario Premier Mitch Hepburn during the King administration).

As the defeat of the Republican cause neared, the Mac-Pacs tried to get back to Canada. While the American and British governments gave some assistance in repatriation, Canada, as usual, hesitated, leaving the Canadians stranded in Spain after the Americans and British had left. Eventually, the dying Spanish government paid $20,000 to the CPR to pay passage home for the Canadians. Funds were also raised among ordinary Canadians. By February, 1939, most of the surviving Mac-Pacs were home. Madrid fell on March 31. Six months later, Hitler invaded Poland.

CHAPTER TWELVE

The Dandy Dan Traps a Rat

IN JULY 1938, Commissioner Stuart Wood decided to formalize Frank Zaneth's status as the RCMP's top trouble shooter. Zaneth was, on paper, transferred to headquarters Criminal Investigation Branch in Ottawa, although he remained based in Montreal. Wood sent a memo to Officers Commanding, for transmission to all Sub-Division and CIB officers, ordering them to provide Zaneth with "full cooperation" and "access to all files" and noting "His requests for assistance in the way of men, transport etc. are to be complied with."

In December, Zaneth got an assignment he relished: another crack at Rocco Perri. He was assigned by the RCMP and the minister of national revenue, to interview and develop key Crown witnesses in an inquiry into a new smuggling empire that Perri had set up. The case apparently involved the whole-sale corruption of Canadian Customs officials. Zaneth was delighted to help in a new investigation that promised to finally break the power of his nemesis, the hitherto untouchable King of the Bootleggers. Perri had a new common-law wife and partner in crime, Annie Newman, who had replaced Bessie within three years of Bessie's grisly execution, as the brains behind the Perri mob. (Rocco Perri, it seemed, needed a strong woman behind him in organizing his most successful rackets.) Though Zaneth had been tenacious in his attempts to bring Perri and his mob to justice and while his intelligence information on the Perri mob was reasonably good, he could never assemble enough evidence to actually charge the leadership of the Perri gang with a major crime. Now Zaneth was coming in as a senior Mountie with special interrogation skills and special powers under the Customs Act to force witnesses to testify. (Zaneth was so good at breaking down potential witnesses, he was sent in January, 1939 to lecture at the Canadian Police College in Regina on "Interrogation of Witnesses.")

Zaneth interviewed Milton Goldhart, one of Rocco Perri's drivers and a key potential Crown witness. Two junior RCMP officers had tried unsuccessfully to break him down. One of them, a corporal named Woods, a tall, husky, intimidating man, had used physical intimidation as an interrogation method. According to Goldhart, Woods "put his hands around my shoulders and almost crushed me." Not exactly the subtle, psychological approach of a Frank Zaneth.

Zaneth came in as the "good cop" in his handling of the tough, street-smart Milty Goldhart. In contrast to his aggressive colleague, Zaneth appeared almost gentle, though unremitting. Goldhart later said he never became a "fink," but only answered Zaneth's relentless questions to "get him to lay off me." Milty Goldhart broke under the pressure of Zaneth's continuous cross-examination. Zaneth simply used classic "good cop" psychology on Goldhart by helping him to find a way out of a serious problem. Zaneth wanted Goldhart both to come clean and to abandon his criminal life. Hard as he was on Goldhart, Zaneth was gentle after Corporal Woods' more aggressive interrogation.[46]

Goldhart vividly remembered Frank Zaneth, whom he described as "a dandy Dan with spectacles . . . a little shit and a liar" of a Mountie "He called me a rat the first time I met him, and I was going to zap him," Goldhart recalled. He added that Zaneth was a smart guy who had tricked him into his confession. Zaneth had been psychologically deft in his handling of Goldhart. He had taken advantage of his special powers under the Customs Act, but for Goldhart he added the Zaneth touch. He told him that Goldhart faced penalties for contempt of court for not answering questions put to him in the name of

"King George VI, By the Grace of God, King of Great Britain, Ireland and the British Dominions Beyond the Seas, King, Defender of the Faith and Emperor of India." Goldhart said he was particularly intimidated by Zaneth's use of King George's other titles, especially the Emperor of India and the specter Zaneth had raised of up to six months in jail for every question he didn't answer.

Goldhart answered as many questions as he could with "I don't remember" or a simple yes or no. However, he gave Zaneth and the RCMP a detailed outline of the smuggling activities of Annie Newman and Rocco Perri and their network of corrupt customs officers. By the time Zaneth was through with him on July 24, 1939, Goldhart had given, under oath, a twenty eight page statement signed by Zaneth. Later, Goldhart refused to sign an affidavit confirming that this confession was true and voluntary.

Goldhart had been brought into the criminal family of Rocco Perri by Annie Newman in 1937. Goldhart had known Perri from Hamilton before Newman recruited him to work for the Perri mob. He drove her to Detroit and Chicago in 1937 and arranged to bring back regular loads of bootleg American alcohol into Canada. This was well after Prohibition had ended in both countries. Rocco Perri had figured out that with the high Canadian taxes and the heavy-handed restrictions on Canadian booze which was sold only in tightly controlled provincial government outlets. There was a huge profit to be made in illegally importing cheap American alcohol. Perri purchased alcohol from mob associates in Chicago and sold it in Ontario and Quebec. It was a smuggling/bootlegging in reverse mob racket — smuggling liquor *into* Canada rather than the other way around.

Annie Newman, had come to Canada from an obscure village in Poland with her family. In 1939, she was a very good-looking woman in her early forties, petite, with a great figure, beautiful, sparkling gray-blue eyes, sleek and polished silver hair, a perennial tan and a soft, slightly accented, voice. She was always elegantly dressed, she loved to dance, play cards and have a good time. She was also tough, wily, and sharp. According to those who knew her well, "you couldn't put anything past her." While Goldhart "wouldn't have minded crawling into her pants," to use his expression, he detested the woman. "She was a rotten, greedy bitch — a hunk of garbage," Goldhart reminisced about his one-time boss.

On Goldhart's very first trip with Annie in 1937, he met Customs officer Dave Armaly of Walkerville (part of Windsor). Armaly had been the principal agent of the corruption among the Customs officers who were in the employ of the Perri mob in the late 1930s. Goldhart later referred to Armaly contemptuously as "the squealer" and "that shit." Armaly had been working as a Customs officer at the Walkerville ferry which ran between Detroit and Windsor. He was a compulsive gambler, and in 1933, to pay off a heavy gambling debt to Sam "Fan" Miller, a Rocco Perri associate and the gambling boss of Windsor at the time, Armaly had agreed to wave certain cars go through customs. Armaly admitted that between 1935 and 1936 he let more than 200 cars through customs. In 1936, he began to work directly for Annie Newman on behalf of Rocco Perri and his gang.

Armaly made sure that Perri's bootleg booze made it unmolested through Customs at Windsor and Walkerville. Then he was caught red handed allowing parts for stills through customs for the Perri mob. He then admitted he let in some roulette wheels for Montreal gambling czar Max Shapiro. Armaly was dismissed from Canada Customs in 1936. He continued to work for Newman and Rocco Perri as the liaison between the Perris and the customs officers. He arranged to payoffs so they would look the other way when Goldhart and other Perri drivers came through. In addition to his regular salary from the Perri mob, Armaly kept a share of the payoff money for each officer for himself. Armaly made over twenty trips to Chicago himself picking up the Perri liquor from the Chicago mob and getting it to Detroit, where another driver took over the load to smuggle it into Canada. Armaly also continued to drive for Miller until 1938. Eventually, Newman set him up in a Perri owned drugstore in Windsor, conveniently located just past the Ambassador Bridge. It was there he made his payoffs.

The first big break for Zaneth and his colleagues came in early 1939 when the local RCMP in Windsor raided Sam Miller's gambling establishment and found a little red notebook. The RCMP division then routinely dispatched an officer to question David Armaly, whose name appeared in the book. To the officer's surprise, Armaly broke down and confessed about an entirely separate issue — his working relationship with Rocco Perri and Annie Newman. He outlined all his criminal dealings with the Perris. The confession was totally unexpected, but the RCMP were prepared to make the most of it.

Armaly said he had met Milton Goldhart at Sam Miller's gambling club in Windsor in the early thirties. Goldhart told Armaly that he was working for Rocco Perri and Annie Newman. In the early part of 1936, Goldhart asked Armaly to help him bring in alcohol for Perri. Goldhart then took Armaly to a parked car. In the car was Annie Newman who took Armaly for a ride. She told Armaly that she was working with Perri, "the best man in the alcohol racket." Armaly said he then recruited many of his colleagues at customs. He named Edward Mansell, Carl Gough, Wilfred Fletcher, and Norman Le Pain as collaborators.

As a result, a new RCMP investigation of the Perri rackets began, under the watchful guidance of RCMP troubleshooter Frank Zaneth.

Reluctantly, Goldhart had agreed to Zaneth's suggestion that he act as a Crown witness against Rocco Perri and Annie Newman. Goldhart always maintained that "I was never a rat" and he "only answered questions to get them [the RCMP] to lay off me. My lawyer advised me that I had no choice under the circumstances."

The RCMP were under no illusions. There had been two recent attempts on Perri's life; they reminded everyone that people in Perri's league played for keeps. In July 1939, Superintendent Vernon Kemp insisted that the three chief witnesses be placed in protective custody in secret locations, with the RCMP picking up the full tab. Armaly and his wife and four children were put in a summer cottage outside Ottawa. Goldhart was placed with the Lindsay, Ontario, detachment and, like the other informers, he was put on an RCMP expense account. A third informer, Victor Bernat was put up by the RCMP detachment in Amherstburg.

On August 26, 1939, Commissioner Wood ordered the immediate arrest of the "principal co-conspirators Rocco Perri and Anne Newman before they go into hiding." The arrests climaxed Zaneth's eight month investigation. Perri and Newman were charged with bribing customs officers and with conspiracy to breach the Customs Act. In Windsor on August 27 and 28, six Customs officials were arrested and charged with bribery and corruption in the performance of their duties. Two of Perri's bootlegging and gambling associates, Sam Motruk and Sam Miller were also arrested. The story of the arrests was carried prominently in all the major newspapers in the country. The trial was scheduled for early January, 1940.

In an exclusive story on September 1, 1939, headlined, MOUNTIES LAUNCH DRIVE TO CRUSH GANGLAND IN ONTARIO, the Toronto *Telegram*, described a coming RCMP sweep against organized crime in the Ontario. It began: "After years of intensive investigations, methodical planning, and a quiet tiding up of pertinent evidence, the Royal Canadian Mounted Police are ready to rip the cover from Ontario's underworld." The *Telegram* described the arrests of Rocco and his co-conspirators, then gave its scoop: "This is but the first step in a concerted drive by the RCMP to bring gangland leaders to justice and strike a crushing blow to the forces of lawlessness."

On the same day, the Germans invaded Poland. The RCMP's planned attack on the underworld was to be limited, for the time being, to the arrests made in the Perri case.

The three Crown witnesses, David Michael Armaly, Victor Bernat, and Milton Goldhart had all taken a direct part in the Perri bootlegging business, Armaly as a Customs officer and driver and Bernat and Goldhart as drivers. Armaly was the key

Crown witness. He could tell how he had recruited his fellow officials before he was dismissed from his post. Bernat had been a driver and though considered insignificant, he was able to offer some corroborating testimony for Armaly's story. Goldhart's testimony was considered to be the more damaging, because he had dealt directly with Annie Newman and had been driving with Rocco and Annie for more than two years. All three men were crucial to the successful prosecution of the Perri case. The federal deputy minister of justice admitted in a confidential letter to the attorney general of Ontario, "there is little or no direct Police evidence."

The police were not the only ones aware of the slender nature of the Crown's case. RCMP informers in the underworld reported that Perri's arrest had caused "a violent furor amongst the underworld as far away as Chicago." In an urgent memo, Superintendent Kemp, the commanding officer of O Division, advised the Commissioner that the witnesses might be tampered with or eliminated.

Armaly and Bernat were hardly paragons of virtue. Before the trials were over, Armaly had confessed to forgery, illegal gambling, cheating on welfare, taking bribes and fraud, among other illegal acts. Bernat had a long criminal record and was equally disreputable.

The stories the three informers had to tell were certainly worth the price of keeping them safe. For the first time in his criminal career, Rocco Perri faced the real possibility of ending up behind bars for many years for some pretty serious crimes. Armaly, Bernat, and Goldhart represented a real chink in Perri's otherwise impenetrable armor.

There is some evidence in the files of an internal inquiry by customs that Zaneth's strategy with Armaly was to make him "operational" between April and August 1939 to entrap some of the other customs officers who were charged. Zaneth felt that with Armaly, Goldhart and Bernat testifying, the case against Perri and Newman would be easy to make, but that the charges of corruption against some of the customs officers needed to be shored up. He had RCMP officers listen in on

Armaly's discussions with these customs officials after the charges were made public. Customs officer Carl Gough said that two Mounties were watching at one point in the summer of 1939 when he was talking with Armaly, and later, customs officer Eddie Mansell testified that Armaly had called him at the Ambassador Bridge in August 1939. He assumed the phone call was tapped by the Mounties.

Zaneth's strategies began to fall apart when one of the RCMP's most important witnesses disappeared. While he was living under RCMP protective custody, Goldhart managed to get a message to his good friend and one-time boss, Rocco Perri. Milty Goldhart had always had a good working relationship with Perri, whom he looked up to and admired. "Roc was the finest person — a Prince — the best person I ever met in my life," Goldhart enthused. *

Goldhart explained that Perri took care of everything himself, giving instructions to Goldhart in a series of pay phone to pay phone conversations. Goldhart disappeared before the trials began and ended up in New York. "Roc was the only one who knew where I was. I called him from a pay phone in NYC by pre-arrangement." Goldhart then went to Chicago to work at a mob distillery. The RCMP thought he was dead, and after a time, Goldhart went on to England where he joined the Royal Air Force, ironically serving his country in a way the RCMP had neither desired nor anticipated.

The Mounties were never to find out what actually happened to Goldhart though he returned to Canada after the war to become a stunt man and later a millionaire entrepreneur. He died peacefully of a heart attack in Toronto in 1987. He had had the last laugh at Zaneth's expense.

Some of the relevant parts of Goldhart's reluctant statement to Zaneth, which the jury did not get to see, have survived in RCMP files. In his statement, Goldhart said that Annie Newman offered him a job driving alcohol from Chicago via Windsor to Hamilton starting at twenty-five dollars a trip. (Later this went

---

* During a 1987 phone interview.

up to one hundred dollars a trip plus expenses.) On many occasions Goldhart drove with Annie Newman to Windsor and Chicago. Newman would be with Goldhart in the car from Chicago to Detroit; then she would cross into Canada by herself and meet Goldhart on the Canadian side. She would fix things with customs so that Goldhart's car was not searched. The two then drove to Dundas, Ontario where they met with another car, which took the load of alcohol.

When Goldhart was arrested by the OPP in Chatham, Ontario, with a load of alcohol, Annie Newman bailed him out of jail. Goldhart also said that there were four or five Customs officers who would pass the car at different times while he was working for Annie Newman and Perri. He was never nervous when he went through Canadian Customs with a load, as he knew that passage "in each case it had been fixed by Armaly." Each time he went through customs, Annie Newman gave Goldhart an envelope containing money to deliver to Armaly.

In his statement, Goldhart had stated that Anne Newman was involved in all aspects of the bootlegging, she went down to Detroit with him, arranged for the payoff of customs officials, arranged contacts in the United States, arranged for the disposition of the bootleg liquor in Canada. In all things connected with the bootleg trade Newman acted to insulate Rocco Perri. Annie, according to Goldhart, was the principal organizer and front for Rocco. Without Goldhart's testimony the Crown's case was seriously weakened.

Rocco was confident throughout the proceedings. He knew that Goldhart would not appear. He had made all the arrangements for the disappearance himself. In the end, Goldhart had been loyal, even though he had been forced by Zaneth to outline for the police the inner workings of his bootlegging operations.

During the eight-day trial, in January 1940, he maintained an unruffled calm and seemed to enjoy himself as his well paid lawyers went to work on the Crown's remaining two witnesses. Perri's defense team consisted of Joseph Bullen K.C. of Toronto and a young Windsor M.P., Paul Martin, later Minister for External Affairs. Martin made mince meat of the most important remaining Crown witness, David Armaly, by attacking his credibility. Martin presented him as an opportunistic rogue, a mercenary who would fabricate and say anything to get paid. Martin zeroed in on the fact that Armaly was on the RCMP payroll as an informer while he was also collecting welfare from the City of Windsor. Bullen described the defense view of Armaly in this succinct fashion: "I would rather believe a yellow dog grovelling and sniffing for his food in an ash can in the alley than believe this witness."

When Victor Bernat took the stand, Martin was equally unrelenting. He implicated Bernat in a hold-up for which Bernat's brother had been convicted and sentenced to Kingston. He also tried to establish that Bernat was out to "get at all costs" Sam Motruk, a childhood friend with whom he had argued. Martin maintained that this was why Bernat had offered his information to the RCMP. Victor Bernat's character was quickly discredited by the introduction of evidence that he had been involved in smuggling Chinese illegal aliens into the United States.

The demolition of the Crown's case was complete and the verdict was almost anticlimactic. Rocco Perri, Anne Newman and four customs officials were acquitted on February 1. Two more customs officers were acquitted in a separate trial later. Only Perri's unfortunate Windsor lieutenants, Sam Miller and Sam Motruk, were convicted in a third separate trial and sentenced to prison terms up to two years.*

Three weeks after the acquittals, Armaly himself was found guilty of defrauding the welfare department in Windsor and was sentenced to three months in jail.

Rocco Perri had once again successfully frustrated Zaneth's efforts to put behind him bars. But Zaneth had not yet played all his cards.

On May 27, less than a week after charges were dropped in

---

* Ironically, one Crown witness, a young friend of Bernat's, Philip Bucheski, eighteen, was found guilty of perjury on May 20, 1940 for lying in his signed statement to Frank Zaneth. He told Zaneth what his friend Bernat had told him to say about Sam Motruk's bootleg business, because Bernat had promised him a job and money.

the last of the Customs cases, Zaneth had arranged to have Rocco Perri's name put at the top of the list in a top secret RCMP intelligence memo detailing those Italian-born residents of Canada who were suspected of being fascists, fascist-sympathizers or potential subversives. In the very likely case of war with Italy, the people listed in the RCMP memos were to be interned.

Italy declared war on June 10, 1940 and Rocco Perri was picked up by the RCMP in a national round-up of more than seven hundred suspected "subversives," which included known criminals and suspected Fascists, as well as many totally innocent and often respectable Italian businessmen and professionals.

So, in the end, Zaneth did get his man. After three years in internment in Camp Petawawa, Rocco Perri emerged a broken man. Although Perri attempted a comeback, his criminal career was finished. In April, 1944, he disappeared. After an international search, the RCMP concluded that Perri had been murdered by rival gangsters, his body put in a wooden barrel filled with cement and dropped into Hamilton Bay.

"We won't find his body," one RCMP officer concluded in an newspaper interview in 1954, "until the Bay dries up."

CHAPTER THIRTEEN

Zaneth the Commander

IN THE SUMMER BEFORE THE WAR, many North Americans often chose to ignore what was happening in Europe. Europe was far away. At home, things were looking up: some people were going back to work. The prairie dust bowl of the Dirty Thirties was in the past. By late spring, 1939, the prairie farmers knew that the harvest would be good. So did the crooks. On June 4, 1939, two men broke into the office at the United Grain Growers elevator at Rothwell, Manitoba, and blew the safe. The safe was empty. The two tried to get away on a railway gas car but were spotted and stopped. One man, an expert safecracker, was caught and sentenced to three and a half years.

There were more safe breakings. Two Manitoba men were arrested for a safe job in Elphinstone. Safes were blown at the Eaton's store in Brandon, in the Canada West Grain Company in Buchanan, Saskatchewan, at stores in Westaskiwin and Mayerthorpe, Alberta and at the post office in Fort Saskatchewan. The grain elevators were rich with cash. Farmers had little reason to trust Canada's chartered banks, and some smaller towns had no banks. The farmers demanded cash when they brought in the grain and then spent some of the cash at stores in town.

That meant from late summer until Christmas, the grain elevators and the stores were easy targets for travelling safe blowers. RCMP veterans say they were Canada's equivalent to the wandering bank robbers who had become part of the folklore in the U.S. great plains.

In Ottawa, Commissioner Stuart Wood and the RCMP brass decided that the safeblowers would receive increased attention.

On February 4, 1940, Frank Zaneth's father died in Springfield. Ambrose Zanetti was 78. He left his wife, Christina, his sons, Frank and Fred, his three daughters, all married, and three grandsons. There was a requiem high mass at Mt. Carmel Church, which Ambrose Zanetti had helped found, attended by honorary pall bearers from the Italian American Citizens club.

When he returned from the funeral, Zaneth had a new job waiting for him. He was posted to Regina as "Coordinating Officer" for three divisions, D in Manitoba, F in Saskatchewan, and K in Alberta. The job was to stop safeblowing and his responsibilities included supervising the investigations, training the officers and preventing crime.

He began by dividing each province into zones, each which would be the responsibility of a safe-blowing squad. Saskatchewan, for example, had four zones, and squads were based at Swift Current, Regina, Yorkton and Saskatoon. Each squad consisted of two teams of two constables and a sergeant. Half the job was to be preventive: the mounties would teach store owners and elevator operators how to protect their money. The other half of the job was to investigate safecrackings.

As always, Zaneth picked his men carefully, checking their service records. Some men of them he wanted were simply asked by their superiors to join the squad, others were called to Regina to meet Zaneth for an interview and given the option of joining.

Once the men were picked, Zaneth brought them to Regina for training sessions. One of the men was B.D. Peck.

He lectured us, he coached us, trained us, . . . Zaneth would show us photographs of well known and travelling criminals. He would say 'That's No. 1, that's No. 2' and would go on. He was quite dynamic. We were trying to remember faces. He was good at that himself, he could spot people quickly.

He was a tireless man, tenacious. He would lecture for a couple of hours and grill us on what he wanted.

He lectured on explosives and had a good knowledge. He was also particularly good at dusting and examining for fingerprints and good at photography and supervising ident men.

The veterans usually knew who the local crooks were, and could keep an eye on them. The main targets of the safe-blowing squads were the small gangs who would travel across the prairies by car or by riding freight cars. "They'd look like an ordinary hobo in those days," said Don Fraser, who was on a Manitoba safe squad. "They'd look the place over first, usually some fellow who didn't look like a crook, who had no record. He'd carry the nitro and the fuse and the caps." The gang had to check out the town, find the elevator, see if the local agent slept there or in town, and try and get an idea of the police patrols.

The elevators were often out of town along railway tracks, far enough from town that an explosion wouldn't be heard.

There were different kinds of safes. Some were only tin cans or shoe boxes. The simple fire proof box was common. For those the thieves would punch the spindle and knock off the knobs, then open the door. Others would try to "peel a safe" by using a sledgehammer and crowbar. Blowing a safe required more skill. Nitroglycerin was extracted from dynamite to produce what the safecrackers called "soup." The nitro was poured into the cracks around the door near the lock and sealed in with melted, liquefied soap. A detonator was attached to a fuse, the fuse was lit and the safe was "popped." Too much nitro and the safe and its contents were destroyed. Not enough soup and the cracker had to resort to the crowbar.

The bigger grain elevators weren't always concerned about the loss — they were insured and the premiums were considered a cost of doing business. Zaneth and his men, however, were determined to stop a crime wave.

Peck recalled that quite often a safeblower would be recognized by his style, his m.o., and tracked down.

"Lots of time we pinpointed on someone who was in the district," Peck said. "They'd cop a plea which is usual in break and enter cases."

If the suspect wasn't known to a zone squad, a Criminal Investigation Branch sergeant attached to the safe blowing squad would take over, perhaps following one gang across the prairies.

Zaneth emphasized crime prevention. "He was particularly desirous of night patrols and anti-safe blowing work," Peck recalled. Zaneth also used malachite green to mark the money; the chemical left a green stain on the hands of anyone who touched the cash.

By January 1942, the problem had cleared up. The safe blowing squads had put most of the safecrackers behind bars. Other safecrackers had found more gainful employment in the Canadian army. Zaneth was transferred back to Montreal. For most of 1942, he was once more the RCMP's trouble-shooter. C.W. Harvison, whom he had worked with for years, was now the Inspector in charge of the Montreal Criminal Investigation Branch, the job Zaneth had had ten years before. In December, Zaneth was placed in command of the Montreal Sub-Division.

CHAPTER FOURTEEN

The Battle of Heriot Hill

IN THE EARLY 1940S, the RCMP operation in Montreal was run out of two offices, from the barracks in the old mansion on Sherbrooke Street and from the top of a post office building at Place Des Armes. War brought new duties. National Registration Certificates, draft cards, were forged, a hint of the anti-conscription sentiment growing in the province of Quebec. Ration cards were also forged and liquor rationing brought back the moonshiner. Zaneth was named an inspector under the Foreign Exchange regulations, after Canada restricted taking money out of the country. The Montreal detachment also helped handle security for the meeting of Franklin Roosevelt and Winston Churchill at the Quebec Conference.

In November, 1943, Zaneth received word through international channels that his wife, Rita, had died in hospital in Pavia in September, 1942.

Two years after Rita died, on September 23, 1944, Zaneth married again. He was fifty-three. Edith Didsbury, thirty-seven, was a secretary, She had been born in Etobicoke and had lived much of her life in Montreal.

Zaneth's nephew, Bill Rivers said, "Edith was a lovely lady, dainty, very slim, almost thin. She was great for Frank, she was very much in love with him." They were married in Montreal's at the Anglican Church of St. James the Apostle. (Frank Zaneth had left the Catholic church many years before.)

Canada, meanwhile, was edging toward another conscription

crisis, something Prime Minister Mackenzie King had always feared. After Hitler had torn up the Munich agreement in March 1939, King had accepted a proposal from the leader of the Conservative opposition: no conscription for service outside Canada's borders. After Canada declared war, there was enthusiastic recruitment, but after the first wave, King introduced a form of conscription, the National Resources Mobilization Act, which drafted men for home defense. The draftees who stayed in Canada, who did not volunteer for overseas service, were quickly dubbed the "Zombies."

Early in the war there was growing pressure for conscription from English Canada. King saw this as a disaster. In 1942, he called for a plebiscite asking the people of Canada to release him from his pledge of no conscription for overseas service. It was when he was discussing the vote that King uttered his most famous phrase: "Conscription if necessary but not necessarily conscription." Overall Canada voted two to one in favor; Quebec voted seventy-two per cent against.

The crisis came in late 1944, after D-Day, when Canadian soldiers were fighting on French soil. Casualties were high and replacements were needed for the foot slogging infantry. King made General Andrew McNaughton minister of national defence and sent him out as a recruiting sergeant to persuade the Zombies to volunteer for overseas service. The idea failed, and after some political and military prodding King introduced another compromise motion: he proposed sending sixteen thousand overseas. The motion passed the House of Commons 143 to 70. Quebec nationalists were outraged. Some MPs and MLAs broke from the old parties to found *Le Bloc Populaire*, and there were large anti-conscription demonstrations. The first ten thousand men were told get ready; by January 1945, 7,800, not all from Quebec, had deserted or gone absent without leave.* It was the job of the RCMP to round them up. The

---

* The final figure showed that of 14,500 ordered overseas by April 1945, 4,000 draft evaders were unaccounted for, about 2,500 from Quebec and 1,000 from the prairies.

number of draft evaders in Quebec in the winter of 1945 was estimated at twenty-five thousand.

By February 1945, the RCMP was coordinating raids with the Canadian Army Provost Corps, searching for draft evaders and deserters. Zaneth planned a major raid on the textile town of Drummondville in the Eastern Townships, northeast of Montreal, to take place on Saturday evening February 24. That morning, Zaneth drove to Drummondville to survey the town. He planned to keep his identity quiet.

When he got there, he found, to his surprise, that he was expected. A constable at the local detachment told him that Larry Conroy, police reporter for the Montreal *Gazette* had shown up, asking for Zaneth.

In the afternoon, Zaneth found himself alone in a hotel lobby with Conroy, who told him that he knew from the "highest authority" that Drummondville was to be raided. Conroy assured Zaneth that he was the only person who knew about the plans. Zaneth could only hope that the leak was limited to one reporter.

By evening, Zaneth's plans for the raid were ready. He divided the fifty RCMP officers and forty Provost into eleven squads, each headed by an experienced member of the RCMP. As usual, Zaneth's planning was detailed and meticulous. Each squad had a target, the Drummondville Arena, pool rooms, a dance hall, restaurants and grills.

Zaneth was waiting at the RCMP detachment at 11:00 that night as the Mounties in blue Chevrolet police cars rendezvoused with army trucks outside town. As they entered the town, Zaneth reported, about a hundred people began screaming. Zaneth did not believe there had been a leak, but "a certain element had organized a system whereby residents could be aware of our presence." The raiding parties spread around the town, while Zaneth and some other Mounties, expert in the new National Selective Service Mobilization Regulations, waited in the RCMP office to inspect papers. A few young men were brought in for checks, "although a bedlam was raging outside." Zaneth kept those who said they had forgotten their papers in the small office; deserters or men whose status was unclear were taken out the back door and put in an army truck.

The raiders were holding some young men in front of the Capitol Theatre. The movie, *The Climax*, starring Boris Karloff, was just letting out, and the patrons gathered around the raiders and their prisoners.

"*Maudits anglais*," shouted someone.

"*Ca prend des Canadiens français pour venir chercher nos Canadiens français,*" * someone else grumbled.

One teenage prisoner had been with two girlfriends, who tagged along, jeering, swearing and inciting the crowd to attack the Mounties. Someone in the crowd threw a Coke bottle, which hit a constable in the back of the head. A crowd — Zaneth estimated at between five hundred and seven hundred — followed the raiders along rue Heriot back to the RCMP office.

Zaneth knew the crowd was "bent on serious trouble." Rue Heriot had just been cleared of snow and there were piles of broken ice on both sides of street. Zaneth sent the men outside under the command of a sergeant to form a line in the street. Only noncommissioned RCMP officers loaded their revolvers. Zaneth told the sergeant "that firearms were not to be used; not to reply to the jeers of the people, not to break rank, and should people throw missiles to avoid them as well as possible and not retaliate."

The rioters held the high ground, rue Heriot went up a hill to the Manoir Drummond.

The police and soldiers kept dodging but three men were seriously injured. One man was struck in the eye; a second was hit on the head with a heavy piece of wood. Zaneth called a local doctor for help but, "he definitely refused to render professional assistance." The phone kept ringing as people tried to tie up the line.

The riot raged over seven blocks; the crowd grew, evaporated and then grew again. Conroy reported in the *Gazette* that:

---

* "It takes French Canadians to come and get our French Canadians."

Roaring defiance at the police and the army, cries of vengeance mixed with the shrill screams from young boys and girls, which followed the mob at times, the milling group of 1,500 at time flowed across . . . and down Heriot street to the Mounted Police detachment office where it was turned back by a determined charge of the mixed police and army forces.*

Richard Daigneault, a reporter from the *Gazette*, Earl Banner of the Boston *Globe* and Conroy were in midst the melee. Daigneault was pushed to the ground and kicked in the head; Conroy was attacked by men yelling "Stoolies." Banner was rescued by one man who lifted him away from rioters determined to beat up "stool pigeons."

Zaneth decided: "Our men could no longer hold their position without clashing with the mob." He ordered the Provost men to leave. An RCMP corporal took charge of the truck with the prisoners. Zaneth told him to go to the outskirts of town, and release all those who had complied with the regulations. He was then to go on to Montreal with the prisoners. Zaneth reported:

When the men broke formation in an effort to reach the cars and trucks which were parked on both sides of the street, facing the highway to Montreal, the crowd rushed them and attacked them with everything they could lay their hands on. During the fracas a rioter, who seems to have been the leader, received a blow on the head and before he had the opportunity to get away, our men picked him up bodily and carried him into the office.

Zaneth stood on the balcony of the detachment to make sure that none of his men were left in the street. The mob attacked three of the remaining police cars, smashing the windows with rocks and lumber. One car was turned over.

---

* Zaneth does not mention the charge in his reports.

Conroy reported: "A few Mounties who failed to get away and Insp. Zaneth, who stayed in the office, faced the mob for a long period while it vented its anger on the overturned cars." Zaneth reported, "The crowd remained in front of the office until 2:30 a.m. all the while shouting and throwing ice and rocks at the cars and at the office building. A large piece of frozen clinker was thrown through the glass door leading to the balcony. All kinds of missiles were thrown at the building in an attempt to break all the windows." The RCMP called the local police for help, but they didn't appear until 2:45 and by then most of the crowd had dispersed. Four of the rioters who had been held in the station were released, as were five men suspected of breaking draft regulations. Eight men had been taken into Montreal for further questioning.

The *Gazette* called it the Battle of Heriot Hill.

The riot sparked an immediate internal RCMP investigation; initial reports went to Commissioner Wood and through him to the Minister of Justice, Louis St. Laurent. By Monday, the riot was news across North America. The *Gazette* had personal experience stories on the front page, Banner's story was on page one of the Boston *Globe*. The story also made page one of the *New York Times*, sharing the spotlight with the fall of Manila and the U.S. Marines fighting their way across a Pacific island called Iwo Jima. *Time* and *Newsweek* both picked up the story.

News reports noted that before the raid there was bad feeling between the people of Drummondville and the Provosts. There had been fights on the street, and on a previous occasion a man had been "rescued" from a Provost squad. On Tuesday, February 27, André Laurendeau, anti-conscriptionist leader of the nationalist *Bloc Populaire* rose in the Quebec legislature on a question of privilege to request an emergency debate on the Drummondville riot. Laurendeau accused Prime Minister King of employing "methods worthy of barbarous times" and said that if the government wanted to enforce its "unjust" conscription law, it shouldn't "act as if the province of Quebec were occupied by an enemy power."

Robert Bernard, the Union Nationale member for Drummond, said the raid was "under the direction of an inspector of the RCMP of the name of Zaneth, of an unknown racial origin, with no knowledge of the French language." In a long and fiery speech, Bernard called the raid an attack on the "peaceable and industrious population . . . is worthy of the Gestapo of Hitler."

Bernard quoted a Radio Canada report that the RCMP was holding an investigation. "At Drummondville," he said, "we do not expect justice from Inspector Zaneth and we had our own investigation made by the local police." He claimed that Zaneth had tipped off the newspapers, that because no French language reporters were tipped, the tip was racist, and the coverage from the Montreal papers to the Toronto *Star* and the *New York Times*, "has surpassed the propaganda organized in Germany by Goebbels."

Bernard's accusations widened the RCMP internal investigation. Commissioner Wood assured St. Laurent that all RCMP members of the raiding party were bilingual. The Officer Commanding of C Division, Superintendent Josaphat Brunet spoke to reporter Larry Conroy. Brunet said that Conroy "would not tell me that he had been advised by anyone of this Force of our proposed action . . . He had been following our actions since the first raid conducted in Montreal."

The day after Brunet talked to Conroy, the rival Montreal *Star*, in its lead editorial, called the attack on Zaneth a "cheap tactic." "The officer thus assailed has been a distinguished member of the RCMP for twenty-five years and speaks French as fluently as does the member who thus glibly raises a race cry he would be the first to condemn had it been raised elsewhere."

On March 1, Wood sent a complete report to St. Laurent: six hundred men were checked for draft papers during the raid. Thirty-three were detained, of these thirteen were quickly released and twenty were taken to the station. Of the eight taken to Montreal, one was a deserter, three had broken draft regulations and the other four were released and given a ride back to Drummondville.

Zaneth did confirm one of the reports, that one of the arrested men had been beaten up.

When the riot was at its peak, a member of the Provost Corps brought to the office a man and as soon as he entered the office pushed him down on a chair and slapped him across the mouth and at the same time saying, "It's dirty cock-suckers like you . . ." I immediately stepped forward and reprimanded the man in presence of this young man. One of our Constables escorted the Provost out of the room and told him we did not allow such treatment to prisoners in our case . . . The young man in question was allowed to go shortly after.

A constable at the border detachment at Rock Island reported that an Unemployment Insurance Commission official in Sherbooke told him that everyone in Drummondville knew about the raid on Friday, the day before, and the arrival of the reporters had only confirmed it.

Insp. Harvison made a discreet visit to George Carpenter, managing editor of the *Gazette* trying to discover the newspaper's sources. Carpenter replied in a two-page, tongue-in-cheek letter to Wood:

In Larry Conroy, The Gazette prides itself having one of the best police reporters in America. Being such a reporter he makes it his business to have as many sources of information as possible . . . He is an accomplished mathematician, particularly in working out the proposition that two and two are more often that not equal to four . . .

Carpenter said Conroy had overheard "a snatch of conversation in a downtown elevator." When Conroy decided to go to Drummondville, the *Gazette* had sent Daigneault to back him up. When Earl Banner had dropped by the office, Carpenter said, "I told him that if I were a young man who had been sent from Boston to get a story and had nothing better to do than visit other newspaper offices, I would catch the next train for Drummondville."

On March 29, the debate moved to the House of Commons.

Joseph Choquette, the *Bloc Populaire* member for Stanstead, rose during Question Period to ask, "Was Inspector Zaneth . . . authorized to give advance information to certain newspapermen? What is the country of origin of Inspector Zaneth? What is his racial origin? Has he been naturalized? How long has he been a member of the Royal Canadian Mounted Police? Does Inspector Zaneth speak French and English fluently?"

Justice Minister St. Laurent answered the questions, provided by the RCMP. In a separate letter, Wood informed the Justice Minister that in April, 1944 Choquette "ran foul of this force" for smuggling American cigarettes into Canada. The MP was released on voluntary payment of $100 and the cigarettes confiscated. Wood stated "As Inspector Zaneth is in charge [of the Montreal subdivision] . . . there may be some connection . . ." The smuggling story had also been leaked to the Montreal papers.

The Montreal *Star* responded with a second editorial:

A GOOD CITIZEN

The Bloc Populaire Member for Stanstead carried this campaign of vilification a step further by asking questions in the House of Commons as to the nationality of Inspector Zaneth . . . Zaneth, the Minister said was born in Italy, came to Canada in 1911, was naturalized four years later and has been a member of the RCMP for more than twenty-seven years. He speaks both French and English fluently.

Inspector Zaneth's status as a citizen is as good as that of the man born here, and he has rendered to his country of adoption, more loyal and distinguished service than his detractors permit themselves to offer.

The RCMP internal investigation revealed that small, inconspicuous raids or routine spot checks were the standard procedure for the force and the Provost Corps. Many raids had been successfully carried out in Quebec and Ontario. There had been some larger raids, on February 22, for example, thirty RCMP and

Provosts had gone through Valleyfield, Quebec. The next day, twenty-five had raided the Auditorium Dance Palace in Montreal. According to Wood, "The reason for the strength of the detail [at Drummondville] being a little larger was due entirely to the serious incidents which had occurred when the Provost Corps visited the town on previous occasions."

The files on the Drummondville riot end with intelligence reports on reactions from extremists on both sides, a anti-Quebec, anti-Catholic editorial from Toronto's *Gospel Witness* newspaper, and a public meeting in Montreal which accused the RCMP of being the "Gestapo." There were no more serious incidents, the war was drawing to a close.

CHAPTER FIFTEEN

New Glasgow

ON OCTOBER 1, 1945, Frank Zaneth was promoted to superintendent and transferred to Ottawa to take Command of A Division. There is an interesting coincidence to the posting. In September, Igor Gouzenko, the cipher clerk at the Soviet embassy, defected, bringing with him documents that described a Soviet spy ring in Canada. Within days, the Mounties were unravelling the spy ring. Zaneth had no part in the investigation. A senior source, however, said that in the days after Gouzenko's defection, Commissioner Wood was covering all bases. Zaneth was due for the promotion to command a division and he would be most useful in Ottawa; he might have been brought there in case he was needed. There is no record he was.

After about two years in Ottawa, Superintendent Zaneth was transferred again, to command the Regina sub division. Safe-blowing was a problem once again. The war was over and the crooks back at work. Zaneth assisted the officers involved in coordinating the safe squads that he had pioneered. As well, he was involved in an experiment dreamed up by the RCMP and the National Research Council. A small amount of a radioactive liquid was placed in a glass bottle in a safe, in the hopes that if the safe was blown, the money would become hotter than the thieves intended and could be traced with a Geiger counter. The thieves, unfortunately, never tried to blow the safes or steal the cash boxes that concealed the radioactive tracer.

On May 1, 1949, Zaneth became the first Italian Canadian to be named an Assistant Commissioner of the RCMP. He was transferred to Ottawa and named Director of Training of the Force. His responsibilities included overseeing recruit training at Depot Division in Regina and N Division in Ottawa and the advanced courses taught to senior officers from Canada and other countries at the Canadian Police College in Regina. Zaneth travelled to Montreal and Toronto to give his own courses, based on his experience, on such topics as conspiracy and interrogation of witnesses.

In February 1951, he took six months' leave and officially retired from the RCMP on August 11, 1951. Frank Zaneth had been a Mountie for almost thirty-four years.

Frank and Edith moved to Toronto, then in 1954, to Miami Beach. They didn't like the retirement life there, and at the end of September, 1956, they returned to Montreal.

John Marrett was in Montreal at the time. Marrett had been a former police superintendent in Jamaica. In 1956, he was working for Foundation Company, a subcontractor for Western Electric which was building the Distant Early Warning (DEW) line for the U.S. Air Force and the Canadian Department of Defence Production. Marrett's job was to conduct security checks for the various organizations involved in construction.

Marrett found that his expense account had been boosted by someone. He followed it up and discovered corruption. "To put it mildly, they were selling jobs on the DEW line. It cost a month's salary to get a job up there."

He asked a security contact in the Department of Defence Production for help and the man replied, "You need someone like Frank Zaneth."

"Frank came into my life and protected my good name," Marrett said. Zaneth remained in Montreal, working with Marrett for a year while he was travelling in the Eastern Arctic.

"Frank was very, very intelligent. It did not take him more than a moment to catch on to anything," Marrett said. "He protected my backside when I had to investigate the selling of jobs by some senior officials."

After a year, both men left the DEW line job. Marrett worked for Bell Canada, then became the security chief for the International Civil Aviation Organization (ICAO).

In June, 1959, Frank and Edith Zaneth moved to New Glasgow, Quebec, a tiny village east of St-Jerome. They bought and fixed up a white gingerbread house on a hill overlooking the village. Edith had fond memories of New Glasgow; she had spent some time when she was younger.

For the next decade, the Zaneths spent living quietly in New Glasgow. They kept pretty much to themselves. Edith was somewhat active in the Ladies Auxiliary of the tiny St. John's Anglican church. A couple of times a month, she would drive to Montreal to attend her bridge club.

Frank or Edith would walk along Achigan Road East each day, taking along their big bull dog. A long time neighbor, Jesse Hesse, says Frank Zaneth would say hello to her as he passed walking the dog. "We'd talk about the weather, you know," Hesse recalled in 1989, "You never got into a real conversation."

John Marrett and his family were also frequent visitors to the New Glasgow house. At one point Frank gave John an old Meerschaum pipe with a carving of a lion grabbing a gazelle. Frank and Edith were godparents to John's daughter Penny.

As a little girl, Penny Marrett found that Edith, like her husband, paid attention to detail. "The house was meticulous," she says, "I remember the stairway. I swear Aunt Edith must have polished it by hand, the bannister, was just always gleaming and the windows, they were bright, bright, bright.

In the mid-sixties, the bulldog died after a bone stuck in its throat. The Zaneths soon had another. It was a bigger dog, and not as well trained, a problem as the couple got older. "Edith used to take him on a walk and it would be him pulling her, she would be at a half run," Hesse said. "I think the dog would pull him too, he was getting on in years."

There were visitors, mainly retired RCMP veterans. One was Clifford Harvison, who had become Commissioner in 1960 and retired in 1963. His wife Doris also liked the New Glasgow area.

Zaneth's nephew, Bill Rivers, from Springfield was also an occasional visitor.

Frank Zaneth would seldom talk about his years with the RCMP, despite the urging of his relatives and friends.

Jesse Hesse remembers Frank did try and take on one rather wild 12 year old boy whose mother had died. "He told me "I think I'm succeeding, he listens to me,' " she remembered.

In later years, Frank Zaneth's health began to fail. He had prostate problems, high blood pressure and a minor heart attack. It was Edith who took care of Frank. "She was so dainty, yet she took care of him," Bill Rivers said. "Edith wore herself out, taking care of him." Jesse Hesse agreed, "She used to carry his tray up to him in bed. I think that's what killed her, carrying up the trays and things. She was only a little bit of a thing."

On April 15, 1971, Edith woke early as usual. "The sun room was gorgeous," Bill Rivers said. "It was her habit to get up early and make coffee or something good and check on Frank, if he had a bad night. Then she would go into the sun room, sit down and read." Frank came down around 11 a.m.; there was a television program he liked to watch.

"He called her and she didn't answer and he came downstairs and he found on her on the couch," Rivers said. "She was still alive, because later he was telling how she died in his arms." Edith Zaneth was sixty-five.

Zaneth called a neighbor for help. The neighbor called Rivers in Springfield. By the time his nephew arrived, Frank was sicker. "He had gone from bad to worse. He would fall out of bed at night, and I had to get him back in. Just caring for him, I knew that we had to do something, he just wore me out in four days."

All the villagers in New Glasgow, and their friends gathered for Edith's funeral at St. John's Anglican Church. Penny Marrett was fourteen at the time. "It was almost packed to overflowing . . . I remember Uncle Frank had difficulty walking, he was much slower at that point. [Afterward] Uncle Frank was so weak."

Rivers was trying to get Zaneth into a veterans home. In the meantime, he had to return to Springfield, the nearest neighbors promised to look after Frank. Seventeen days after Edith, on May 2, 1971, at the age of eighty, Frank Zaneth died.

Rivers was once again summoned from Springfield. "Those two weeks were the worst two weeks of my life, I don't remember an awful lot. As soon as the funeral was taken care of, I was ready to pack up and get out of there."

There were few reminders of Zaneth's long career in the cottage. There was no red serge uniform. But Rivers found that Zaneth had continued, in retirement, to use the small notebooks he had used so meticulously as an investigator.

"It included 'stove,' " Rivers said, "then such and such a date, and where he bought it, how much he paid for it, if he had any repair work done on it. It had the names of plumbers and stuff like that. It was the sort of thing everyone should do and most of us don't — when bills were due, when they were paid."

Only a few people gathered in the old cemetery in New Glasgow, on the morning of Wednesday, May 9, 1971, for the funeral of Frank W. Zaneth. There were no obituaries in Canadian newspapers, just a simple death notice in the Montreal Star.

It was not the funeral one would expect for a retired Assistant Commissioner of the Royal Canadian Mounted Police.

The cemetery was small, bounded by Highway 158 to St-Jerome, a barnyard and a woodlot. Among the modern polished red or black granite headstones were many older bleached, weathered marble memorials dating back to 1831, when the first of the Scots settlers were buried.

The service was held across the highway in the small, wooden, barn-red St. John's Anglican Church. The mourners included neighbors from New Glasgow, the officer commanding the Montreal detachment of the RCMP, two constables in red serge and a few gray haired veterans who came down from Ottawa.

After the funeral, Bill Rivers found other notebooks, ones that Zaneth used as reminders. One included Lincoln's Gettysburg

Address; others held small bits of information, quotes, philosophy, the names of the then forty-eight United States and their capitals, legal definitions in both English and French. Another notebook had a quote from George Washington. "I hope I shall always possess firmness and virtue, enough to maintain what I consider the most enviable of all titles, the character of an Honest Man."

Frank Zaneth was never a red-coated rider of the plains. He never wore a parka in the high Arctic. When he joined the force in 1917, such men were already legends; Superintendent James Walsh, one of the few white men trusted by Sitting Bull, Inspector Charles Constantine, who guarded the Chilcott Pass; Sam Steele, who kept the Yukon peaceful during the Klondike Gold Rush — all wore the red serge. Frank Zaneth wore a trench coat and fedora. He was a city cop. His fancy McLaughlin Buick is as important to RCMP history as the dog sled.

Frank Zaneth was a loner. He is seen only through his own reports, the conclusions of his superiors and the distant memories of those who knew him. In some ways, he is better known as a operative than a person, as author John Robert Colombo quipped. Zaneth was an impressive character actor, always on stage. In the small force of the 1920s and 1930s, he had to jump in and out of character, from gangster undercover to official policeman. He was a superb police technician as he gathered evidence, little piece by little piece, then put it together into a case. He had something special, for out of hundreds of officers who served in the Silent Force during the twenties, thirties and forties, he is the one of the few who is remembered.

Frank Zaneth, like all cops, had failures and successes. He had to face the xenophobia and racism of some Canadians. He never hesitated to take on the Mafia. Some of his RCMP superiors may have had political motives in their orders, but Zaneth was equally diligent, "without fear, favor or affection," in his search for evidence against the left and against the wealthy Bronfmans.

Zaneth is as much a Mountie trail blazer as Walsh, Constantine or Steele, for if their contribution to Canadian history was the peaceful settlement of the prairies and the north, Zaneth, undercover or preparing a brief for court, was the first modern Mountie. He was the link between the prairie patrol and the commercial crime and international narcotics squads of the Royal Canadian Mounted Police of the 1990s.

He remained silent to his death. The low-key funeral in May, 1971, was something Frank Zaneth would have thought appropriate. After all, he had been the RCMP's most secret operative.

APPENDIX

Operative No. 1 and Al Capone

ON JUNE 9, 1930, there was a murder in Chicago. This was not unusual in a city where there was a gangland murder almost daily. But the lunchtime assassination of Chicago *Tribune* reporter Alfred "Jake" Lingle, was one of the events that led to the fall of Al Capone, the boss of the city's south side.

Frank Zaneth may have been of significant assistance in the investigation.

Lingle was the *Tribune*'s legman, a reporter who kept in touch with the street, who passed on information to the rewrite desk. He had started on the *Tribune* in 1912, at age twenty, as a copyboy. A few weeks later, he was a junior police reporter. In 1930, Lingle was not known to the public; he never got a byline. For eighteen years, he was valuable source to the *Tribune* in the highly competitive era made famous by the play *The Front Page*, a time when the gangs were the top news story in Chicago. He couldn't write — he called stories to the rewrite desk — and his salary was sixty-five dollars a week. He was also a heavy gambler.

On June 9, Lingle left his plush suite at a downtown hotel and walked over to the *Tribune* to talk to the city desk. He told them he was checking out rumors of "something brewing" in Bugs Moran's Northside gang. His first aim, however, was to catch a special train to the track. He never made it.

Lingle walked into a pedestrian subway. Behind him was a tall, blond, nattily dressed young man. He took a revolver from his pocket, aimed it inches from the back of Lingle's head and pulled the trigger. The reporter fell to the pavement, a lit cigar still in his mouth, one hand clutching a *Racing Form*.

Colonel Robert McCormick, the outspoken publisher of the *Tribune*, had never heard of Lingle, but within hours, the paper portrayed him as a martyr, a reporter slain by gangsters in the line of duty. Lingle had had contacts on both sides of the law, he had access to Al Capone and was best friends with Chicago Police Commissioner William Russell. He knew all the cops in town and everyone from the governor of Illinois to alky cookers who brewed booze for the mob and other small fry. There was a huge funeral as the city paid tribute to Lingle. McCormick offered a $25,000 reward for the killer. Rival newspapers added money to the reward until it totalled $55,725.

McCormick also offered to underwrite the investigation into Lingle's death. Three men led the investigation, Pat Roche, chief investigator for the Cook County State's Attorney's office, a *Tribune* lawyer named Charles Rathbun and a reporter named John Boettiger. Boettiger's memoir of the case, *Jake Lingle, or Chicago On the Spot*, was published later that year. It detailed each step in the investigation. Although some critics have called it a whitewash for the *Tribune*, the book remains one of the most accurate and vivid accounts of that momentous year in Capone's Chicago.

The team soon came up with bad news for McCormick. Lingle was no martyr, but a corrupt fixer, the liaison between the gangs and the police. He had more than $63,000 in the bank. He had five stock-market accounts, one held jointly with the Police Commissioner.

McCormick decided that there would be no coverup and told his investigative team to keep trying to find the killer. The murder had come at a time when the pendulum had just started to swing against Al Capone. The gangs were still taking in six million dollars a week from bootlegging, drugs, gambling and prostitution. Capone got about two million of that. Suspicion was aimed equally at Bugs Moran's Northsiders and Capone's mob.

Rathbun and Roche began to harass all the gangs, supported by other men who wanted to stop Capone. President Herbert Hoover had ordered the Treasury Department to get the "Big Fellow." The Treasury Intelligence Service's tax investigation on Capone had been under way when Zaneth met Arthur Madden and Converse in the summer of 1929. A group of wealthy businessmen had formed the Secret Six, with the aim of bank rolling anti-gang activities probably including the Garage Cafe speak-easy that had provided the cover for Frank Zaneth as Arthur Anderson. The Six had also hired their own private investigators, led by Alexander Jamie, and were helping to finance other anti-gang activities. The *Tribune* arranged with an honest judge to haul men on the Public Enemies list, including Capone, into court on vagrancy charges. Jamie's brother-in-law, Elliot Ness, and his "Untouchables" took on Capone's breweries and distilleries. High bail was set for men rounded up on the vagrancy charges. Their detention caused disruption to the business at a time of the Ness raids. It all began to make a small dent in the Capone organization.

In late September or early October, 1930, a wealthy and apparently respectable businessman approached Rathbun and Roche at their office. He had a message, "The Big Fellow wants to see you."

That was one way Capone operated. He had safe meetings with his legitimate opponents. Frank Loesch, of the Chicago Crime Commission, the man who had originated the idea of the Public Enemies list, had met Capone in the autumn of 1928, to ask for an honest municipal election. Robert Randolph, the founder of the Secret Six, would meet with Capone in February 1931.

Roche wasn't impressed with the offer of a meeting. As Boettiger related in his book, Roche replied, "We don't want to see Capone. We want to drive him out of town."

"But it can't do any harm for you to see him," the business-man insisted. "He wants to see you. It may do you some good."

"He can't do anybody any good."

After a long debate, Rathbun and Roche decided they would

not meet with Capone themselves, but they would send a go-between. The only record of that meeting is contained in Boettiger's book. He says that the identities of the two agents were kept secret and "There was never even a memorandum made of what transpired with the gang czar, so closely was the secret guarded, and the date is fixed only through recollections of other events of that time." Boettiger called the agent "Operative No. 1."

Was Frank Zaneth Operative No. 1?

The answer is: possibly. Boettiger says that the investigative team kept no records of the meeting. Zaneth's personnel file contains some hints of his activities during the crucial period.

The key is Zaneth's relationship with Pat Roche. When Zaneth arrived in Chicago during the Rocco Perri drug operation, he was looking for Roche, whom he knew.

Could Zaneth and Roche have worked together in the mid-1920s? Roche was almost the American counterpart of Zaneth. He had come from Ireland when he was seventeen and spent some time working as a railway clerk; then joined the Chicago police. It was soon apparent that young Roche was, like Zaneth, a natural, with an instinct for solving crimes. After a couple of years, Roche was asked to join the Treasury Intelligence Service. Roche started off looking at tax fraud, and then was promoted into investigating corruption in other U.S. federal agencies, especially the Bureau of Prohibition. Undercover in New York, Roche became a junior Prohibition officer, took $100,000 in bribes and handed it over to the Justice Department.

Roche's next big case, in 1925, was tracking corruption in the narcotics division of the Bureau of Prohibition in Chicago. Roche charged Will Gray Beach, chief of the Chicago narcotics bureau, and three top agents with graft. Two of the agents pleaded guilty; the third was convicted. Beach was acquitted but retired. The woman behind that drug racket, Kitty Gilhooley, was charged under narcotics laws and convicted. Roche's next target was the oriental drug traffic in the Windy City. If the newspaper reports are correct and Zaneth did work undercover on narcotics in Chicago in 1926 and 1927, his talents would have been known to Roche.

When John Swanson was elected State's Attorney for Cook County in 1928, he asked Roche to become his chief investigator and help clean up the city. Since the RCMP and those U.S. authorities they trusted often cooperated, and since Zaneth was always being sent by the Commissioner on some mission, it would have been easy to bring Zaneth down from Toronto for two weeks.

On or about October 21, 1930, Operative No. 1 was driven to meet Capone who was still wanted on the vagrancy warrant. The driver took several precautions to make sure he wasn't followed. The meeting took place at the suburban home of the wealthy businessman who originally contacted Roche. Operative No. 1 was ushered into the drawing room. There was Al Capone. The businessman then left the room.

As Boettiger later told the story, Capone got right to the point. "Here's want I want to tell you, and I won't be long about it. I can't stand the gaff of these raids and pinches. If it's going to keep up, I'll have to pack up and get out of Chicago."

"So far as I can tell you, the gaff is on for keeps. This town has been burning up since Jake Lingle was murdered."

"Well, I didn't kill Jake Lingle, did I?"

"We don't know who killed him."

"Why didn't you ask me?" Capone said. "Maybe I can find out for you."

"Maybe you can," replied Operative No. 1.

"I don't know what the fellow that killed Jake looks like," Capone said. "I know none of my fellows did it. I liked Lingle, and certainly I didn't have any reason to kill him."

Operative No. 1 gave Capone the description of the killer — something valuable to Capone if he was genuinely looking for the killer or wanted to know if his triggerman had been fingered. Capone then told Operative No. 1 his theory why Lingle was murdered.

The Capone mob had been operating two dog tracks, the Moran gang a third, which had somehow burned to the ground.

A Canadian named Thomas Duggan had been trying to promote dog racing at Chicago Stadium, but then the Capone racetracks had been closed by injunction and the Illinois state courts had ruled that dog racing was illegal. Capone said that the Northside mob had been behind Duggan's plan for dog racing at the stadium and had given Lingle $30,000 to pay off the state's attorney and the police. Roche, one of the few Chicago law enforcement officers who couldn't be bought, had warned the owner of the stadium that it would be raided if he allowed dog racing.

"When the gang saw that they could not go," Capone said, sitting in an easy chair beside a crackling fireplace, "they blamed Jake Lingle and I think's that's why he was pushed. But I don't know who they used to do the job, it must have been some fellow from out of town. I'll try to find out."

"You can do this if you want to, Capone," replied Operative No. 1, "but I don't think it will help you with Roche.

In closing the meeting, Capone mentioned that Bugs Moran and Joseph Aiello, both of the Northside gang, had made peace overtures. "He wants to join up with me," Capone said of Moran, "and maybe I can trade off with him for a bit of information on the Lingle murder. I might take him in if he will tell me who killed Jake."

If you have any more information to give, Operative No. 1 told Capone, have the businessman contact Roche. Then Operative No. 1 was driven back to downtown Chicago. Two days later, Aiello was machine-gunned to death when he emerged from hiding in a house on Chicago's West Side.

A few days later, Operative No. 1 met with the businessman. Boettiger's account continues.

"The Big Fellow has made inquiries throughout the gangs," he said "and he has been unable to find any man who answers the description of the killer. It seems that he has been well covered up. Al has got 50 men working on the case, and he hopes to dig up something definite."

There was a final meeting with the businessman, two weeks after Operative No. 1 met Capone.

"Al wants to know, will you take the killer of Lingle dead?" was the question.

"You can tell Capone that he has been bluffing and that he can go to hell," was the reply. That was the last meeting. While Capone had been making his proposal to Operative No. 1, federal agents, through an undercover informant had learned that Capone had held a strategy meeting with some of his top lieutenants where he revealed that the offer was a trick. In the meantime, Capone had brought in hitmen from New York to kill Pat Roche, Madden, another IRS investigator and a U.S. Attorney — a scheme the feds soon put a stop to, forcing the hit team to leave town in a hurry.

Eventually, in December, 1930, Roche and his men captured Leo Vincent Brothers, a St. Louis hood who got his start as a labor racketeer. In April 1931, Brothers was convicted of Lingle's murder and sentenced to 14 years. "I can do that standing on my head," was his only comment. He served eight years then returned to St. Louis, where he was rewarded with a franchise in a mob run taxi business.

Even after sixty years, there are still questions about the Lingle murder. The most common conclusion is that Capone ordered the hit and that Leo Brothers took the fall, did his time and got his reward.

Was Operative No. 1 Zaneth? Zaneth was in Windsor in mid-September, 1930. A number of undercover agents, informants and detectives were involved in various aspects of the effort to get Al Capone. Boettiger, in one reference, says Operative No. 1 was on Roche's staff.

Boettiger also says, however, that in the investigation "Roche and Rathbun and their men travelled from Montreal to Havana, in their efforts to find proof for the motive in the Lingle murder." So there was a Canadian connection.

It's just one more mysterious spot in the career of Operative No. 1., but given Zaneth's ability, his reputation in both the RCMP and with U.S. agencies, and his contacts in Chicago, there is a high probability he was Operative No. 1 in the case of Al Capone.

AFTERWORD

The Secret Files

FOR MORE THAN SEVENTY YEARS, the secret files on the Winnipeg General Strike, a pivotal moment in Canadian history, were missing. For years, the Liberal and Conservative governments and the Royal Canadian Mounted Police refused to confirm or deny that the files existed. Historians suspected that documents had survived, but requests for information were routinely denied.

There were scraps of information, — Royal North-West Mounted Police headquarters files in the National Archives in Ottawa, records from the Labour department and others scattered here and there. In Winnipeg, the transcripts of the trials had long since disappeared. A law firm had donated a transcript of one preliminary hearing to the Manitoba Archives and there were copies of seized or intercepted letters and telegrams.

There were tantalizing clues that the RNWMP had been doing a lot during those key months in 1919. One hint is a coded telegram, from N.W. Rowell, the minister responsible for the Royal North-West Mounted Police, to A.A. MacLean, the Comptroller (then civilian administrator) of the RNWMP on June 16, 1919, as the police prepared to arrest the leaders of the strike in Winnipeg:

> Very important that adequate secret service force be maintained in Winnipeg, Vancouver, Calgary and Edmonton to trace out and look after all undesirables. Stop. You are

authorized to employ all additional men you require for this purpose.

There was obviously a lot going on, and not just in Winnipeg. In 1986, the Conservative government of Brian Mulroney was attempting to bring in a new law to tighten, rather than open, the security and secrecy provisions governing documents deposited in Canada's National Archives. It was part of reforms updating the Public Archives Act, which had been passed in 1912. During the debate on Second Reading of the new National Archives Act, in June 1986, Lynn McDonald, then the New Democratic Member of Parliament for Broadview Greenwood, said, "We know that the RCMP keeps, as confidential, files on the Winnipeg General Strike of 1919, a very long time ago. It is difficult to imagine that there are current security matters which could be jeopardized from files dating back to that period of time. Certainly we have agencies which are excessive in how they define what material has to be kept away from the Public and the Archives."

As result of extensive lobbying by the academic and artistic communities, the government withdrew the worst provisions of the bill, saying it would find "other means" to make sure national security was maintained.

While the Commons was debating the new Archives Act, we had already begun to uncover the cases of Frank Zaneth, the RCMP's Operative No. 1.

We had discovered Frank Zaneth in the Archives in Ottawa. There was one file in Record Group (RG) 18, Records of the Royal Canadian Mounted Police, about the undercover drug investigation in 1929 against the Perri mob. Leafing through reports, typewritten on thick legal-size paper or on flimsy carbon copies, we read that Zaneth was assigned to the case of Rocco Perri. Little was known about Zaneth's undercover work in the West during the time of the Winnipeg strike. He had been attacked in the jury summations by two defendants, William Pritchard and Fred Dixon, and was recorded by the Canadian left as the infamous agent provocateur of the Winnipeg strike.

We dug further into files that hadn't been seen in fifty years, not in the RCMP records, but in other federal divisions, immigration or pensions and national health. We checked references in the National Archives in Washington. We filed requests under Canada's Access to Information Act and the U.S. Freedom of Information Act.

All but the most routine documents were marked "secret."

In Canada, we had to work through two agencies, the Royal Canadian Mounted Police and the Canadian Security Intelligence Service.

RCMP annual reports mentioned a few of Zaneth's criminal cases. We routinely applied under the Access to Information Act for those files. If they existed, the files, with the censoring required by the act, were released.

When we tried to uncover Zaneth's security cases, his early work in the west, we faced what appeared to be an unsurmountable problem: the blanket and total secrecy that has surrounded the RCMP operations in Winnipeg during the strike since 1919.

We filed a series of requests with CSIS. Some material was released, that dealt with Zaneth's undercover work with the One Big Union in Montreal between 1920 and 1923. Most of this material had already been cleared by CSIS and released to other, earlier researchers.

As for Zaneth's work in the west, CSIS replied to our letters, "We conducted a review of files pertaining to subversive activities in the Prairie Provinces and could not locate any report submitted by Frank W. Zaneth." The word "submitted" would later become very significant.

Under one special section of the Privacy Act, we requested and received from the RCMP Zaneth's personnel file. There were the plans for infiltrating the IWW and the Communist Party in the United States. The RCMP had checked with CSIS before clearing political material; it had cleared criminal content itself.

Once again we filed access requests with CSIS. We got the familiar answer. "No information on Zaneth."

We filed two appeals to the Information Commissioner; one

on the withholding of material by csis, the second on national security material withheld from the personnel file.

Then, on January 9, 1990, the government ordered csis to dispose of files "not relevant to the service's mandate."

Under the provisions of the new National Archives Act, csis had to transfer 3,500 files of "correspondence, memoranda, reports, briefs, clippings and other printed material related to individuals and organizations involved in the labour movement, including protests, demonstrations and strikes in Canada, covering the period 1919–1988."

While our first appeal was being processed, we filed a new Access request, this time to the Archives, requesting any material relating to Frank Zaneth in the new Record Group 146, rcmp/csis Labor files.

The office of the information commissioner replied that csis files "did not contain any Zaneth records pertaining to those . . . topics" covered in the first appeal.

"In addition," we were told, "csis confirmed in writing to us . . . that it had made a substantial search with a view to locating Zaneth's records" pertaining to the two areas we had chosen.

Information Commissioner John Grace added, "The issue of whether 70-year-old material would be injurious to the detection or prevention of subversive activities is not a consideration because I am satisfied that no record was located . . . I should point out that, regardless of the age of certain records, an injury may exist. It is my policy to arrive at such a decision on a case-by-case basis following an investigation. Let me say, here, that it would require the most compelling of arrangements to justify the withholding of 70-year-old information."

That, we thought, was that.

Then, in late December 1990, an archivist's box arrived from Ottawa. It contained thirteen files, hundreds of pages of memos, and reports and lists, all stemming from the 1919 strikes. Just part, perhaps, of the famous Winnipeg files that the government, the rcmp and csis had either denied existed or refused scholars permission to see.

On top was the rnwmp intelligence file on left-wing activities in Calgary. We discovered that Zaneth's reports were oral. So, in fact, there were few written reports *submitted* by Constable Zaneth, but there were his undercover adventures, as he had related them to his controllers.

The box contained many of the long lost files about the Winnipeg General Strike, including frightening plans for nationwide raids.

The police watch continued long after the Winnipeg arrests. One file contains the reports of an undercover operative assigned to be a spectator in court; the operative watched and made lists of those who attended the trials.

Specific material we requested on the iww, the British Columbia Federation of Labour and the machinists and miners unions is apparently long gone. But much more may remain. If the Calgary material can suddenly surface after seventy years, it is probable that more of the actual Winnipeg files are now in the custody of the Archives.

As we were completing the manuscript we were notified that the information commissioner had upheld our appeal on the personnel file. Fifty new pages arrived, containing Zaneth's story about how he went to New York to infiltrate the Communist party.

Why were the files kept secret for seventy years? Some of the files actually reflect favourably on the rcmp.

Most likely it was the bureaucratic tendency within the Silent Force to keep secret all that it could. RG 146 shows that the rcmp and then csis kept an eye on the labour movement right up until 1988. The need for secrecy builds upon itself. A file is opened on an individual and then kept up to date. Such a system is a waste of taxpayers' money. It's also a threat to democracy.

Continual pressure to make the secret files of a police or security service public is one way a democratic society puts a check on their operations.

The Frank Zaneth Papers

AIA = Files obtained under the Access to Information Act
FOI = Files obtained under the U.S. Freedom of Information Act

All Chapters

RCMP File O 284, Frank Zaneth's RCMP Personnel File AIA
RCMP Annual Reports

Chapter One: Frank Zaneth and the Royal Northwest Mounted Police

SASKATCHEWAN ARCHIVES
Homestead Files 2723076, 2710666
CITIZENSHIP CANADA AIA
Naturalisation File 3577121, Frank Zanetti
U.S. IMMIGRATION AND NATURALIZATION SERVICE, FOI
Zaneth's Green Card File
MOOSE JAW ARCHIVES
Local History Files
REGINA PUBLIC LIBRARY
Prairie History Room files
SPRINGFIELD, MA. PUBLIC LIBRARY
Local History Collection

Chapter Two: The Calgary Stoolpigeon

NATIONAL ARCHIVES OF CANADA RG 146 CSIS LABOUR FILES, AIA
"Winnipeg General Strike and Riot 1919"
Sympathy Strike-Calgary, Alberta File 175/670
NATIONAL ARCHIVES OF CANADA RG 33 ROYAL COMMISSION RECORDS
Vol. 95 Royal Commission on Labour Relations transcripts Microfilm
M1980
NATIONAL ARCHIVES OF CANADA RG 18 RCMP RECORDS

Vol 581 files G.477 Edmonton and Calgary Strikes
Vol 581 File 485 Letters from Ottawa re Labor situation
Vol 550 File 128 Strike at Drumheller Coalfields
Vol 552 File 167 Strike at Drumheller Coalfields
GLENBOW-ALBERTA INSTITUTE
M 861 James Moodie Papers
CHICAGO HISTORICAL SOCIETY LOCAL HISTORY FILES
Industrial Workers of the World

Chapter Three: Zaneth Agent Provocateur

NATIONAL ARCHIVES OF CANADA RG 146 RCMP/CSIS LABOUR FILES, AIA
"Winnipeg General Strike and Riot 1919"
Execution of Search Warrants in Connection with the Strike Leaders.
Wpg. File 175/1164
Correspondence, 1919–1920
"Strike at Drumheller" 175/684
NATIONAL ARCHIVES OF CANADA RG 27 LABOUR RECORDS
Vol. 313 F 151 Calgary Strike

Chapter Four : Zaneth and the Communists (I)

MANITOBA ARCHIVES RG 4 A1 MANITOBA COURT RECORDS 1919–1920
Exhibits King vs William Ivens
MG 10 VOL. A 14 KING VS WILLIAM IVENS-LAWYERS FILES
Transcript of Preliminary Hearing
NATIONAL ARCHIVES OF CANADA RG 18 RCMP RECORDS
File 3314 Winnipeg General Strike
Vol 83–84/321 Box File 2–6 (1951)
Absorption of Dominion Police into RNWMP
NATIONAL ARCHIVES OF CANADA RG 24 MILITARY INTELLIGENCE RECORDS
Vol 4472 File-20–1–44 Montreal Socialists
CANADIAN SECURITY INTELLIGENCE SERVICE FILES
Michael and Rebecca Buhay AIA
Socialist Party of Canada, Montreal AIA
French Socialist Communist Party, Montreal AIA
One Big Union, Montreal AIA
RECORDS of MT. CARMEL CATHEDRAL, Springfield, Ma.

Chapter Five: **Operative No. 1 and the Tangled Web**

NATIONAL ARCHIVES OF CANADA RG 76 IMMIGRATION BRANCH
Volume 340, File 357484, Parts 1, 2 & 3
Investigation by the Royal Canadian Mounted Police of
the forgery of the name of Thomas Gelley, (Division
Commissioner of Immigration and Colonization, Winnipeg,
Manitoba) Italian Immigration Cases, 1929
NATIONAL ARCHIVES OF CANADA RG 13 DEPT. OF EXTERNAL AFFAIRS
C 1 Vol. 999 File 1928/855
Extradition of Flavio Masi
U.S. NATIONAL ARCHIVES RG 59 STATE DEPARTMENT RECORDS
1929, Visa Office, 150.4269 Capello, Antonio

Chapter Six: **Operative No. 1 Undercover Against the Mob**

NATIONAL ARCHIVES OF CANADA RG 18 ROYAL CANADIAN MOUNTED
POLICE
File 3313 Rocco Perri Opium and Narcotic Drug Act
ARCHIVES OF ONTARIO RG 23 ONTARIO PROVINCIAL POLICE
Series E File 93–1.9 Wood Alcohol Poisoning
RCMP FILES AIA
Tony Roma, Opium and Narcotic Drug Act

Chapter Seven: **Everywhere and Nowhere**

RCMP FILES AIA
Tony Roma, Opium and Narcotic Drug Act

Chapter Eight: **Modus Operandi**

NATIONAL ARCHIVES OF CANADA RG 29 HEALTH PROTECTION BRANCH
Vol. 230, File 323–12–13, Smuggling of narcotics in bulbs from Holland
ARCHIVES OF ONTARIO RG 4 RECORDS OF THE ATTORNEY GENERAL
c3 1926–1928 Wood Alcohol Poisoning
ARCHIVES OF ONTARIO RG 23 ONTARIO PROVINCIAL POLICE
Series E File 93–1.9 Wood Alcohol Poisoning

Chapter Nine: Zaneth and the First "French Connection"

RCMP FILES AIA

Harry Davis, Opium and Narcotic Drug Act

U.S. NATIONAL ARCHIVES RG 59 STATE DEPARTMENT RECORDS

Pincus Brecher Extradition File U.S. to Canada, 1933–34

Jacob Pollakowetz Extradition file France to U.S. 1933–34

Narcotics Intelligence files 1930–34

Elias Eliopoulis

Jacob Bloom

Charles Wimmer Joseph Bernstein

Drugs on board *Ile de France,* the *Beregenaria* and *Majestic*

Jacob Pollakowetz

NATIONAL ARCHIVES OF CANADA RG 32 PERSONNEL RECORDS

Vol 232 1881.09.29 Charles Henry Ludovic Sharman

NATIONAL ARCHIVES OF CANADA RG 13 EXTERNAL AFFAIRS

C 1 Vol 1009 File 1933/1382

Extradition of Pincus Brecher

UNIVERSITY OF PENNSYLVANIA, PATTEE LIBRARY: Harry Anslinger Papers

Chapter Ten: Zaneth and the Bronfman Conspiracy

RCMP FILES AIA

1933 HQ -768- (C series, 5 Volumes) (Q series)

"The Bronfman Conspiracy,"

"Province Wide Conspiracy, Québec/ Nova Scotia"

U.S. NATIONAL ARCHIVES RG 59 STATE DEPARTMENT RECORDS

Bootlegging intelligence files 811.114 Canada 1930s

"Smuggling Along the St. Lawrence River" 1933

"United States Tax Liabilities of the Bronfman Brothers"

"Prosecution of the Bronfman Brothers"

"I'm Alone Arbitration"

Files on various bootlegging vessels including *Isabel H.*
and *Yvonne Joanne*

Bootlegging intelligence files 811.114 Newfoundland

U.S. NATIONAL ARCHIVES RG 26 COAST GUARD RECORDS

"Logs for RCMP"

Seized vessel files

"Estimate of the Smuggling Situation Subsequent to the

Repeal of the 18th Amendment"
Bootlegging intelligence files
U.S. NATIONAL ARCHIVES RG 60 DEPARTMENT OF JUSTICE
File 23–4581 Atlas Shipping

Chapter Eleven: Zaneth and the Communists (II)

CANADIAN SECURITY INTELLIGENCE SERVICE
Transcript Rex. vs Tim Buck Nov. 3, 1931
Recruiting for Spain by the Communist Party of Canada AIA

Chapter Twelve: The Dandy Dan Meets a Rat

RCMP FILES
Irregularities of Customs Officers AIA
NATIONAL ARCHIVES OF CANADA RG 16 CUSTOMS RECORDS
B-1 1003, Windsor Customs Corruption Inquiry
Books #1, #2
NATIONAL ARCHIVES OF CANADA RG 18 ROYAL CANADIAN MOUNTED
POLICE
Internment files

Chapter Thirteen: The Battle of Heriot Hill

RCMP FILES AIA
Disturbances re Deserters and N.S.S.M.R. Evaders,
Drummondville, Québec AIA
NATIONAL ARCHIVES OF CANADA LOUIS ST. LAURENT PAPERS MG 26-L
Volume 2, Files 11–12
Disturbances at Drummondville

Chapter Fourteen: New Glasgow

U.S. IMMIGRATION AND NATURALIZATION SERVICE,
Zaneth's Green Card file FOI

Appendix: Operative No. 1 and Al Capone

CHICAGO CRIME COMMISSION
Index files
CHICAGO HISTORICAL SOCIETY LOCAL HISTORY FILES
Organized Crime in Bootlegging Era

Endnotes

End reference notes have been kept to a minimum, usually to acknowledge published sources, or to highlight information that adds to the main text. Material has been integrated from many sources, and academic reference notes would be too extensive. Where necessary readers are referred to the bibliography.

1 D'Amato, Donald, *Springfield, 350 Years. A Pictorial History* (Norfolk, Virginia. The Donning Company/Publisher, 1985.)

2 It was a sort of half-citizenship. An applicant became "naturalised as a British subject, and is within Canada, entitled to all political and other rights . . . to which a natural born British subject is entitled . . . with this qualification, that he shall not within the limits of the foreign state of which he was a citizenship . . . be deemed a British subject unless he ceased to be a citizen of that State, in pursuance of the laws thereof."

3 Zaneth's citizenship application says he crossed the border on April 1, 1912, but since he was already on a homestead by November, 1911, we have assumed there was a typographical error.

4 In 1869, the Canadian government divided the prairie lands into a series of townships, each six miles square and divided in thirty-six sections. Each section included four 160 acre quarter sections. Townships were numbered north from the U.S. border, and ranges ran east and west from the first meridian which went through Fort Garry, Manitoba. North-south roads were one mile apart; east-west roads were two miles apart. A similar system was adopted for homesteading in the United States.

5 No other records could be discovered that mention a child. One old-timer had a vague memory of a Zanetti daughter, but could not remember what happened to her. Very little is known about Rita Scevola Ruscollotti Zanetti. Frank's surviving relatives and colleagues say he never talked about her, and only the most basic records exist.

6 In the Moose Jaw Public Library archives.

7 Accounts of recruitment and training are based on the experiences

of C.W. Harvison, who was recruited two years later, in 1919, and who related his experiences in *The Horsemen*, pp 12–15. (For complete reference see Bibliography).

8 Horrall, Stan "The Royal North-West Mounted Police and Labour Unrest in Western Canada 1919;" Pinkerton, William A. "The Bolsheviki," (pamphlet in Moodie Papers, Glenbow Institute); Report to Sir Robert Borden from Perry, Aug. 7, 1919 (RCMP Records, National Archives of Canada)

9 The Industrial Workers of the World was founded in Chicago in 1905, under the leadership of three people: miner William "Big Bill" Haywood, Eugene Debs, a leader of the American Socialist Party and Mother Jones, a 75-year-old labor agitator. The IWW aimed at drawing all workers into "one big union," so that a general strike would bring down the capitalist system and see the birth of a "Workers Co-operative Republic." In 1912, the IWW had organized a strike of construction workers on the Grand Trunk Pacific and Canadian Northern railways. The union had conducted what it called free-speech campaigns in Victoria and Vancouver and had tried to organize the woodworkers in British Columbia. It did not stop at English-speaking workers. During the Grand Trunk strike in the Fraser Canyon, IWW leaders had made a special effort to organize Italian laborers, using Italian speaking organizers and printing their literature in Italian. Although IWW activity had slowed with the start of he war, the term "IWW" had come to be used about any labor radical.

10 Raven was a veteran of the hunt for Almighty Voice in 1897. Almighty Voice was a Cree wanted for the murder of Sergeant C.C. Colebrook in 1895. Raven was wounded in a gunfight with Almighty Voice in a poplar grove near Duck Lake, Alta., in May of 1897. Almighty Voice was killed by police the next day.

11 Much of the description of the life of the miners is based on David Bercuson's accounts, supplemented by local histories of the Drumheller valley. See Bercuson, *Fools and Wise Men: The Rise And Fall of the One Big Union*. 12–14.

12 According to a Pinkerton agent who stayed at the Rosedale mine until December 1919, quite a few veterans did get jobs in the mines at Drumheller, but many soon tired of the hard, dirty work and the "foreign element" who had been pushed out got their jobs back.

13 *The Searchlight* Dec. 12, 1919.

According to his extensive RNWMP profile, P.F. Lawson claimed to have worked for large papers such as the *Christian Science Monitor* and the Chicago *Examiner*, but he spent most of his life on very small papers. He was on the *Galesburg Evening Mail* in Illinois for eight years, then he worked in eastern Canada for seven on the *Co-operative News* and the *Berwick News*, both in Berwick, in the Annapolis valley of Nova Scotia before moving to the Halifax *Herald*. One RNWMP source, known only as "H.B.," said "P.F. Lawson is the 'king-pin' agitator [in eastern British Columbia] . . . none of the others have the influence and weight he has. . ."

14 Based on Zaneth's testimony in the Winnipeg General Strike trials in December, 1919, February, 1920.

15 The material on the conference is based on accounts in the Calgary *Herald* and the official transcript of the conference *The Origin of the One Big Union*

16 Events reconstructed from Zaneth's reports and later testimony

17 Based on the official transcript of the Calgary session.

18 Based on Longstreth's account in *The Silent Force* pp 307–308

19 *Searchlight* Dec. 12, 1919

20 "Lenine" was the accepted spelling at the time.

21 The FBI has no records on Ambrose Zanetti, so it is highly unlikely that he had any radical connections.

22 The RNWMP detachment in Fernie reported on the strike there in May, 1919. It was "a miniature Winnipeg affair, minus the riots," run by Lawson, "who more or less constituted himself as dictator."

Why then did Lawson leave Fernie for Calgary? Lawson's outline of his career seems to indicate he quickly tired of being a big fish in a very little pond.

23 Based on trial accounts appearing in the Manitoba *Free Press*, the Winnipeg *Evening Tribune* and the *One Big Union Bulletin*

24 According to Zaneth's report of July 24, even the One Big Union members wondered why Joe Knight had not been arrested. An Access request to the Canadian Security Intelligence Service produced no file on Joe Knight. Sources in CSIS claim that if there was a Personal History file on Knight, it disappeared, like many others, years ago. But then CSIS also told us early in our research that Zaneth's reports did not exist. We obtained those reports after they were transferred to the National Archives.

25 Spalding's mole on the *Searchlight* staff was still at work. A "Secret and Confidential" memo from Spalding to Perry quoted a letter the Winnipeg defendant, Rev. William Ivens, had sent to Lawson in late January, 1920. The RNWMP's agent had copied the letter and sent it on to the inspector, along with copies of the newspaper. Ivens had sent Lawson a proposed article, outlining a history of the Winnipeg General Strike, and asked the editor, "My only request is that you do not use my name, because I am one of the accused, and I have still to face trial . . . In any case it is yours to do such as you see fit, use it or burn it." Neither man knew a copy went to the RNWMP, as Spalding noted, "It would, of course, be impossible to refer in Court to the original of this article, without uncovering our source of information ■ ■ ■"

26 After the Winnipeg strike ended, Prime Minister Borden had summoned Commissioner A. Bowen Perry to Ottawa in August. He expressed his concern about unrest around the world, then asked for Perry's opinion on the future of federal policing in Canada. In a report submitted to the prime minister two days later, Perry said he no longer trusted the municipal police forces. He considered both the Vancouver and Winnipeg forces, "disloyal" and "unreliable." Perry believed that the Mounted Police, with its cavalry tradition and with its new corps of detectives, was the solution.

As far as special agents, Perry said the Dominion Police relied too much on American detective agencies. "It has been urged that they are in a position to supply the most expert operators, but this has not been my experience. The result of the policy adopted is that no large body of loyal expert detectives has been created by the Dominion Police; Canadian in nationality and sentiment, whose services would be invaluable at this time."

Borden accepted Perry's recommendation that the jurisdiction of the Royal North-West Mounted Police be extended throughout Canada, that they absorb the Dominion Police. They would have a new headquarters in Ottawa. In November 1919 Parliament acted and a new police force came into being. The name of the new force was changed to the Royal Canadian Mounted Police.

27 David Bercuson, *Fools and Wise Men* Chapter 7. The earliest record Bercuson has of the OBU in New England is two years later during a textile strike in Lawrence, Massachusetts. The IWW had been behind the famous Lawrence strike in 1911. The IWW reasserted itself and swallowed up the

New England OBU in 1924.

28 The Labor College was founded, but in our research we have been unable to confirm that Soviet funds were involved. The OBU later sold Soviet made toys to raise funds for the money-strapped college. Along with a later memo, Zaneth included the Labor college's prospectus: Its cafeteria advertised "bourgeoisie food at proletarian prices." He sent the brochure onto Ottawa without comment.

29 This incident gave Rees a reputation as a "Communist Party organizer" in one RCMP file. Although Rees was a socialist and union militant, he opposed the efforts of the One Big Union.

30 George Benjamin, of Belleville, Ontario, was the first Jew to be seated in a Canadian assembly when he was elected to the Parliament of the Province of Canada in 1857.

31 Based on information from Harvison in *The Horseman* and the Montreal RCMP narcotics files from the 1920s which survive in the National Archives of Canada

32 The building still exists; today it is a fast food restaurant and a gym.

33 Veitch was interviewed in August 1988. He was at age eighty-eight.

34 One of the necessary documents was a passport for Zaneth. To obtain it, Zaneth had to upgrade his citizenship. He filled in new forms and was granted a new certificate of naturalization in June 1928.

35 The Associated Press story got almost everything wrong.

NEW YORK, Nov. 30 – AP – Canadian Mounted Policeman F.W. Zambeth arrived here today on the liner Conte Blancamano from Pescara Italy, with an extradited prisoner, Flavio Masi, former fruit merchant of Hamilton, Ont.
Masi, who had lived in Canada many years, was charged with forging immigration permits for about fifty-five Italians, illegally brought into Canada and is alleged to have received $250,000 from Canadian farmers for importing labor. The laborers are said to have complained of not being paid by the farmers.

The AP story was a surprise to the Toronto press. The Toronto *Globe* checked out the story. It was also a surprise to local officials in Hamilton, although *Globe* sources did report that "immigration inspectors" had undertaken the investigation, an indication that Zaneth's cover had worked. The story was also headlined in Zaneth's hometown papers in Springfield, Mass.

"MOUNTIE" WHO JOURNEYED TO ITALY TO "GET HIS MAN" WAS FORMER SPRINGFIELD RESIDENT

During his career as a "mountie" Zanetti has had a good many thrilling experiences and on one occasion trailed a man from Quebec to Boston but to date he has never failed to get his man. About two months ago he was put on the trail of Flavio Masi, a former fruit merchant from Hamilton, Ontario, who was charged with forging immigration permits . . . Zanetti followed his man over the larger part of Canada and then to Italy where he arrested him.

36 For a more detailed account of this investigation and of Rocco Perri's life, see our book, *King of the Mob: Rocco Perri and the Women Who Ran His Rackets,* Penguin, 1987.

37 Zaneth even checked to see if Paul Clement was in Chicago.

38 The RCMP checked with Montreal police who could find no record that they wanted Tony Roma.

39 There was another dog story told about Zaneth, recounted by Clifford Harvison. When Zaneth was a senior officer in Ottawa in the late forties, there was demonstration of dog handling at N Division. The dog handler constable asked for an object. Zaneth gave the constable his wallet, which the constable placed in the middle of the parade ground. The dog sniffed Zaneth and then went down wind sniffing for the wallet. Then it bounded to the wallet, stopped, sniffed, lifted its leg and marked the wallet.

40 The RCMP took that report very seriously. "possibly a case of forgery could be proven if this list is submitted to the Dominion Government . . . if false signatures could be proven."

41 Montreal organized-crime historian and writer Jean-Pierre Charbonneau in his 1975 book *The Canadian Connection* called Davis "one of the barons of the Montreal underworld."

42 A letter from the bank's lawyers on June 28, 1932 stated:

With regard to the cheques negotiated by the Bank, the situation is as follows.

(a) Mr. Bronfman tells us that the parties from whom his Company receives these cheques, do not wish to negotiate them in the United States for two reasons —

(i) They wish to avoid any chance of prosecution for violations of the liquor laws of the United States.

(ii) They wish to prevent the exposing of their incomes to the United States authorities, and consequently to prevent or minimize the possibility of any income tax prosecution.

(b) Mr. Bronfman states that very few, if any, of the cheques in question are forgeries and that in any event the Bank is only taking the ordinary banking risk in cashing these cheques, and that it has the endorsement of its customer, Atlas Shipping Company Limited as its protection in that regard.

(c) Mr. Bronfman states that the amount of these cheques constitute about 21.45 per cent of the total business done with the Bank in connection with the account in question since first of January last. Mr. Oliver tells us that this statement is correct.

(d) Mr. Bronfman states that it is impossible to have these cheques made payable to a named person or registered entity, in view of the manner in which the customers of his Company obtain these cheques.

43 The *Tremblay* was the most famous barge in Canadian history. It was used to smuggle alcohol back into Quebec from St. Pierre as early as 1924 and in November of that year, Quebec Liquor Commission officers seized its load of sixteen thousand gallons at St-Sulpice. When the *Tremblay* docked at Montreal, the barge was boarded by Joseph Bisaillon, Montreal's Chief Preventive officer (then still part of the Customs Service). Bisaillon, a federal official, ordered the Quebec men off, then allowed the crew to escape. As a result, Bisaillon was charged with conspiracy, along with the crew. A check of his bank account showed it contained $69,000 of government money. Bisaillon was acquitted, but the *Tremblay* publicity caught the eye of Canadian businessmen worried about smuggling and their investigator soon found corruption going all the way to the Customs Minister, Jacques Bureau, who had been shielding Bisaillon. Bureau got an appointment to the Senate and the new Customs minister, George Boivin, sold the sixteen thousand gallons to Dominion Distilleries cheap. Dominion Distilleries was run by a former Liberal MP

who sold the alcohol across the border into the United States. The result was revelations in the House of Commons, a Commons committee investigation, the fall of King's government, the King-Byng constitutional crisis and the Royal Commission on Customs Excise.

44 U.S. Coast Guard and State Department intelligence files show that the *Isabel H*, under several owners, was smuggling as late as 1940. She was tracked near Bermuda in February, 1936, with sixteen hundred cases of alcohol on board. When she went into Hamilton, Bermuda for repairs, the Coast Guard cutter *Mendota* was sent to Hamilton for a "visit," leading to a diplomatic incident. For a while *Isabel H* was in legitimate trade, but by 1937, the vessel was smuggling once again. This time it was suspected that illegal Chinese immigrants were being carried alongside the rum. After a joint investigation by the Mounties and the Coast Guard, the new owners and crew of the *Isabel H* were charged with conspiracy, only to be acquitted by a Cape Breton jury in June, 1940. The judge had only one comment: "Gentlemen, I am amazed!"

45 Three weeks later, two U.S. investigators met with Sam and Allan Bronfman and Lazarus Phillips. Their aim was to threaten the Bronfmans with criminal prosecution for tax evasion in order to produce a settlement in a planned civil case for back taxes. Wesley Frost, the Consul, was hoping for a criminal prosecution. In his covering report on the meeting he said, "The success of the Bronfmans in defrauding the American Government is well known throughout both countries, and if it continues indefinitely will encourage other operators to follow similar methods. On the other hand their conviction would constitute a moral and psychological triumph, similar to the conviction of Capone and would stiffen the forces for the enforcement of law and order throughout the United States . . . Furthermore it would remove from active 'hostilities' the fertile brain and evil genius of Sam and Allan Bronfman." Lazarus Phillips maintained to the U.S. agents that the treaties between the United States and Canada "constituted a set of rules" that Distillers Corporation followed, so his clients "had no feeling of guilt."

In his report, one of the investigators reported his amazement when "Sam Bronfman, at one point during the interview stated that the American government should be indebted to him, as his organization and the Canadian distillers generally, by reason of the fact that their product had found its way into the United States, had kept alive there the market for

American type whiskey; that had it not been for this fact the revenue now accruing to American distillers might be flowing out of the United States to Scotland or to some other country."

The United States would eventually claim a total of one hundred million dollars in back taxes and duties against all Canadian distillers. In May, 1936, the United States and the distillers settled for a payment of just under three million dollars.

46 Goldhart spoke to James Dubro in interviews in 1987.

Acknowledgements

We found out about Frank Zaneth during our research on the life of prohibition gangster Rocco Perri for the book *King of the Mob: Rocco Perri and the Women Who Ran His Rackets*.

Our investigation began, thanks to Kitson Vincent, of Stornoway Productions, who provided research funds in 1987. That permitted us to do the initial work in the National Archives of Canada, and gave us the background on Zaneth's career.

A Canada Council Non Fiction Grant in 1989 permitted further work in the National Archives of Canada, and trips to Washington, to the U.S. National Archives, to Chicago, Winnipeg, Regina, Moose Jaw, Calgary, Drumheller, Montreal, St-Jerome, Boston and Springfield.

John Robert Colombo provided early support and encouragement, then evaluated an early draft and provided essential advice. Thanks, John, for all your help.

Special thanks also to Guy Bannerman and John Yoannou.

Stan Horrall and Bill Beahen in the RCMP History office were always willing to supply substantial information and check minor points. Malcolm Wake and his staff at the RCMP Museum in Regina helped by providing background and information and pointing to interview subjects. Chief Superintendent D.C. McCormick, Inspector J.A. Fontaine, Sergeants Bernie Lettre and E.A. Ypma and the staff of the RCMP Access to Information office were helpful and patient with our numerous requests. Retired RCMP officers who assisted included the late Commissioner Len Higgitt; Bill Kelly, Jim Lemieux, Andrew Veitch, Jack Chester, B.D. Peck, J. Don Fraser, John Stevenson, Don Taylor and C.T.W. Wallace.

Thanks to Eldon Frost and the Access staff of the Government Archives Division at the National Archives who found the Zaneth files — after the government transferred them to the Archives — that the Canadian Security Intelligence Service couldn't find!

Thanks to Joycelyn Béland, the investigator at the office of the Information Commissioner who handled our appeals and the Information

Commissioner, John Grace, for his favorable ruling.

Thanks also to David A.G. Reid, Access Coordinator at Multiculuralism and Citizenship and the Miami FOI office of the U.S Immigration and Naturalization service.

Bill Rivers, Zaneth's nephew, and Bill's wife, Ellen, were always helpful during a visit to Springfield and later.

Milton Goldhart provided a very colourful viewpoint from the other side of the law.

Archivists and librarians were always helpful. At the National Archives of Canada, over several years, Judith Roberts Moore, Rod Young, Tina Lloyd, Cathy Bailey, John Smart and Danny Moore were invaluable.

Thanks also to Bill Sherman at the National Archives in Washington; Susan Kooyman, Glenbow Museum; Linde Turner, Drumheller Public Library; Karon Speizer, Moose Jaw Public Library; Sharon Maier, Regina Public Library; Donald Richan, Saskatchewan Archives; and the staff at the Manitoba Archives, the Archives of Ontario and the newspaper microfilm section at the Metro Toronto Reference Library; Chicago Historial Society, Winnipeg Public Library and the Springfield Public Library.

Thanks also to Leith Knight for her follow-up research in Moose Jaw. Dorothy Murphy was a stroke of luck as a bed and breakfast host in Calgary; her mother, Kathleen McGinn, knew Zaneth when he worked on the Doyle ranch near Moose Jaw. Dorothy also provided information and help. Other B and B hosts went beyond the call of duty with gems of information and sometimes rides to see sources. Thanks to Bill and Jean McDowell in Regina, Robert Rivoire in Ottawa, Jerry Wiebe in Drumheller, Stephanie Peach in Chicago, Betty Bradley in Springfield and Ollie Hillman in Winnipeg.

David Stansbury in Springfield copied the old photographs from the Rivers family collection.

Thanks to John Jemilo and Jerry Gladden at the Chicago Crime Commission, Michael Graham, Chicago; Don Guidolin, Drumheller; Dennis Hoffman, University of Nebraska; John Marrett, Victoria; his daughter, Penny Marrett, Toronto; Sergeant Don Peters, Winnipeg Police; Jesse Hesse, St-Jerome; John Whyte; Whyte Museum of the Canadian Rockies; Patterson Smith; Jean Panko, Moose Jaw; John Griffith and Janet Torge, Montreal; Charles Weckworth, Springfield College; W.A.B. Douglas, the

Department of National Defense historian; and Edna Barker.

Robert J. Sawyer was always willing to give advice on Wordstar and thanks to James Burton at WordStar International and to Julie Rosenberg for their quick efforts as we converted text.

For their encouragement and support, special thanks to our agent Jan Whitford, our publisher Michael Murton and to Doug Webb, Larry Rose, Rob Roy, Martha Porter, Bill Macadam, Dick Nielsen, Martyn Burke, David Ostriker, and Lee Lamothe at the Toronto *Sun*, and Peter Edwards at the Toronto *Star*.

Bibliography

Books and Magazines

Allen, Ralph. *Ordeal by Fire: Canada 1910–1945* Doubleday, Garden City 1961

Anslinger, Harry and Will Oursler. *The Murderers*. New York: Avon 1961

_____ , and Dennis Gregory. *The Protectors: Our Battle Against The Crime Gangs*. New York: Farrar, Straus and Company, 1964

Arlachi, Pino. *Mafia Business: The Mafia Ethic Business and the Spirit of Capitalism*. Trans. by Martin Ryle. London: Verso, 1983.

Avakumovic, Ivan. *The Communist Party in Canada: A History*. Toronto: McClelland and Stewart, 1975.

Betcherman, Lita-Rose. *The Little Band: The Clashes between the Communists and the Canadian Establishment 1928–1932*. Ottawa: Deneau 1982

Bercuson, David. *Confrontation at Winnipeg*. Montreal: McGill-Queen's University Press 1975.

_____ . *Fools and Wise Men: The Rise and Fall of the One Big Union*. Toronto: McGraw Hill Ryerson 1978.

Boettiger, John. *Jake Lingle or Chicago On the Spot*. New York: E.P. Dutton & Co. Inc. 1931.

Canada: Royal Canadian Mounted Police *Annual Reports* 1919–1951.

Caragata, Warren. *Alberta Labour: A Heritage Untold*. Toronto: James Lorimer & Co., 1979.

Charbonneau, Jean-Pierre *The Canadian Connection*. Translated by James Stewart, Ottawa. Optimum Publishing Company, 1976.

Dubro, James. *Mob Rule*. Toronto: Macmillan 1985.

_____ . *Mob Mistress*. Toronto. Macmillan, 1988.

_____ , and Robin Rowland. *King of the Mob: Rocco Perri and the Women Who Ran His Rackets*. Toronto, Penguin 1987.

Gosch, Martin, and Richard Hammer, *The Last Testament of Lucky Luciano (The Luciano Testament)*. London: MacMillan, 1975.

Gray, James. *Booze: The Impact of Whisky on the Prairie West*. Toronto: Macmillan, 1972.

_____ . *Red Lights on the Prairies* Toronto: Macmillan, 1971.

Harvison, C.W. *The Horsemen*. Toronto: McClelland and Stewart, 1967.

Hoffman, Dennis E. *Business vs. Organized Crime: Chicago's Private War on Al Capone, 1923–1932*. Chicago: Chicago Crime Commission Monographs, 1989.

Horrall, S.W. *The Pictorial History of the Royal Canadian Mounted Police*. Toronto: McGraw Hill Ryerson, 1973.

_____ . "The Royal North-West Mounted Police and Labour Unrest in West Canada, *Canadian Historical Review* LXI, 2, 1980.

Howard, Victor with Mac Reynolds *The Mackenzie-Papineau Battalion: The Canadian Contingent in the Spanish Civil War*. Ottawa, Carleton University Press, 1986.

Kelly, William & Nora. *The Royal Canadian Mounted Police: A Century of History*. Edmonton, Hurtig, 1973.

Kemp, Vernon. *Without Fear, Favour or Affection: Thirty-five Years with the Royal Canadian Mounted Police*. Toronto: Longmans, 1958.

Kobler, John *Capone: The Life and World of Al Capone*. New York: G.P. Putnams Sons, 1971.

Kornbluh, Joyce L. (ed.) *Rebel Voices: An I.W.W. Anthology*. Expanded Edition. Chicago: Charles H. Kerr Publishing Co., 1988.

Kyuig, David E. (ed.) *Law, Alcohol and Order: Perspectives on National Prohibition* Contributions in American History, #110, Westport Ct., 1985.

Lipton, Charles. *The Trade Union Movement of Canada, 1827–1959*. Montreal: Canadian Social Publications Ltd, 1966.

Longstreth, T. Morris. *The Silent Force: Scenes from the life of the Mounted Police of Canada*. New York: The Century Co., 1927.

Miller, Scott, "The Assassination of Jake Lingle." *Chicago Reader*, 20 March 1981, v̄10 #24.

Nelli, Humbert S. *The Business of Crime: Italians and Syndicate Crime In The United States*. Chicago: University of Chicago Press, 1976.

Ness, Elliot, with Oscar Fraley, *The Untouchables*. New York: Pocket Books, 1987.

Newman, Peter C. *Bronfman Dynasty: The Rothschilds of the New World*. Toronto: McClelland and Stewart, 1978.

One Big Union. *The Origin of the One Big Union: A Verbatim Report of the Calgary Conference, 1919*. Winnipeg: One Big Union, N.D.

Penner, Norman. *Winnipeg 1919: The Strikers Own History of the Winnipeg General Strike*. Second Edition. Toronto: James Lorimer & Co., 1975.

Ryan, Oscar. *Tim Buck: A Conscience for Canada*. Toronto: Progress Books, 1975.

Williams, Jack. *The Story of Unions in Canada*. Toronto: Dent 1975.

Wilson, R.S.S. *Undercover for the RCMP*. Victoria: Sono Nis Press 1986.

Unpublished Theses

Askin, William R., "Labour Unrest In The Edmonton District and Its Coverage By The Edmonton Press, 1918–1919" M.A. Thesis, University of Alberta, 1973.

Damji, Alimohammed, "Militancy to Passivism: The Calgary Labour Movement 1919–1924." M.A. Thesis, University of Calgary, 1987.

Warrian, Peter J. "The Challenge of the One Big Union Movement of Canada 1919–1921." M.A. Thesis, University of Waterloo, 1971.

Magazines and Newspapers

British Columbia *Federationist*

Boston *Globe*

Calgary *Albertan*

Calgary *Herald*

Hamilton *Spectator*

New York *Times*

Montreal *Herald*

Montreal *Gazette*

Montreal *Star*

Montreal *Standard*

Moose Jaw *Times*

RCMP Quarterly

Springfield [Mass.] *News*

Springfield [Mass.] *Union*

Toronto *Globe*

Toronto *Globe & Mail*

Toronto *Telegram*

Toronto *Star*

Winnipeg *Free Press*

Winnipeg *Tribune*

Winnipeg *Western Labour News*

Index

Marseilles 107
Martin, Paul 245–46
Masi, Ernestina 110
Masi, Flavio 109–11, 113–17, 119–20, 122–26, 170
Masi, Nicola 109, 114
Mathers, T.G. 50
Mathewson, Hugh 104, 130–31, 133–36, 147, 155
Mayerthorpe 248
McCormick, Robert 270
McDonald, Lynn 277
McInnes, R.S. 205–06
McIntosh, Cameron 122
McNaughton, Andrew 253
Mead, Fred 56, 59, 178, 194, 204, 217, 230
Medellín cocaine cartel 15
Meighen, Arthur 119
Memphis 124
Meriden 150
Metcalfe, (Justice) 74, 83
Miami Beach 263
Michelangelo 84
Milan 123, 159
Milford 150, 159
Military Service Act 49
Miller, Sam 240, 242, 246
Monette, Gustave 184–85, 187, 189
Montcalm 179
Montclair 183
Montreal 12–13, 46, 65, 74, 87, 91–94, 101, 131, 138, 141, 146–47, 160, 165, 170, 175–76, 179, 182–85, 187, 189, 194–96, 202, 213–14, 220, 222, 224, 229,
231, 233, 237, 251–52, 254, 258, 261, 263–64, 278
Montreal *Gazette* 254–55, 257, 259
Montreal *Star* 104, 258, 260, 266
Moodie, James 30–31, 37
Moose Jaw 12, 19–20, 22–23, 51, 231
Moran, George "Bugs" 136, 269–70, 273–74
morphine 16, 131, 135, 146, 155, 177–78, 181, 184–85
Motruk, Sam 242, 246
Mulroney, Brian 277
Murder Inc. 191
Murphy, Jim 144, 146
Murphy, Pat 145
Mussolini, Benito 105, 122
Mutual Steamship Agencies 124, 167

Nanaimo 44
Naples 123
narcotics traffic 129–33, 135, 138, 146, 153, 160, 165, 176–79, 184, 191
Nassau 208
National Archives Act 277, 279
National Archives of Canada 277
National Research Council 262
Nelson, Raymond 133
Ness, Elliot 271
New Amsterdam 165
New Brunswick 11, 175, 193–94, 198
New Democratic Party 277
New Glasgow 264–65

Poles, Frank 142–43
Pollakowitz, Jacob 178–79, 182–83, 185
Pool 208
Price Waterhouse 204, 218
Price, G.B. 94
Prince Edward Island 175, 194, 225
Pritchard, William 44–47, 57–59, 61–62, 73, 75, 84–85, 277
Privacy Act 278
Prohibition 14, 100, 102, 129, 193, 202, 208, 239

Q, Agent
    See Curwood, James
Quebec 11, 46, 107, 158, 193–94, 198, 214, 239
Quebec City 27
Quebec Liquor Commission 292
Queen, John 59, 73, 85

Radio Canada 258
Ramsay, C.A. 107, 109–10, 112, 167
Ramsley, Fanny 37
Rand School of Social Science 89
Randolph, Robert 271
Rathbun, Charles 270–71, 275
Raven, C.C. 28, 287
Raymond, Jean 188
Reames, Albert 40
Reckel, William 121
Reed, John 88
Rees, David 43–45, 69, 95–98, 290
Regina 12, 17–18, 24, 29, 34, 38,
51, 56, 73, 210, 231–32, 238, 249, 262–63
Reilly, Sidney 13
Revolutionary Age 70
Riel, Louis 21
Rinaldi, Michele 111–12, 117, 120
Ripstein, Hyman 208
Rivers, Bill 159, 252, 265–66
Rivett-Carnac, Charles 230–31, 233
Rivière du Loup 214
Roche, Pat 139, 270–75
Rochester 155
Rock Island 259
Rocky Mountain Park 37
Roger, Bray 73
Roma, Tony 131–33, 148–53, 155, 291
Rome 112, 123
Romeo, Frank 134–36
Roosevelt, Franklin 252
Rosedale 29–30, 32, 34, 36, 287
Ross, Frank 132–37, 168
Ross, Tony 134, 136–37, 168
Rothstein, Arnold 153
Rothwell 248
Rowell, Newton W. 34, 276
Royal Air Force 244
Royal Canadian Mounted Police 11–12, 16, 83, 105, 129–32, 153, 156, 165, 189, 192, 229, 233, 235–36, 241–42, 244, 246, 249, 253, 258, 262, 267, 276, 278
    intelligence services 87, 100, 230, 247
    Marine Section 194
    provincial policing 175, 194

True Crime from
M&S Paperbacks

WOMEN WHO KILLED
Stories of Canadian Female Murderers
by Lisa Priest

Eleven stories of murders committed between 1975 and 1990, by the award-winning author of *Conspiracy of Silence*.

"Lisa Priest at her best." – *The Globe and Mail*

"This collection has rewards on every page." – *The Toronto Star*

0-7710-7153-1 $6.99 8 pages b&w photos

FATAL CRUISE
The Trial of Robert Frisbee
by William Deverell

The critically acclaimed inside story of the 1985 shipboard murder of a wealthy widow by her seemingly passive manservant. Written by the killer's lawyer — and the author of *The Dance of Shiva* and *Needles*!

"The real goods from an ultimate insider . . . Gorgeously written. " – Jack Batten, *Books in Canada*

0-7710-2668-4 $6.99 16 pages b&w photos

UNKINDEST CUT
The Torso Murder of Selina Shen and the Sensational Trials that Followed
by Doug Clark

Four years after the body parts of beautiful Selina Shen were found scattered throughout south-eastern Ontario, her former lover was convicted of her murder. By the co-author of *Billion-Dollar High*.

0-7710-2117-8 $7.99 16 pages b&w photos

**True Crime from
M&S Paperbacks**

M&S

TERROR'S END
Allan Legere on Trial
by Rick MacLean, André Veniot and Shaun Waters
Through much of 1989 New Brunswick was gripped by a
reign of terror. Four people were brutally murdered during
that period, and in 1991 Allan Legere, already convicted of
an earlier murder, was found guilty in those deaths. The
complete, definitive story by the authors of the best-
selling *Terror*.
0-7710-5595-1 $6.99 16 pages b&w photos

THE DEATHS OF CINDY JAMES
by Neal Hall
Was it suicide — or murder? That's the mystery police
faced when the decomposing body of a Vancouver nurse
was found beside an abandoned house in 1989.
"Well-documented and well-written . . . Intriguing." – *The
Ottawa Citizen*
0-7710-3784-8 $2.99 8 pages b&w photos

CONSPIRACY OF SILENCE
by Lisa Priest
The powerful, award-winning best-seller about racism,
murder, and apathy in a Manitoba community. Basis of
the acclaimed CBC-TV movie. From the author of *Women
Who Killed: Stories of Canadian Female Murderers*.
0-7710-7152-3 $5.99 Photos